# XP-ADJUNCTION IN UNIVERSAL GRAMMAR

OXFORD STUDIES IN COMPARATIVE SYNTAX
Richard Kayne, General Editor

# XP-Adjunction
# in
# Universal Grammar

## *Scrambling and Binding in Hindi-Urdu*

*Ayesha Kidwai*

**OXFORD**
UNIVERSITY PRESS

2000

# OXFORD
UNIVERSITY PRESS

Oxford   New York

Athens   Auckland   Bangkok   Bogotá   Buenos Aires   Calcutta
Cape Town   Chennai   Dar es Salaam   Delhi   Florence   Hong Kong   Istanbul
Karachi   Kuala Lumpur   Madrid   Melbourne   Mexico City   Mumbai
Nairobi   Paris   São Paulo   Singapore   Taipei   Tokyo   Toronto   Warsaw

and associated companics in
Berlin   Ibadan

Published by Oxford University Press, Inc.
198 Madison Avenue, New York, New York 10016

Oxford is a registered trademark of Oxford University Press.

Library of Congress Cataloging-in-Publication Data
Kidwai, Ayesha, 1967–
XP-adjunction in universal grammar : scrambling and binding in
Hindi-Urdu / Ayesha Kidwai.
p.   cm. — (Oxford studies in comparative syntax)
Includes bibliographical references and index.
ISBN 0-19-513251-3. ISBN 0-19-513252-1 (pbk)
1. Grammar, Comparative and general—Syntax.   2. Hindi language—
Syntax.   3. Urdu language—Syntax.   I. Title.   II. Series.
P291.K477 1999
415—dc21   99-10145

1 2 5 7 9 8 6 4 2

Printed in the United States of America
on acid-free paper

For my mother,
AMINA KIDWAI

And in the memory of my father,
TAUFIQ KIDWAI

# Preface

This book offers an investigation of leftward argument scrambling and therefore addresses many of the controversies surrounding the exact status of the operation in the theory of grammar. It argues that, contrary to the by-now-standard assumptions, leftward argument scrambling must be given a uniform characterization as an XP-adjunction operation, and that it is neither semantically vacuous nor entirely optional. I suggest that scrambled constructions must be analyzed as belonging to the class of positional focus constructions in natural language. Although the data for this claim is drawn mainly from Hindi-Urdu, there is mounting evidence that the crosslinguistic link between scrambling and focus may be more pervasive than was initially assumed. This work is therefore located in the tradition that investigates the 'purely' syntactic properties of scrambling as well as in the tradition that investigates both the properties of focus in natural language and the link between focus and linear order.

To advance the thesis that leftward argument scrambling is an XP-adjunction operation, I adopt a strategy that is the reverse of what is traditionally brought to bear upon it. Rather than taking the apparently contradictory binding-theoretic data in different scrambled orders as evidence for the impossibility of a uniform syntactic analysis, I suggest that the contradictions in the data arise from the fact that the binding theory and the weak crossover filter are themselves imperfect in formulation. This strategy then ties the issue of a syntactic description of the scrambling to a reworking of the binding theory and the account of weak crossover effects. This is in itself not a novel strategy, but the implementation I suggest is distinct because it not only provides an explanation for the cases of apparent binding from XP-adjoined positions, it also constructs a theory of binding and coreference that eliminates the need for special statements about weak crossover as well as the mechanism of reconstruction.

Because the discussion uses the minimalist program as its theoretical framework, the book can also be seen as an investigation of XP-adjunction, binding, and reconstruction in the grammar. As this book draws extensively on my 1995 dissertation, much of the discussion makes reference to Chomsky (1992) and only occasional reference to more recent developments. While it is possible to see my claim that XP-adjunction is a morphosyntactically driven operation as contrary to recent suggestions (Chomsky 1995, Zubizarreta 1998) that relegate derived XP-adjunction to the PF component, my current thinking on the matter suggests that this conclusion could be premature. Although many issues are involved in an analysis of scrambling as (uniformly) XP-adjunction in the PF component, the key features of my analysis are actually not entirely incompatible with it. For example, the suggestion that the coreferential interpretations available in scrambled configurations are the result of the computations of a separate coreference component rather than of the binding theory can be of use to a PF-movement account of scrambling if it is ensured that the coreference component can access configurations involving PF-movement. If similar reinterpretations of the other aspects of my proposals are possible, then this book can be seen as a contribution to the debate on the special status of derived XP-adjunction in Universal Grammar.

The other proposals regarding the architecture of a minimalist Universal Grammar are, however, relatively unaffected by subsequent developments. Many of the proposals considerably simplify existing conditions and mechanisms in the grammar. The proposals I make eliminate the need for copy-deletion at LF to create the operator-variable pair, the ordering between this deletion and the application of the binding theory and the need for a reference to the L/L-bar distinction in the binding theory and copy-deletion mechanisms in the grammar. The proposals also provide for a simplification of the economy condition of Full Interpretation and some extensions of its role in the grammar.

In the course of the book, I examine various aspects of Hindi-Urdu syntax. I advance novel proposals regarding the hierarchical positioning of the AGR-oP projection in UG and argue that the double object construction involves overt Case checking by the IO in a position broadly L-related to AGR-o. I also investigate the nature of Hindi-Urdu topicalization, and advance an analysis of the -to particle. In the discussion on the proper formulation of the binding theory, I examine the binding domains relevant for Hindi-Urdu possessive reflexives and pronominals and suggest the means by which the LF-raising approaches to these categories can be made compatible with minimalism as well as the crosslinguistic facts. This book can, then, also be seen as contributing to a study of the core syntax of Hindi-Urdu.

This book has benefited tremendously from discussions with Tanmoy Bhattacharya, Priyanka Bhattacharya, Noam Chomsky, Nomi Erteschik-Shir, Pritha Chandra, Jacqueline Gueron, K. A. Jayaseelan, Liza Joseph,

B. N. Patnaik, Jean-Yves Pollock, Srija Sinha and Rachna Sinha. My intellectual debt to Anvita Abbi and Probal Dasgupta extends far beyond this book and the thesis upon which it is based, and I thank them for their continuing engagement with my work. This book is also dedicated to the memory of Teun Hoekstra, whose example as a teacher I can only hope to emulate. I am particularly grateful to an anonymous referee who not only made insightful criticisms but also suggested the way they may be tackled. Many of the proposals in this book are deeply influenced by her/his suggestions.

The people who have perhaps felt the most burdened by this book are my friends and family, and I am grateful to them for their tolerance, sympathy, and skepticism. A special thanks also to Dr. V. L. Bhargava, and most of all to Rahul, without whom nothing would ever be complete.

*Jawaharlal Nehru University, New Delhi*       A. K.
*July 1999*

# Contents

# XP-ADJUNCTION IN UNIVERSAL GRAMMAR

# Chapter 1

# Issues in the Study of Scrambling

This book investigates the syntactic and interpretive properties of the leftward argument scrambling operation in Hindi-Urdu,[1] and through it, the status of derived XP-adjunction in the model of Universal Grammar (UG) conceived of in the minimalist program (Chomsky 1992, 1993, 1995, Chomsky and Lasnik 1993). The study of argument scrambling has, over the past decade or so, made this leap from empirical fact to theoretical conjecture quite distinctly its own, mainly because the (leftward) argument scrambling operation crosslinguistically exhibits a puzzling variety of properties that resist description in more traditional terms of reference.

## 1.1 Empirical Issues

Hindi-Urdu is a predominantly head-final, WH- in situ, Modern Indo-Aryan language, which normally patterns with other SOV languages in arranging its constituents in the default order SUBJECT–INDIRECT OBJECT–DIRECT OBJECT–ADJUNCT(S)–VERB–AUXILIARIES. This order is, however, less than rigid, and arguments may appear dislocated to the left as well as to the right of the verb. Thus, an example such as (1) can have (at least) any of the word order variants in (2):[2]

(1)  nur-ne      ənjʊm-ko    kɪtab      di        (SU-IO-DO-V)
     Noor(SU)   Anjum(IO)   book(DO)  gave(V)
     'Noor gave Anjum a book.'

(2)  (a) ənjʊm-ko nur-ne kɪtab di (IO-SU-DO-V)

     (b) kɪtab nur-ne ənjʊm-ko di (DO-SU-IO-V)

     (c) nur-ne kɪtab ənjʊm-ko di (SU-DO-IO-V)

     (d) ənjʊm-ko kɪtab nur-ne di (IO-DO-SU-V)

    (e)  kɪtab ənjʊm-ko nur-ne di (DO-IO-SU-V)

    (f)  nur-ne ənjʊm-ko di kɪtab (SU-IO-V-DO)

    (g)  nur-ne di ənjʊm-ko kɪtab (SU-V-IO-DO)

    (h)  ənjʊm-ko kɪtab di nur-ne (IO-DO-V-SU)

    (i)  nur-ne kɪtab di ənjʊm-ko (SU-DO-V-IO)

    (j)  nur-ne di kɪtab ənjʊm-ko (SU-V-DO-IO)

Native speakers usually judge these orders to be entirely optional and discourse-driven, judgments that suggest that the most reasonable syntactic explanation of their origin is one that derives them from an XP-adjunction operation. A closer look at the syntactic properties of these constructions, however, apparently defeats such intentions. For one, the data appears to divide into two classes, where the orders in (2f–j) appear to be the products of base-generated XP-adjunction. Although the leftward scrambled orders in (2a–e) do exhibit the properties of syntactic movement, this set is such a mixed one that a uniform analysis of the leftward scrambling operation appears impossible. For example, as (3) shows, leftward scrambling, unlike configurations derived by XP-adjunction, crosslinguistically has the ability to positively affect binding configurations and override Weak Crossover (WCO) effects (Gurtu 1985, Mahajan 1990, Pandit 1985, Saito 1989, 1992, Sengupta 1990, Webelhuth 1989, etc.):

(3)    (a)  Uski$_i$    bɛhen      kɪsko$_{*i}$    pyar kərti hɛ
            his     sister(SU)  who(DO)  love  does  is
            'Who$_i$ does his$_i$ sister love?'

        (b)  kɪsko$_i$     Uski$_i$  bɛhen     t$_i$  pyar kərti hɛ
            who(DO)  his     sister(SU)     love  does  is
            'Who$_i$ does his$_i$ sister love?'

The illegitimacy of the coindexation in (3a) derives from the fact that after WH-raising to [Spec, CP] at LF, the example is ruled out by the WCO filter formulated in (4). As (3b) demonstrates, the scrambling of the DO WH-phrase somehow conspires to exempt the configuration from this filter. If the leftward scrambled DO in (3b) is held to occupy an (XP-adjoined) operator position at S-structure/Spellout, we have no explanation for the fact that WCO effects are actually overridden in this configuration—because the pronominal and the variable are in the classic WCO configuration in (4),[3] this coindexation should be impossible.

(4)    WCO FILTER
      *[... Operator$_i$ [[ ... Pronoun$_i$ ... ] ... Variable$_i$ ...]]

Traditionally, the only type of movement that is exempt from the WCO filter is Case-driven NP-movement, and it therefore appears that a syntactic description of scrambling could typologize it with Case-driven NP-movement rather than WH-movement or derived XP-adjunction.[4] This conclusion is supported by the data in (5), where scrambling putatively licenses reflexive-binding as well. In (5b), the scrambled DO licenses a subject-contained reflexive and receives a substantially improved judgment with respect to Principle A than does (5a).

(5)  (a) *$\text{əpne}_i$  bəccõ-ne      mohən-ko$_i$   $g^h$ər–se    nɪkɑl  diyɑ
         self's   children(SU)   Mohan(DO)   house-from   threw   gave

     (lit.)'Self's$_i$ children threw Mohan$_i$ out of the house.'[9]

     (b) ?mohən-ko$_i$  əpne$_i$  bəccõ-ne      $t_i$  $g^h$ər–se    nɪkɑl
         Mohan(DO)   self's   children(SU)        house-from   threw
         diyɑ
         gave

     (lit.)'Self's$_i$ children threw Mohan$_i$ out of the house.'

Example (5b) cannot, however, be considered conclusive proof for the analysis of leftward scrambling as NP-movement, not only because Case-driven movement is typically obligatory but also because the evidence from the binding theory is not uniform in this regard, as (6) and (7) demonstrate:

(6)  (a) nur$_i$      əpne-ap-$_i$-ko  pyɑr  kərti  hɛ
         Noor(SU)   self(DO)      love   does   is
         'Noor loves herself.'

     (b) əpne-ap-ko$_i$  nur$_i$      $t_i$  pyɑr  kɑrti  hɛ
         self(DO)      Noor(SU)        love   does   is
         'Noor loves herself.'

(7)  (a) *$\text{əpne}_i$(ap)-ne  mohən$_i$-ko    mɑrɑ
         self(SU)          Mohan(DO)   hit
         'Self hit Mohan.'

     (b) *mohən$_i$-ko  əpne$_i$(ap)-ne  $t_i$  mɑrɑ
         Mohan(DO)   self(SU)          hit
         'Self hit Mohan.'

     (c) *ek  dusre$_i$-ne  [mohən  ɔr  sitɑ]$_i$-ko   mɑrɑ
         each other(SU)  Mohan  and  Sita(DO)   hit
         'Each other hit Mohan and Sita.'

     (d) *[mohən  ɔr  sitɑ]$_i$-ko  ek  dusre$_i$-ne  $t_i$  mɑrɑ
         Mohan  and  Sita(DO)   each  other(SU)        hit
         'Each other hit Mohan and Sita.'

A uniform analysis of leftward scrambling as NP-movement would require that all instances of leftward scrambling be immune to reconstruction
(Barss 1986), but as (6) demonstrates, this is not the case. In (6b), the
scrambled reflexive must reconstruct if the absence of the Principle A violation is to be correctly accounted for. The examples in (7) demonstrate
that the ability of leftward scrambling to license reflexives is limited only to
possessive reflexives, as leftward scrambling in (7b) and (7d) cannot repair
the Principle A violation by the complex reflexive in (7a) or the reciprocal
in (7c).

Example (8) casts still further doubt on the validity of an NP-movement
analysis of leftward scrambling based on data like (3), as it demonstrates that Hindi-Urdu pronominals pattern with Norwegian and Russian (Hestvik 1992, Avrutin 1994) in that they must obviate from the
closest c-commanding subject. If leftward scrambling in (3b) is actually
NP-movement to the specifier of the highest functional projection in the
clause, and if that is the syntactic definition of subject, we would expect
the pronominal embedded in the subject to obviate from the scrambled DO.

(8)  (a) sita$_i$  Uski$*_{i/j}$  gaṭi  layi
         Sita    her        car    brought

     'Sita brought her car.'

     (b) sita$_i$-ne  Uske$*_{i/j}$  piċ$^h$e   dek$^h$a
         Sita       her        behind  looked

     'Sita looked behind her.'

The other syntactic and semantic properties of leftward scrambled arguments are equally befuddling. For instance, scrambled constructions are
highly infelicitous discourse-initiators, partly because, as (9) shows, scrambled XPs receive a presuppositional interpretation quite like that of topics:

(9)  (a) mẽ-ne    ram-ko    film      dɪk$^h$ayi
         I(SU)    Ram(IO)   film(DO)  showed

     'I showed Ram a/the film.'

     (b) fɪlm$_i$      mẽ-ne    ram-ko    t$_i$  dɪk$^h$ayi
         film(DO)   I(SU)    Ram(IO)       showed

     'I showed Ram the/*a film.'

In (9b), the scrambled DO is interpreted as *familiar/specific*, and this
fact could be taken to suggest that leftward scrambling shares some of
the semantic properties of topicalization (e.g., Gambhir 1981, Jayaseelan
1989/1995). However, the fact that leftward scrambling affects the relative scope of quantifiers in the Hindi-Urdu example (10b) puts paid to a

uniform analysis of leftward scrambling as topicalization. Ordinarily, the topicalization of quantified DPs is not licit, as shown by (11):

(10)  (a)  hər    admi      kɪsi    ɔrət-ko      pyar   kərta   hɛ
           each   man(SU)   some    woman(DO)    love   does    is

           'Every man loves some woman.' (*unambiguous*)

      (b)  kɪsi    ɔrət-koᵢ    hər    admi      tᵢ   pyar   kərta   hɛ
           some    woman(DO)   each   man(SU)        love   does    is

           'Some woman, every man loves.' (*unambiguous*)

(11)  *[everybody else]ᵢ we told his wife that we had called tᵢ

Due to the fact that Hindi-Urdu, like Japanese and Chinese, encodes the relative scope of quantifiers in terms of their linear order, (10a) is unambiguous, with the universal quantifier taking wide scope over the existentially quantified DO. Surprisingly, leftward scrambling in (10b) has the ability to alter the scopal interpretation, with the wide scope reading being accorded to the scrambled DO. This would suggest that rather than topicalization, leftward scrambling targets a scope-taking position at S-structure; that is, leftward scrambling is a Quantifier Raising (QR) operation at S-structure. Scrambled quantifiers thus occupy operator positions at S-structure, and should exhibit WCO effects. As (12b) demonstrates, this is not the case, as here the leftward scrambled DO quantifier can license a bound variable reading of the pronominal in the subject DP:

(12)  (a)  Uskiᵢ   bɛhen-ne     hər    lərke*ᵢ-ko   dekʰa
           his     sister(SU)   each   boy(DO)      saw

           'Hisᵢ sister saw each boy*ᵢ.'

      (b)  hər    lərkeᵢ-ko   Uskiᵢ   bɛhen-ne     tᵢ   dekʰa
           each   boy(DO)     his     sister(SU)        saw

           'Each boyᵢ was seen by hisᵢ sister.'

Leftward argument scrambling thus exhibits a mixture of the properties of (at least) NP-movement, WH-movement, XP-adjunction, topicalization, and S-structure QR—in short, a movement that defies a uniform description. The most pervasive reaction to these facts has been to deconstruct the very term scrambling itself (e.g., Mahajan 1990) so that it characterizes a *set* of operations. Depending on analyses, the membership of the set of scrambling operations may contain either all or some of the movement operations listed previously. Presumably, the fact that rightward scrambling exhibits none of these properties implies that base-generation is also a member of the set of scrambling operations.

Although I have no disagreement with a characterization of rightward scrambling as base-generated XP-adjunction, such an account of leftward scrambling, henceforth simply scrambling, constitutes something of a retreat in the face of complex empirical data. My difficulty with this position is not so much that all it effects is a restatement of the problem itself as its solution, but with the fact that it must necessarily fix as constant all other assumptions about the architecture of UG and allow only a bare minimum of interaction between the various modules of the grammar and the scrambling operation. Take, for example, the unquestioning acceptance that the WCO effect is an unambiguous diagnostic for the type of movement, Case- or operator-driven, involved. As Lasnik and Stowell (1991) demonstrate, the topicalization, appositive relatives, clefts, and parasitic gap constructions in (13) exhibit only mild, if any, WCO effects, even as they are clearly the constructions of a movement type that is not Case-driven.

(13)   (a)  Himself$_i$ he$_i$ likes t$_i$

    (b)  The man$_i$ who$_i$ his$_i$ mother likes t$_i$

    (c)  It's him$_i$ that he$_i$ thinks that Mary likes t$_i$

    (d)  Who$_i$ did you speak with t$_i$ before his$_i$ wife could speak to t$_i$

The problem with the WCO filter is its strict adherence to the binary typology of movement types and landing sites given by the A-/A-bar distinction, by which any A-bar position is definitionally held to be an [operator] position, from which binding is illicit. As the facts in (13) demonstrate, what is required is a more nuanced definition of which A-bar elements actually count as operators, and a theory about how the lack of operator status for certain A-bar elements actually improves the possibility of pronominal coreference with them.

These observations suggest that the scrambling data in which WCO effects are overridden should rightly be discussed along with the facts in (13) (i.e., in an inquiry into the proper definition of operators and the reformulation of the WCO filter). The avenues for a uniform analysis of the scrambling operation as XP-adjunction are thus not closed; rather, such an analysis is made contingent upon a proper reanalysis of WCO and other instances of putative binding from A-bar positions. I suggest in chapters 2 and 4 that the proper definition of operator must make reference to whether the morphosyntactic feature that is checked in the A-bar position is a quantificational one or not, and the binding theory must be rendered sensitive to this distinction. The basic result is that nonquantificational A-bar elements do not count as binders for pronominals in A-positions, and hence the absence of WCO effects in the previous examples.

The improprieties in the formulation of the WCO Filter also entail that an adequate characterization of the syntactic properties of the scrambling operation must find independent corroboration from areas of the grammar other than the binding theory. Thus, if the characterization of scrambling as a mixed type of movement is to be upheld, only evidence that demonstrates that each type of scrambling actually exhibits the syntactic motivation and locality constraints of NP-movement, WH-movement, topicalization, etc., is admissible.

As demonstrated in chapter 2, the evidence from the theory of movement actually arraigns itself against an identification of scrambling with NP-movement, WH-movement, topicalization, or S-structure Quantifier Raising (QR), and for an analysis of it as derived XP-adjunction. The instances in which such scrambling appears to share the properties of either topicalization or S-structure QR must then arise from interactions of other principles and components of the grammar. In chapter 5, I suggest that the fact that scrambled XPs and topics share a presuppositional interpretation follows from Diesing's (1990, 1992) analysis of the relationship between the semantic effects of hierarchical positioning outside the VP at Spellout. Chapter 2 demonstrates that the scope-freezing effects in scrambled constructions cannot be derived from an analysis of it as S-structure QR but, rather, from the way the theory of scopal relations of Aoun and Li (1993) interacts with XP-adjoined positions.

In effect, then, I advocate that the appropriate strategy for the study of scrambling is quite the reverse of the one that yields the characterization of it as a mixed movement. Given my contention that there is strong syntactic evidence that scrambling is a uniformly derived XP-adjunction operation, I assume that to be the constant and examine how its intrigues with a network of principles and mechanisms yield the set of (superficially contradictory) properties of the scrambling operation.[5]

## 1.2 Some Minimalist Background

The claim that scrambling is a derived XP-adjunction operation cannot be maintained without elaboration in the minimalist framework (Chomsky 1992, Chomsky and Lasnik 1993). Although I address the issues that will concern us as we go along, a brief outline of its main features (Chomsky 1992, Chomsky and Lasnik 1993) will facilitate a discussion of the theoretical issues that a minimalist characterization of scrambling as XP-adjunction must address.

The relevance of the minimalist program to the generative enterprise is best characterized by a historical analogy with the conceptual shift from the Extended Standard Theory to the *principles-and-parameters* (P&P) framework. This shift marked the move away from a system of rules to a system of grammatical principles and generalized constraints on grammat-

ical outputs. The change of framework resulted in a stricter formulation of
the universal nature of UG, where the notion of parameter entailed greater
empirical coverage without a profusion of rule systems. The successes of the
P&P model notwithstanding, it could be argued to exhibit an increasing
complexity of design and mechanism at odds with the oft-stated objectives
of the theory—a model of UG that is characterized by an economy of design
and mechanism.

Chomsky (1992) suggests that the proper view of UG should commit
itself to a derivational model in which the workings of the grammar are
guided by a principle of indolence rather than industry, i.e., by a principle
of *least effort*. According to this principle, the grammar is designed to make
only the minimum effort, and so it does only as much work as is necessary
to ensure the optimal convergence of its outputs. Moreover, it makes these
efforts only in the *last resort*, i.e., only when not making them will cause an
illegitimate output. Hence, it must minimize derivations by constraining
overt movement and eliminate all superfluous steps and symbols from these
derivations. Minimalism can therefore be seen as an attempt to constrain
the UG constructed by the P&P framework. Simultaneously, minimalism
also transcends this very limited objective as it builds on the successes of
the P&P model in its attempt at higher-order generalizations of the results
already attained.

The primary aim of the minimalist approach to UG is to reduce the
starting assumptions regarding the structure of UG to "virtual conceptual necessity," so as to weed out unwanted and superfluous assumptions
about its form and content. Take, for example, the issue of the generative procedure called language. Intuitively, we know that this procedure is
constrained by at least the *external interface levels* of LF and PF, where
sound is paired with meaning in a rule-governed manner. The P&P model,
even while it accepted this understanding, posited two additional *internal
interface* levels where the legitimacy of this pairing was to be checked as
well—the levels of D-structure and S-structure. Chomsky (1992) argues
that minimalist assumptions do not countenance the existence of the internal interface levels, given that there is no direct evidence from the primary
linguistic data that confirms their 'reality.' In fact, only the external interface levels of PF and LF are observable realities, as these two levels
interface with the performance systems by "providing the instructions for
the articulatory-perceptual [A-P] and conceptual-intentional [C-I] systems,
respectively" (Chomsky 1992:3).

Suppose, then, the first step in a minimalist reappraisal of the shape of
UG must necessarily be the elimination of the two internal interface levels
via a restatement of their requirements as LF/PF conditions. Consider then
each language to determine a set of pairs $(\pi, \lambda)$, where $\pi$ is drawn from

PF and λ from LF, as its formal representations of sound and meaning. The part of the computational system that is relevant only to π is the PF component, while the part that is relevant only to λ is the LF component. The parts of the computational system that are relevant to both are the overt syntax. Though the computation from the selections from the lexicon to LF is uniform, the application of the operation *Spellout* at any point in the computation to LF forces a switch to the PF component. After Spellout, neither the phonological nor the subsequent computation (the covert component) can have further access to the lexicon. Each derivation is evaluated for legitimacy at the two external interface levels, where each member of the pair $(\pi, \lambda)$ must optimally satisfy, i.e., *converge* with respect to, interface conditions.

The set of interface conditions is then the locus of current research into UG. Minimally, such a set must include a definition of which interface objects can be legible to the performance systems, where a failure to satisfy this definition must result in nonconvergence at the interface. Chomsky (1989, 1992, 1993) formulates this definition as an economy of representation principle in (14):

(14) FULL INTERPRETATION

> PF: Elements that have a uniform, language-independent interpretation in terms of universal phonetics.

> LF: Each object a chain CH($=\alpha_1, \ldots, \alpha_n$): at least with CH a head, an argument, a modifier, or an operator-variable construction.

Beyond this minimal interface condition, matters get more complicated. Considerations of economy and virtual conceptual necessity would require restraint to be exercised in the postulation of interface conditions. Therefore, the elimination of D-structure and S-structure cannot merely entail a wholesale relocation of the conditions that evaluated derivations at those levels to the LF and PF interfaces, but, rather, it is incumbent upon research to find ways in which these conditions may be pared down and unified with other conditions. Thus, the minimalist program scrutinizes the exact status of D-structure requirements like the Projection Principle and the θ-criterion as well as S-structure conditions like Subjacency, the ECP/Relativized Minimality (Rizzi 1990), the (morphological) Case Filter, the binding theory, the WH-movement parameter, etc., in the grammar. In addition, it also requires a reappraisal of the mechanisms and principles that were held to apply only at LF (and PF) as well, because any bid to unify what was formerly a D-/S-structure condition with an LF one is bound to affect both parties equally. Of the LF mechanisms that are bound to be affected are those of covert movement and reconstruction, as well as the ECP.

Because my objective is to provide merely a programmatic outline of the research agenda set by Chomsky (1992), the brief discussion that follows focuses only on the broad details of the treatment of D-/S-structure/LF conditions in minimalism.

### 1.2.1   The Projection Principle

It will be obvious that a restatement of the Projection Principle as an LF interface condition is of little value, as its objective was to ensure fidelity to the lexical entry at every point in the course of a derivation rather than only at the interface. As a consequence, the Projection Principle cannot be merely restated as a convergence condition at LF; it in fact needs to be 'hard-wired' as it were into the business of projection itself. Chomsky's (1992) proposals regarding the nature of computation accomplish at least part of this objective.

All projection is held to be undertaken by the generalized transformation GT (originally proposed in Chomsky 1955) in accordance with the X-bar rule schema in (15), and makes reference to an array of choices from the lexicon, the *numeration* (Chomsky 1995:225–27):

(15)   (a) [X]

   (b) [$_{X'}$ X YP]

   (c) [$_{XP}$ [$_{X'}$ X YP]]

GT as projection is essentially a binary substitution operation that, targeting a phrase-marker K, takes a phrase-marker $K^1$ and inserts it in a designated empty position $\emptyset$, forming a new phrase-marker $K^*$, in satisfaction of X-bar theory. The empty position $\emptyset$ is inserted by the GT itself, and must necessarily be *external* to the targeted phrase-marker K. At any point in the derivation, the operation Spellout may be applied, which switches to the PF component. After Spellout, computation may continue, but with the further stipulation that GT no longer has access to the lexicon. The resulting phrase-marker is evaluated at both interface levels, and if it does not constitute a single phrase-marker, the derivation fails to converge. GT as movement, on the other hand, is a singularly substitution operation that maps K to $K^*$. This operation works exactly as the earlier operation, except that instead of inserting a phrase-marker $K^1$ drawn from the lexicon, this operation *adds* a phrase-marker $\alpha$, which must necessarily be a phrase *within* the targeted phrase-marker K itself. This operation leaves behind a copy of $\alpha$, forming the chain ($\alpha$, $\alpha$). Copies are subject to deletion in the PF and LF component.

Both types of substitution operations are constrained by the *extension condition*, by which all substitution operations necessarily extend the phrase-marker they target, even though the extension of K to $[K+\emptyset]$ is an invisible operation. This derives the prohibition against raising to the complement position, earlier captured by the Projection Principle. Thus, if we have a structure of the form $[_{X'} \text{ X YP}]$ we cannot insert ZP into X' to yield $[_{X'} \text{ X YP ZP}]$, where ZP is either internal or external to X'. In either case, GT will violate X-bar theory, and the structures will be ruled out.

The mechanisms of GT sketched out here also provide an explanation for the Larsonian analysis of ditransitives in (16):

(16)

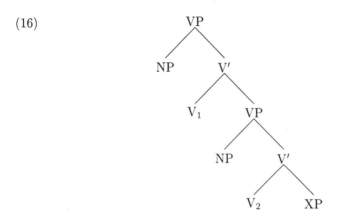

Larson (1988) proposes that the D-structure representation of ditransitives is (16), where the verb is base-generated in the position of $V_2$ and undergoes substitution into $V_1$. This analysis of ditransitives such as *give* actually undermines the very notion of D-structure itself, because the theory of D-structure as a pure projection of lexical properties could not possibly countenance the projection of an empty lexical head $V_1$, except by stipulation. GT now provides a natural way of obtaining this structure. Assuming that projection is necessitated by the lexical properties of the verb and that projection always conforms to X-bar theory and binary branching, faced with the third (Goal) argument of a ditransitive predicate, GT has to project an empty head position to accommodate this argument in accordance with X-bar theory (see also Watanabe 1992).

### 1.2.2   Movement and Language Variation

A major consequence of the elimination of the internal interface level of S-structure is that together with it, we lose the means for describing the crosslinguistic variation with respect to such movement rules as WH-movement. This is not an undesirable result, as it forces an appraisal of whether the concept of parameter actually has any independent explanatory force or whether it exists solely to implement observations about language variation. It appears that at least for the movement parameters, the charge of mere description does hold, and therefore the guidelines behind minimalist inquiry encourage the elimination of parametric statements in the grammar. Like the Projection Principle, the only solution is to somehow build the notion of parametric variation into the theory of movement itself. Chomsky's (1992) proposal that all movement is driven by the narrow requirements of feature checking allows parametric variation to follow without any further stipulation.

Chomsky suggests that the view of UG as simultaneously guided by the principle of least effort and last resort derives the distinction between overt and covert movement. In general, the principle of least effort, in the shape of the economy principle *Procrastinate* in (17), prefers covert movement to overt, as covert movement does not target the PF component and thus minimizes computational effort.

(17)  PROCRASTINATE
      LF-movement is cheaper than overt movement.

Overt movement thus has to be forced, and last resort would entail that the binary GT could raise α only if the failure to raise will result in nonconvergence at the interface(s). This intuition is formalized as the economy principle *Greed* in (18):

(18)  GREED
      Move raises α to a position β only if the morphosyntactic properties of α itself cannot be otherwise satisfied in the derivation.

Chomsky's (1992) claim that such raising is for the purposes of *checking* of morphosyntactic features, rather than the P&P affixation, allows us to capture the intuition behind parameters. Checking theory views the licensing of a lexical element α in terms of a matching of its morphosyntactic features such as [accusative], [+WH], etc., against those on the functional head that is typically associated with licensing them (see chapter 3 for a fuller discussion of the checking relation). Morphosyntactic features may be [strong] or [weak]. Whereas [strong] features force movement in the overt syntax, [weak] features allow the satisfaction of their requirements in the covert syntax. Overt raising for the satisfaction of [weak] features fails Procrastinate, which can be overridden only by the convergence requirements of [strong] features. The difference between English main verbs and auxiliaries with respect to raising to Tense and/or AGR-s then follows from this distinction, as does the difference between English and French main verbs (Pollock 1989). English main verbs and auxiliaries differ in that the [tense] and [AGR] features of auxiliaries are [strong], and hence auxiliaries raise in the overt syntax. The [tense] and [AGR] features of English main verbs, on the other hand, are [weak], and hence Procrastinate postpones English main verb raising to LF. The fact that these features are [strong] for both French main verbs and auxiliaries derives the difference between French and English, as French main verbs must raise in the overt syntax, overriding Procrastinate, precisely because their morphosyntactic properties cannot be satisfied covertly. Parameters are therefore reducible to morphosyntactic properties of lexical items and need no independent statement in the grammar.

Another consequence of the principle of least effort is that it must view with skepticism an account of chain formation that necessarily mimics the actual derivational process. If least effort can be seen as implementing a fewest steps requirement, then the P&P–style chain-formation will simply be too expensive. Consequently, Chomsky proposes that chains are actually formed all at once, and that "we take the basic transformational operation to be not Move-α but *Form-Chain*, an operation that forms the required chain in a single step" (Chomsky 1992:24).

### 1.2.3 Derivational Economy

One of the major consequences of the elimination of S-structure is that there is no longer a site available at which derivations can be evaluated for legitimacy with respect to constraints on movement such as Subjacency, the ECP, and/or relativized minimality (Rizzi 1990). The intuitions behind these constraints, however, need to be captured as they enforce least effort by ruling those derivations as optimal that make the shortest move, keep links minimal, and in general proscribe computational complexity. Current research suggests that these principles need to be intrinsically associated with movement in the grammar, either as global economy conditions constraining movement or as built into the defining characteristics of movement itself (Chomsky 1992, 1995).

Although proposals vary as to the exact formulation of these intuitions, it will be clear that the commitment to a derivational view of UG demands that representational conditions such as the ECP and/or relativized minimality need to be restated as derivational constraints. Chomsky and Lasnik (1993) suggest that the basic intuition that these two principles are intended to capture is that Move-α always seeks to construct the shortest link. Derivations that have longer links fail to converge, either because some intervening landing site has been skipped (as in the cases of relativized minimality violations) or because it is possible to construct a convergent derivation that involves both shorter links and fewer steps. This latter condition attributes a certain evaluative power to the economy of derivation, by which it may *choose* between convergent derivations, and is formalized by Collins (1994) as (19):

(19) ECONOMY OF DERIVATION

    (a) A derivation is optimal if there is no shorter derivation yielding the same legitimate objects, and

    (b) Derivation $D_1$ is shorter than derivation $D_2$ if either $D_1$ traverses less nodes than $D_2$ or $D_1$ involves less operations than $D_2$ (e.g., Form-Chain).

## 1.3    Theoretical Issues

The status of overt derived XP-adjunction in the minimalist UG is at best unclear. Although the framework maintains the distinct phrase-structure status and domination relations of XP-adjoined configurations (Chomsky 1986a:7–9) in (20), economy principles pose significant problems for the characterization of XP-adjunction (and therefore leftward scrambling) as syntactic movement, given the P&P descriptions of it as an entirely 'optional' operation that is often 'semantically vacuous' in its effects. This luxury is no longer afforded by current assumptions, as all movement has to serve Greed, and it may be overt only if the features that drive this movement are [strong].

(20)    (a) $[_\beta\ \alpha\ [_\beta...]]$

    (b) $\alpha$ is dominated by $\beta$ iff it is dominated by every segment of $\beta$.

    (c) $\alpha$ excludes $\beta$ if no segment of $\alpha$ dominates $\beta$.

Now, if XP-adjunction operations are truly optional, XP-adjunction will have to be characterized as immune to Greed, because morphosyntactic imperatives cannot be allowed only sporadic satisfaction. Procrastinate should then postpone all such XP-adjunction operations to LF, thereby exiling constructions involving derived XP-adjunction from phonetic output. A similar conclusion is reached by the Economy of Derivation that chooses the least expensive derivation from a set of convergent derivations. If derivations involving derived XP-adjunction originate from the same numeration as ones without, they must be considered as yielding the same output as the default word order, but by traversing more nodes and involving more operations. The Economy of Derivation will then always reject the XP-adjoined variant as uneconomical, and derivations involving derived XP-adjunction will therefore never exit PF.

If exempting XP-adjunction from economy principles in the grammar is hardly a tenable solution, the principal means of rescue lies in motivating the operation to be morphosyntactically driven. In terms of technology, nothing much is required, as XP-adjoined positions have to be *excluded* from the checking relation only by stipulation, otherwise the definition of checking domain in Chomsky (1992) in fact allows feature checking from such positions. The descriptive advantages of such a postulation are significant—for example, if XP-adjunction involves feature checking then speculations about its optionality are without basis, as the derivation in which XP-adjunction does not take place really belongs to a different numeration from the one that does.

As far as scrambling is concerned, the morphosyntactic imperative can be resurrected from footnoted observations in the literature that such orders typically involve 'focus' and 'emphasis.' Properly characterized, in a scrambled construction, the element that occupies the immediately preverbal position is interpreted as the focus of the utterance. Because Hindi-Urdu is a syllable-timed language, this focusing does not have any discernible correlates in terms of stress, but the immediately preverbal element is interpreted as the asserted element in the configuration, as demonstrated in the examples in (21). Example (21b) is infelicitous because the discourse that follows the scrambled order attempts to pick out the presupposed element as a focus of contrast:

(21)  (a)  kɪtab$_i$      **sita-ne**    t$_i$  pəʈ$^h$i  t$^h$i,  ram-ne  nəhĩ
          book(DO)    Sita(SU)      read  was  Ram    not
          'Sita was the one who read the book, not Ram.'

   (b)  **#kɪtab**$_i$   sita-ne    t$_i$  pəʈ$^h$i  t$^h$i,  kɔmɪk  nəhĩ
          book(DO)    Sita(SU)      read  was  comic  not
          'It was the book that Sita read, not the comic.'

As example (22) shows, this preverbal position is also the position in which WH-phrases are preferentially placed. In an SU or IO question, leftward scrambling is necessarily involved.

(22)  (a)  kɪtab     **kɔn**       layega
          book(DO)  who(SU)   will bring
          'The book, who will bring?'

   (b)  ram          kɪtab  **kɪse**  degaa
          book(DO)  Ram    who    will give
          'Who will Ram give the book to?'

The link between scrambling and this preverbal focusing can be seen on a closer perusal of (21) and (22). Both these examples involve scrambling of

an argument, in comparison with the normal order in (1), where there is neither scrambling nor a necessary assumption that the DO is the focus of the
utterance. It is my claim in chapter 5 that herein lies the morphosyntactic
imperative for scrambling—scrambling is needed to *activate* the preverbal
focus position in Hindi-Urdu. Such head-activation is necessarily an overt
phenomenon because focusing is a discourse-relevant strategy and hence
scrambling must take place before the branching to PF.

Recall now that the XP-adjunction analysis of scrambling is actually
contingent upon a proper formulation of the WCO filter, the way the term
operator is to be defined and a theory of how only true operators can qualify as binders for the binding theory. The issues involved in a minimalist
(re)formulation of these intuitions are too numerous to list in this introductory discussion, so consider here only the general questions.

The minimalist program permits an extremely restricted range of options for the (re)formulation of the binding theory and the WCO Filter.
Standardly (e.g., Chomsky 1981), the binding theory makes reference to
the typology of movement and its landing sites given by the A-/A-bar distinction (in its various recensions), but in a theory of grammar that holds
this typology to be derivative from the kind of features that are checked
in each position, the binding theory should not make reference to anything
but morphosyntactic features. Similar concerns also hold for the WCO Filter, with the additional note that guidelines of virtual conceptual necessity
actually necessitate an elimination of the account of WCO effects in terms
of filters, linearity conditions, and the like.

Furthermore, because the minimalist program conceives of movement
as a copying and deletion process, it is also necessary that the binding
theory exhibit a sensitivity to copies. Chomsky (1992:58) suggests that the
deletion of copies is different at each interface, for although PF rules delete
intermediate and tail copies as a matter of general rule, copy-deletion at LF
has a somewhat different character. Chomsky suggests that copy-deletion
at LF is driven to construct the operator–variable pair, and it targets for
deletion the referential parts of copies in operator positions. Because this
derives the effects of the P&P phenomenon of reconstruction, the binding
theory applies after such copy-deletion takes place. Finally, this deletion
being constrained by other convergence conditions, Chomsky chooses to
phrase the mechanism as a preference principle, as in (23):

(23)  PREFERENCE PRINCIPLE FOR RECONSTRUCTION
      Do it when you can, i.e., try to minimize the restriction on the
      operator position.

The binding theory I propose meets these constraints in a way that is
quite distinct from Chomsky's, in that I hold the binding theory to apply

before copy-deletion takes place. As discussed in chapters 4 and 6, I hold the legitimacy of A-bar binders to be determined by the kind of features they check, with the result that quantificational elements can never legitimately bind pronominal expressions inside the IP. The illegitimacy of WCO and SCO effects is traced to the fact that they involve such binding. Because nonquantificational A-bar elements and quantificational elements that have undergone covert raising from a Spellout A-bar position do not qualify as binders, coreferential uses of pronominals (in the sense of Reinhart 1986, 1991) with such nonquantificational elements is permitted.

This formulation completely eliminates the need for an independent phenomenon of 'reconstruction' for determining coreferential interpretations. As a consequence, it raises important questions about the mechanisms that induce the deletion of copies in the grammar. I argue in chapter 6 that copy-deletion is driven by the requirement to construct the *variable* part of a chain. My proposal that copy-deletion eliminates all intervening copies between the head and the lexical link of the chain allows for an elimination of special operations to construct the operator–variable pair, and facilitates a reformulation of Full Interpretation that does not give operator–variable constructions a special status in the economy of representation.

## 1.4   Organization

This book being as much about the theoretical status of XP-adjunction and the theories of binding and coreference in a minimalist UG as about the proper analysis of Hindi-Urdu scrambling, it is perhaps better to speak of its organization in terms of three distinct 'books' and to describe how each chapter contributes to a fuller understanding of our three central concerns.

Consider, first, how the study of the syntactic properties of scrambling proceeds. Chapter 2 initiates a characterization of scrambling as derived XP-adjunction by examining, in turn, whether scrambling can be uniformly characterized as either Case-driven NP-movement, WH-movement, topicalization, or S-structure QR. It demonstrates that scrambling does not share either the intrinsic motivation or locality constraints typical to either of these movements. In such a scenario, the fact that such scrambling appears to share in some of the binding properties of movements such as Case-driven NP-movement and WH-movement can, at best, be taken as a mandate for the reformulation of the binding theory itself. Chapters 3 and 4 can be seen as a consequence of an adoption of this strategy, where chapter 3 defines the basic structural configurations to which the binding theory makes reference and chapter 4 formulates a theory of binding and coreference that can explain coreference with XP-adjoined positions. Having thus removed the only obstacles to an analysis of scrambling as XP-adjunction, chapter 5 considers the motivations for this operation and why it must be necessarily overt. It argues scrambling to belong to the class of focus constructions. The chapter also provides a final argument for the independence of the scrambling operation, as it shows that the presuppositional interpretations of scrambled XPs arise as a consequence of the way rules of semantic interpretation interpret hierarchical positioning at LF, and not necessarily from their interpretation as topics.

The second 'book' contained herein is the one that discusses the status of derived XP-adjunction in a minimalist UG. One of the major proposals here is that derived XP-adjunction is an operation that is driven by the narrow concerns of formal feature checking like any other movement in the grammar. This book contains three distinct instances of feature-driven XP-adjunction: (i) dative-shift as the feature-checking of structural Case in a position broadly L-related to a VP-internal AGR-oP in chapter 3, (ii) X-self reflexive-licensing as agreement from a position broadly L-related to the functional head that bears the features of its antecedent in chapter 4, and (iii) the transmission of a [FOCUS] feature to Tns and $F^0$ by a category XP-adjoined to the TP/FP in chapter 5.

A major consequence of this assimilation of XP-adjunction to the morphosyntactic imperative system is that we must now necessarily assume a multiple typology of A-bar movement, not only with regard to motivations but also with regard to their behavior with respect to binding and reconstruction. The final section of chapter 2 initiates the discussion in this regard and claims there is actually nothing novel here, as the theory has always maintained an internal typology within A-bar movement. The apparent unification of the various A-bar movements being merely the construct of an external typological parameter, such as the L-relatedness distinction, my approach can also derive a similar clustering of properties by an identical reference. The real question, however, is whether we should choose to at all, as this typology has little more than a descriptive role in the grammar, and hence little status in minimalism. Chapter 6 demonstrates that it is indeed possible to eliminate references to this distinction in the grammar.

The 'book' that discusses and develops the theories of binding and coreference in a minimalist UG spans the last three chapters. Chapter 4 presents the basic proposals we make in this regard. The major argument here is for for a distinction between two kinds of coreference, where the coreference that is determined by syntactic binding lies in the domain of the binding theory, but the coreference that holds in its absence is the result of computations of a separate coreference component (Reinhart 1986, 1991, Reinhart and Grodzinsky 1993). The binding theory is proposed to be sensitive to the kind of formal features checked by the participants in coreferential usages determined by it, and incorporates within it the LF raising approach to pronominals and reflexives. The coreference module is shown to interact with the binding theory in allowing coreference with nonquantificational elements in L-bar positions.

As the objective is to eliminate references to the L/L-bar distinction from the grammar in general, and the binding theory in particular, the fact that I analyze dative shift as the checking of structural Case in a position broadly L-related to a VP-internal AGR-oP in chapter 3 problematizes the discussion. Indeed, this proposal demonstrates the inadequacy of substituting references to L-positions with reference to Case-checking positions. As a consequence, the binding theory in chapter 5 retains reference to the L/L-bar distinction, but as chapter 6 shows, a proper analysis of how the binding theory is affected by the analysis that IOs check Case in XP-adjoined positions shows that even allowing all Case positions to be binding positions does not pose significant problems for the empirical coverage of the binding theory. Chapter 6 speculates how the binding theory interacts with the principles of economy of representation and derivation and the theory of last resort deletion in the grammar. I show that the proposal that the deletion of copies is required to construct the tail of the chain provides for a unique definition of legitimate objects at the LF interface.

# Chapter 2

# Scrambling: Syntactic Properties

The mixed syntactic semantic properties of the leftward argument scrambling (henceforth simply scrambling) operation in languages such as Hindi-Urdu, Japanese and German pose significant problems for an adequate syntactic description, in terms of both the trigger for the operation as well as the landing site it targets. As the first chapter demonstrated, the fact that scrambling positively affects binding configurations by overriding WCO effects and licensing reflexives suggests that a characterization of it as Case-driven NP-movement is opportune, but the fact that it is also amenable to reconstruction suggests that the proper description should typologize scrambling with WH-movement or derived XP-adjunction. A consideration of the interpretive effects of the scrambling operation problematizes the description further, as scrambled constituents can exhibit the properties of topics or of such quantificational items as specific (in)definites, suggesting that scrambling may also need to be characterized as topicalization and/or an overt quantifier-raising operation.

The most pervasive reaction to these mixed properties of the scrambling operation has been based on the simplest possible hypothesis: If scrambling does not uniformly exhibit the properties of any one of the known movement types, it must *not* be a uniform operation. Mahajan (1990), for example, suggests that 'scrambling' is actually decomposable into (at least) two distinct operations of Case-driven NP-movement (argument shift) and adjunction to XP. The perception of scrambling as a distinct, mixed type of movement is therefore only an illusion—scrambled configurations where, for example, WCO effects are overridden are configurations in which scrambling-as-argument-shift has taken place, and configurations that show an amenability to reconstruction are the products of a scrambling-as-XP-adjunction operation.

Although an approach along the lines suggested by Mahajan has much to recommend itself, its very simplicity turns out to be problematic. Mahajan's proposals are almost entirely derived from an unquestioning acceptance of the typology of landing sites/movement types found in the literature. A naive use of this typology as a heuristic tool is, however, problematic, as standard formulations of it are insensitive to the way in which a cluster of properties associated with a particular landing site/movement enters the classification—either as an intrinsic property of the movement type or as a property that is usually correlated with the landing site targeted by that movement. An example from the traditional A-/A-bar typology makes the point clear: NP-movement is *intrinsically* a Case-driven movement to a Cased position, but the fact that this Cased position is also typically a position from which reflexive and pronominal binding can take place is only a *correlational* property—a consequence of the movement but not the reason why it is triggered. A use of a typology such as Mahajan's which equates the satisfaction of a correlational property with that of an intrinsic property, yields results in which intrinsically different movements are analyzed as belonging to a single class, as in the case of scrambling that, I will argue, does not share the same morphosyntactic imperative as either NP-movement or WH-movement.

It is therefore necessary that a diagnostic use of the typology of movement types distinguish between instances in which a movement meets the intrinsic typological properties of the movement type and when it meets just the correlational properties. The exclusive use of the intrinsic properties of a movement as the typological parameter not only identifies the necessary conditions a movement must satisfy but also keeps open the option that two intrinsically distinct movement types may share a set of correlational properties. That such an overlap is in fact needed is made evident by (1):

(1)  (a)  Himself$_i$ he$_i$ likes t$_i$

  (b)  The man$_i$ who$_i$ his$_i$ mother likes t$_i$

  (c)  It's him$_i$ that he$_i$ thinks that Mary likes t$_i$

  (d)  Who$_i$ did you speak with t$_i$ before his$_i$ wife could speak to t$_i$

As (1) shows, topicalization, appositive relatives, clefts, and parasitic gap constructions (Lasnik and Stowell 1991) share the correlational properties of the positions targeted by NP-movement in their immunity to WCO effects, even though the movement that derives them differs quite radically from NP-movement in its intrinsic properties.

Thus, in my view, a discussion of the syntactic properties of the scrambling operation must privilege the morphosyntactic imperative for a movement and the locality constraints that the satisfaction of that morphosyntactic imperative entails. This chapter provides evidence that scrambling does not share the intrinsic properties of NP-movement, WH-movement, topicalization, or overt quantifier raising. The series of negative propositions about the scrambling operation in the first four sections of the chapter is intended to simultaneously provide a characterization of scrambling as an XP-adjunction operation. The discussion in sections 2.1–4 therefore assumes a four-way distinction between the landing sites targeted by Move-α—Case checking specifier positions, [Spec, CP], [Spec, TopP], and XP-adjoined positions—rather than the two-way distinction implied by standard formulations of the A-/A-bar distinction. At first blush, however, this assumption appears to be flawed, for research has demonstrated that XP-adjoined, topic, and operator positions exhibit a clustering of shared properties. The concluding section of the chapter addresses this issue, and argues that in fact such a multiple typology of landing sites is not a novel contribution to the theory of grammar. I show that the binary typology assumed in the literature is actually the construction of an external typological parameter, and that the shared sets of correlational properties that a binary typology captures can equally easily be derived by my approach.

## 2.1   Scrambling Is Not NP-movement

One of the most influential sets of arguments to the effect that (some instances of) scrambling is Case-driven movement is that of Mahajan (1990). This section reviews Mahajan's proposals in some detail to demonstrate that there is no real empirical confirmation for the suggestion that scrambling shares the same intrinsic morphosyntactic imperative as Case-driven NP-movement. Once it is recognized that the evidence for the NP-movement analysis of scrambling derives crucially from the (often inconsistent) assumptions it makes about Case and agreement licensing in UG, scrambling must necessarily be considered a distinct movement type, and the fact that it shares some correlational properties with NP-movement must receive an explanation from elsewhere in the grammar. Chapter 4 locates this explanation in the reformulation of the binding theory.

### 2.1.1   Case, Agreement, and Scrambling

It will be apparent that a characterization of scrambling as argument shift crucially depends on the theory of Case-licensing/checking the analysis assumes. For Mahajan, the central concern is to ensure that the mechanisms that license Case (and verb agreement) in Hindi-Urdu are the ones that result in a flexibility of word order. The theory of Case and verb agreement he designs to meet this objective rests on three crucial assumptions. First, Mahajan assumes the articulated IP-structure of Chomsky (1989) and Pollock (1989) in (2), together with the attendant proposal that all structural Case is tied to the AGR system. Therefore, all arguments that need structural Case must move out of the VP to receive structural Case in the specifier positions of the functional projections internal to IP.

(2)

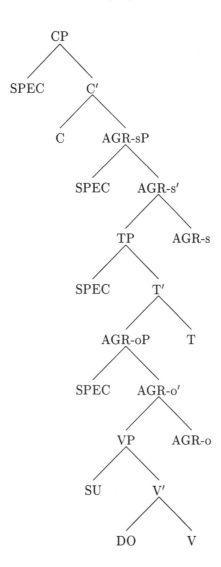

The next two assumptions weaken this strong position on Case-assignment. The first of these suggests that because the role that structural

Case plays in rendering NPs visible for θ-marking becomes relevant only at LF, the S-structure/Spellout Case requirements for arguments may well be weaker, as in (3). Mahajan (1990:99) suggests that lexical Case[1] or structural Case-assignment by the verb is sufficient for S-structure visibility:

(3)    (a)  S-STRUCTURE VISIBILITY
           Every NP must have a Case at S-structure. This Case may be lexical or structural.

       (b)  LF VISIBILITY
           Every NP (or every A-chain with a lexical NP) must have a structural Case.

An important consequence of these proposals is that any argument assigned lexical Case or structural Case by the verb may remain inside the VP at S-structure. S-structure movement out of the VP is compulsory only for those arguments that cannot receive structural/lexical Case inside the VP.

The second assumption that weakens the strict theory of Case-assignment of Chomsky (1989) is that even arguments bearing lexical or structural Case from the verb need to move to a VP-external functional projection by LF. This requirement is held to follow from a generalized view of Case-visibility, where only the Case assigned/licensed by functional heads is considered visible. Thus, at S-structure an argument bearing lexical Case or structural Case from the verb may move out of the VP, although the S-structure visibility condition does not force it to move, it does not proscribe it either. Moreover, because the LF condition requires that argument to be in such a VP-external position at LF, S-structure raising of lexically Case-marked arguments violates no principle of the grammar.[2]

These three assumptions come together to yield an analysis of Hindi-Urdu Case and verb agreement that allows some flexibility in linear order, as they allow an example such as (4) to have not one but two possible S-structure representations—the first, (4a), in which the lexically Case-marked subject raises to [Spec, AGR-sP] at S-structure, and the second, (4b), in which it stays in situ in [Spec,VP].[3]

(4)    (a)  rɑm-ne      roṭi        kʰɑy-i
            Ram(SU)     bread(DO)   ate-AGR
            MSG         FSG         FSG

            'Ram ate bread.'

       (b)  roṭi        rɑm-ne      kʰɑy-i
            bread(DO)   Ram(SU)     ate-AGR
            FSG         MSG         FSG

            'Ram ate bread.'

(5)

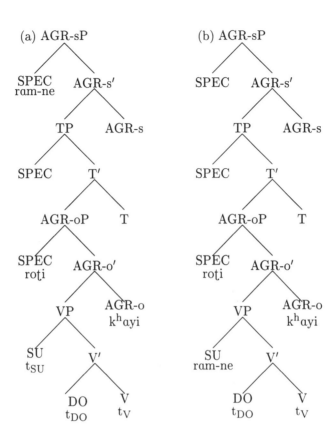

Mahajan suggests that in such instances of object agreement, the perfective participle is *not* a structural Case-assigner (it has the same form as the Hindi-Urdu passive participle), and therefore the DO cannot be assigned even an S-structure visible Case in its base position. To satisfy the S-structure Visibility Condition, the object in (5a) raises to [Spec, AGR-oP] for structural accusative Case, with verb raising to AGR-o accomplishing object-verb agreement. The subject of the clause, being lexically Case-marked, may move at S-structure to the specifier position of functional heads internal to IP, as in (5a). The proposal that the lexically Case-marked subject need not move at S-structure gives us (5b) as a word order variant of (5a).[4]

Only *genuine* Case-driven movement, however, is relevant for the binding theory, which applies at S-structure, because only those arguments that *must* move out of the VP to satisfy the S-structure Visibility condition count as binders. Mahajan (1990:100–6) presents the data in (6) and (7) as confirmation of this prediction:

(6)　kɔnsa　ləɽka$_i$　　Uski$_i$　mã-ne　　　gʰər-se　　　t$_i$　nɪkal　diya
　　　which　boy(DO)　his　　mother(SU)　house-from　　　　threw　gave
　　　'Which boy did his mother throw out of the house?'

(7)　kɔnsa　ləɽka$_i$　　Uski$_{*i}$　mã　　　　gʰər-se　　　t$_i$　nɪkal
　　　which　boy(DO)　his　　mother(SU)　house-from　　　　throw
　　　degi
　　　will give
　　　'Which boy will his mother throw out of the house?'

In (6), the DO cannot satisfy the S-structure Visibility Condition as it is not structurally Case-marked by the verb, because the predicate involved is a perfective participle. Therefore, it has to move to the [Spec, AGR-oP] position and from that position it can bind the pronominal embedded in the subject, because Cased positions are binding positions as well. On the other hand, in (7), the predicate *is* a structural Case-assigner, and so the movement of the DO cannot be for Case reasons. The fact that WCO effects persist despite scrambling demonstrates that the movement here must not be to a Cased position.

The proposals require further extension, given Mahajan's assumption that all arguments generated VP-internally move out to VP-external positions by LF. Consider (8):

(8)　(a)　Uski$_i$　bɛhen　　　kɪsko$_{*i}$　pyar　kərti　hɛ
　　　　　his　　sister(SU)　who(DO)　love　does　is
　　　　　'Who$_i$ does his$_i$ sister love?'

　　　(b)　kɪsko$_i$　　Uski$_i$　bɛhen　　　t$_i$　pyar　kərti　hɛ
　　　　　who(DO)　his　　sister(SU)　　love　does　is
　　　　　'Who$_i$ does his$_i$ sister love?'

The S-structure movement of the direct object to [Spec, AGR-oP] in (8) can be explained by the claim that -*ko* is a structural Case. But the S-structure movement of the subject is also required, as the subject needs nominative Case, and that can only be assigned in the AGR configuration. Thus, the subject too will have to move at S-structure. The two S-structure movements then result in the default word order of the subject and the DO, in that the subject will precede the DO. The question now is how the variant in (8b) comes about—the analysis so far is unable to explain its occurrence. In fact, to achieve the required results, Mahajan must add a *fourth* stipulation, by which the DO may move to a specifier position higher than [Spec, Agr-oP] after the assignment of its structural Case. For (8b), Mahajan proposes that the DO ultimately lands in [Spec, TP], yielding the S-structure in (9):[5]

(9)  [$_{TP}$ kɪsko$_i$ [$_{AGR-sP}$ ʋski bɛhen [$_{AGR-sP}$ t$_i'$ pyɑr kərti hɛ [$_{VP}$ t$_{SU}$ t$_i$ t$_v$]]]]

Now, even within Mahajan's own framework, it is less than clear what the structural Case motivation for this movement of the DO beyond [Spec, AGR-oP] is to be. If -ko is a structural Case assigned in the AGR-oP projection, only the movement to [Spec, Agr-oP] is Case-related; the movement to [Spec, TP] is not. And although it is true that Mahajan's system does not overtly proscribe this movement, it does prohibit the DO in [Spec, TP] from counting as a binder, because its Case requirements were already satisfied prior to its movement to [Spec, TP]. It is therefore unexpected that this configuration will be one in which WCO effects are overriden. Recall that (8b) is one of the core examples that the analysis sets out to explain, so Mahajan's proposals do not meet their own objectives, and with this failure, much of the motivation for the NP-movement analysis of scrambling simply dissolves.

A similar problem is posed by the empty functional projections that the NP-movement analysis of scrambling must countenance. For example, Mahajan argues that in (10b), the IO occupies a functional projection between the AGR-oP projection and the VP. Again, it is unclear what the Case-motivation for overt raising to these empty functional projections may be, but even if such movement is allowed, the positions targeted by definition cannot be binding positions. It is debatable whether this use of empty functional projections is in keeping with the desired objectives of the theory, and there can be little disagreement that it may result in an exponential blow-up of possible derivations available to the child.[6]

(10)  (a)  rɑjɑ-ne     ʋske$_i$    pɪtɑ-ko      kɔnsi   dɑsi$_{*i}$     lɔṭɑ di
           king(SU)    her      father(IO)   which  maid(DO)    returned
           'Which maid$_i$ did the king return to her$_{*i}$ father?'

      (b)  rɑjɑ-ne     kɔnsi   dɑsi$_i$      ʋske$_i$    pɪtɑ-ko       t$_i$  lɔṭɑ di
           king(SU)    which  maid(DO)    her      father(IO)          returned
           'Which maid$_i$ did the king return to her$_i$ father?'

Research has also brought into question the crosslinguistic validity of the NP-movement analysis of scrambling. As den Dikken and Mulder (1991) show, the fact that IOs in Dutch can be scrambled but not passivized is unexpected according to an analysis that attributes a unique motivation to both displacements. Bayer and Kornfilt (1994) show that scrambling out of German infinitivals cannot be characterized as movement for structural Case. Consider the data in (11):

(11) weil     Heinrich [den Wagen]$_i$ versprochen hat [PRO t$_i$ zu
     because Heinrich the  car      promised    has              to
     waschen]
     wash

'. . . because Heinrich has promised to wash the car.'

Bayer and Kornfilt point out that the Case-driven movement analysis of scrambling would force us to assume that the scrambled DO occupies the specifier of an AGR-oP projection in the matrix clause. As they demonstrate, such raising could never conform to the principles governing proper movement in the grammar: Because *zu* is not a proper governor, it cannot L-mark the VP of the embedded clause, where α L-marks β if and only if α is a lexical category that θ-governs β. The VP will then be a blocking category for movement and the infinitival AGR-sP dominating this VP will inherit barrierhood from it. Consequently, object raising across two barriers should be impossible. The only way in which such raising can be executed is by the use of either [Spec, CP] or adjunction to VP and IP as an escape-hatch, but then that would produce an A-chain that has one of its links in an A-bar position, a clear case of improper movement.

Moreover, in Hindi-Urdu there is really no empirical evidence that the Case and verb agreement checking system actually interacts with scrambling in any demonstrable fashion, outside the theory that Mahajan constructs. Scrambling appears to be entirely irrelevant for convergence with respect to Case checking in that there appear to be no cases in which only the scrambled order can converge. Scrambling also does not create new possibilities of verb agreement—for example, the left-scrambling of an unmarked DO does not trigger object-verb agreement, and in no cases is scrambling necessarily required for object-verb agreement. In fact, the evidence that Mahajan produces for this proposal is purely binding-theoretic, because he assumes a strict equivalence between binding and Cased positions. This evidence falls into two types: One shows that scrambling can affect coreference possibilities, and the other (putatively) demonstrates that scrambling does not fully reconstruct.

### 2.1.2  Scrambling, Binding, and Reconstruction

As observed in chapter 1, scrambling positions pattern with Cased positions in terms of their binding properties. Example (8), repeated next as (12), and example (13) show that scrambled DOs can license a bound possessive pronominal and a possessive reflexive in the subject argument:[7]

(12) (a) Uski$_i$ bɛhen kɪsko$_{*i}$ pyɑr kərti hɛ
      his sister(SU) who(DO) love does is
      'Who$_i$ does his$_i$ sister love?'

    (b) kɪsko$_i$ Uski$_i$ bɛhen t$_i$ pyɑr kərti hɛ
      who(DO) his sister(SU) love does is
      'Who$_i$ does his$_i$ sister love?'

(13) (a) *əpne$_i$ bəccõ-ne mohən$_i$-ko g$^h$ər–se nɪkɑl diyɑ
      self's children(SU) Mohan(DO) house-from threw gave
      (lit.)'Self's$_i$ children threw Mohan$_i$ out of the house.'

    (b) ?mohən$_i$-ko əpne$_i$ bəccõ-ne t$_i$ g$^h$ər–se nɪkɑl
      Mohan(DO) self's children(SU) house-from threw
      diyɑ
      gave
      (lit.)'Self's$_i$ children threw Mohan$_i$ out of the house.'

These facts constitute the primary evidence for the NP-movement analysis of scrambling. The assumption of an equivalence between binding and Cased positions is crucial here, as a binding position is held to uniquely identify a Cased position. As we have already seen in the discussion around (1), this is a potentially dangerous strategy as it equates a correlational property of NP-movement with an intrinsic one, and it would force Mahajan to claim that the topicalization, appositive relatives, clefts, and parasitic gap constructions are instances of NP-movement as they too do not exhibit WCO effects despite instantiating the classic WCO configuration.

In addition, there are at least three empirical problems with the claim that the examples in (12) and (13) count as sufficient evidence for an NP-movement analysis of scrambling. First of all, as (14) shows, scrambling can in fact license only the pure 'self' (possessive) reflexive but not the 'X-self' (complex) reflexives or the reciprocal:

(14) (a) *əpne$_i$(ɑp)-ne mohən$_i$-ko mɑrɑ
      self(SU) Mohan(DO) hit
      'Self hit Mohan.'

    (b) *mohən$_i$-ko əpne$_i$(ɑp)-ne t$_i$ mɑrɑ
      Mohan(DO) self(SU) hit
      'Self hit Mohan.'

    (c) *ek dusre$_i$-ne [mohən ɔr sitɑ]$_i$-ko mɑrɑ
      each other(SU) Mohan and Sita(DO) hit
      'Each other hit Mohan and Sita.'

(d) *[mohən ɔr sita]ᵢ-ko ek dusreᵢ-ne tᵢ mara
     Mohan and Sita(DO) each other(SU)    hit

'Each other hit Mohan and Sita.'

Mahajan's proposals do not have the means to account for this divergence between (14b–d) and (13b). In both cases, the verb is a perfective participle, so the DO should be in [Spec, AGR-oP], and therefore able to bind a complex reflexive or reciprocal in the subject in [Spec, VP]. In order to maintain the NP-movement analysis, then, something more needs to be said with regard to the differences between possessive and complex reflexives.

Second, it also appears that Mahajan misconstrues the data on syntactic pronominal binding in Hindi-Urdu. He assumes that possessive pronominals can be bound without exception by a c-commanding antecedent, irrespective of its grammatical function. This runs contrary to native speaker intuitions, because speaker judgments actually exhibit an *anti-subject orientation* of possessive pronominals (see also Gurtu 1985). For example, the DO possessive pronominal in (15) may never be bound by the subject (but may be freely coindexed with the IO):

(15)    (a)   sitaᵢ      Uski\*ᵢ/ⱼ kɪtabẽ     pəʈʰti hɛ
            Sita(SU)   her       books(DO)   reads   is

            'Sita reads his/her/\*her own books.'

      (b)   sitaᵢ-ne   ramⱼ-ko   Uski\*ᵢ/ⱼ/k kɪtabẽ      dĩ
            Sita(SU)   Ram(IO)   her        books(DO)   gave

            'Sita gave Ram his/her/\*her own books.'

These facts identify Hindi-Urdu to pattern with Norwegian and Danish (Hestvik 1992, Vikner 1985) rather than English. Therefore, if the scrambled DO in examples such as (12b) is in [Spec, TP], the NP-movement analysis must explain why it is not considered at par with a syntactic subject by the binding theory, in contravention of all current assumptions regarding the positions of subjects in UG.

Finally, a consequence of the claim that scrambling creates new binding configurations is that certain types of scrambling must be immune to reconstruction. For, if the leftward scrambled DO in, say, (12b) did reconstruct, we should obtain the same judgments for (12b) as we do for (12a). Mahajan claims that the binding judgments reflected in (16) confirm these predictions:

(16)    (a)   ramᵢ-ne    mohənⱼ-ko   əpniᵢ/ⱼ kɪtab     lɔʈai
            Ram(SU)   Mohan(IO)   self's    book(DO)   returned

            'Ramᵢ returned self'sᵢ/ⱼ book to Mohanⱼ.'

(b) $ram_i$-ne    $apni_{i/*j}$    $kitab_k$    $mohan_j$-ko    $t_k$   $lɔtai$
Ram(SU)   self's    book(DO)   Mohan(IO)     returned
'$Ram_i$ returned self's$_{i/*j}$ book to $Mohan_j$.'

(c) $apni_{i/*j}$    $kitab_k$    $ram_i$-ne    $mohan_j$-ko    $t_k$   $lɔtai$
self's      book(DO)   Ram(SU)   Mohan(IO)     returned
'$Ram_i$ returned self's$_{i/*j}$ book to $Mohan_j$.'

Example (16a) reflects a judgment in which the reflexive can be bound by
the subject as well as the IO, but when the DO is fronted over the IO,
as in (16b–c), the reflexive can only take the subject as an antecedent.
To achieve these interpretations under reconstruction, DO reconstruction
must be restricted to a position higher than the IO. This is possible only
if we assume that in (17), the LF representation of (16c), reconstruction is
possible only to the site of $t_1$, which is a variable, and not to the site of $t_2$,
which is the argument trace of the scrambled DO.

(17)   apni kitab [ram-ne $t_1$ mohan-ko $t_2$ lɔtai]

The problem with (16) is that speakers do not accept Mahajan's judgments
regarding the binding of the reflexive by the IO. Hindi-Urdu speakers enforce a strict subject-orientation of reflexives to begin with in (16a). For
these speakers, the examples in (16) actually capture the intuition that
scrambling in Hindi-Urdu undergoes full reconstruction, as all the examples
in (16) receive only the one interpretation where the reflexive obligatorily
corefers with the subject argument. In fact, with the exception of the cases
represented by (12b) and (13b), speakers are unanimous that scrambling
undergoes full reconstruction.

    To conclude, this section demonstrates that an analysis of scrambling as
an intrinsically Case-driven operation is fraught with serious problems of
execution as well as tenability—not only is there no independent empirical
corroboration for the claims that are made, but the internal inconsistencies
forced by the assumption of a Case-motivation result in a situation in which
the analysis fails to meet its own objectives. Even the erroneous assumption of a strict identity between A-binding positions and Cased positions
does not conclusively corroborate the proposals, as the binding-theoretic
evidence for scrambling as NP-movement actually reduces to two isolated
cases in which scrambling has the ability to override WCO effects and license possessive reflexives. In other areas, the binding-theoretic evidence
in fact positions itself against an NP-movement analysis of scrambling. In
the face of such a chorus of problems, it would be more prudent to aban-
don the NP-movement analysis altogether and look for explanations for the
exceptional facts in other areas of the grammar, such as the theory of binding and reconstruction. I return to these issues in chapter 4, so putting the

matter aside for the moment, let us continue the description of the syntactic properties of the scrambling operation.

## 2.2   Scrambling Is Not WH-movement

The conclusion that scrambling does not target argument positions suggests it to be substitution into [Spec, CP] or adjunction to XP. Under a typology that assumes both XP-adjoined positions and [Spec, CP] to share the set of binding properties, each instance where scrambling overrides WCO effects, licenses reflexives, and resists reconstruction counts as evidence against an analysis of scrambling as either WH-movement or derived XP-adjunction. I, however, hold that a unitary characterization of A-bar positions is erroneous, and following Müller and Sternefeld (1993, 1994a, 1994b) (henceforth MS) assume that the landing sites of scrambling must necessarily differ from those targeted by WH-movement, topicalization, or NP-movement, all of which involve substitution into [Spec, XP].

MS's proposals for scrambling as XP-adjunction are articulated within the theory of improper movement in UG. MS suggest that derived XP-adjunction and substitution into the specifier of an operator position are distinguished between by the theory of movement. They propose that proper movement in UG is constrained by the *Principle of Unambiguous Binding* (PUB), by which chains that involve movement from one type of A-bar position to another type of A-bar position are barred (MS 1994a:17):

(18)   PRINCIPLE OF UNAMBIGUOUS BINDING
       A variable that is $\alpha$-bound must be $\beta$-free in the domain of the
       head of its chain (where $\alpha$ and $\beta$ refer to different types of
       A-bar positions).

The NP-movement properties of the scrambling operation listed in the previous section then count as evidence against a WH-movement analysis of the phenomenon. In many languages, the two types of movement diverge significantly in their observance of locality constraints. On the one hand, languages such as German, in (19), allow WH-movement to take a WH-phrase unboundedly far from its base position but restrict scrambling to within the clause; on the other, languages such as Russian, in (20), allow scrambling to be unbounded and force WH-movement to be clause bound.

(19)   (a)   *daß  niemand  [vp Pudding$_i$  sagt  [cp t$_i$'  daß  sie  t$_i$
             that  nobody        pudding     says         that she
             mag]]
             likes

             'That nobody says that she likes pudding.'

(b) [$_{CP}$ Was$_i$ sagt niemand [$_{CP}$ t$_i'$ daß sie t$_i$ mag]]
What says nobody             that she     likes

'What does nobody say that she likes?'

(20) (a) *[$_{CP}$ kto$_i$ stranno [$_{CP}$ t$_i'$ čto t$_i$ nam pomogal]
who is odd               that us helped

'It is odd that who helped us?'

(b) on skazal [$_{CP}$ čto [$_{IP}$ Petrov$_i$ [$_{IP}$ stranno [$_{CP}$ čto
he said          that     Petrov       is odd         that

t$_i$ nam pomogal]]]]
us  helped

'He said that it is odd that Petrov helped us.'

Hindi-Urdu also preserves this pattern. Whereas WH-scope, as (21) shows, is strictly clause-bound in tensed clauses, scrambling, as (22) shows, can cross tensed boundaries:

(21) nur-ko pəta hɛ ki sita kyū ayegi
Noor   knows is that Sita why  will come

'Noor knows why Sita will come.'

≠ 'Why does Noor know Sita will come?'

(22) nur-ko$_i$    mɛ̃ janti hū̃, tUm səb log   t$_i$ bəhət pyar
Noor(DO) I    know am  you all people     lot  love
kərte ho
do   are

'Noor, I know, all of you love a lot.'

This difference in the locality restrictions on scrambling and WH-movement argues that the two cannot target the same landing site of [Spec, CP]. Assuming scrambling to be adjunction to XP and WH-movement to be substitution into [Spec, CP], scrambling in German cannot be long distance because it cannot use [Spec, CP] as an escape-hatch. Long scrambling is possible in Russian because it allows adjunction to CP in the course of a derivation.[8] As WH-movement in Russian cannot proceed successive cyclically, nor can it proceed via adjunction to CP because of the PUB, (20a) is illegitimate. In Hindi-Urdu, the locality constraints on WH-raising at LF have been argued by Dayal (1997) to follow from the fact that finite clauses are extraposed adjuncts and therefore barriers to WH-extraction at LF. Scrambling is allowed out of the same contexts presumably because Hindi-Urdu is similar to Russian in that it allows adjunction to CP in the course of long-distance movement.[9]

The third type of evidence against an analysis of scrambling as WH-movement is the fact that in languages such as German the scrambling of WH-phrases as well as focused phrases is strictly forbidden:

(23) *ich weiß nicht [CP wem$_j$ [IP was$_i$ [IP der Fritz t$_j$ t$_i$
     I    know not       whom     what      the   Fritz

     gesagt hat]]]
     said    has

     'I don't know what Fritz has said to whom.'

(24) *ich glaube [CP daß [IP einer ELEPHANTEN$_i$ [ein
     I     believe      that     an    elephant       a

     Eingeborenor t$_i$ sah]]]
     native       saw

     'I believe that a native saw an ELEPHANT.'

MS use the argument that both focused items and WH-phrases must be in [Spec, CP] at LF to assimilate the violations in (23) and (24) to a PUB account. The scrambling of these operators is prohibited because the chain formed after the LF raising of the operators will violate the PUB, as it will be a WH-chain with one of its links in an adjoined position.

MS are aware that the use of this final argument against an analysis of scrambling as WH-movement may be problematic for such languages as Hindi-Urdu, which, as (25) shows, allows free scrambling of both WH-phrases and foci:

(25)   (a) kıski kıtab$_i$     nur-ne     sita-ko    t$_i$   di     t$^h$i
           whose book(DO) Noor(SU) Sita(IO)      gave   was

           'Whose book did Noor give Sita?'

       (b) ye   kıtab-hi$_i$         nur-ne     sita-ko    t$_i$   di     t$^h$i
           this book-EMPH(DO) Noor(SU) Sita(IO)      gave   was

           'Noor gave Sita THIS BOOK.'

Recall that UG requires all WH-phrases crosslinguistically to be in [Spec, CP] at LF. This would yield an LF representation for (25a) to be the one in (26), one immediately recognizable as a configuration in which a PUB violation should obtain, because the chain of the WH-phrase in [Spec, CP] will contain a link in an adjoined position:

(26) [CP [kıski kıtab]$_i$ [IP t$_i$' [IP nur-ne sita-ko t$_i$ di]]]

Contrary to this prediction, (25a), and its Japanese and Korean analogues, is perfectly grammatical. MS suggest that the difference between these languages and German lies in the fact that "the PUB only restricts the operation Form-Chain, so that the S-structure part of a chain will not be checked again in the course of LF-movement" (MS 1994b:23). MS (1993:507) term such a PUB as *nonprojective*, whereas a PUB that 'checks' overt movement even at LF is termed *projective*. A nonprojective PUB is impervious to S-structure movement, and considers the intermediate trace in (26) to be the 'foot' of the operator chain formed by LF-movement, in which chain no PUB violation obtains.[10]

Although I continue to use the term PUB in the discussion that follows, it is worth speculating about its status in the minimalist program. It appears that this concept of (non)projectivity of the PUB cannot be maintained within minimalism, as it essentially parametrizes what is basically conceived as an economy of derivation principle so that it holds in only a local rather than a global sense. The PUB cannot therefore be incorporated into the minimalist program merely in terms of a reformulation of it as a derivational principle that bars upward movement from one type of A-bar position to another (MS 1994a:18).

I suggest that the minimalist implementation of the PUB is an economy of representation principle. Specifically, assume that it reduces to the Chain Uniformity Condition of Chomsky and Lasnik (1993), by which a legitimate chain at LF must be uniform with respect to the property of L-relatedness. A position is narrowly L-related if it is the specifier or complement of, and broadly L-related if it is adjoined to, a lexical head L or of any of the functional head(s) associated with L. Other positions, such as [Spec, CP], are non–L-related. By the Chain Uniformity Condition, an argument chain is a legitimate LF object because it consists of only L-related positions, but a chain that involves raising from a broadly L-related position to a non–L-related position or vice versa is illegitimate; both results that closely mimic the effects of the PUB.

If this reallocation of the effects of the PUB is licit, the suggestions of Chomsky and Lasnik (1993) with regard to the role of deletion in constructing legitimate LF objects indicate the means by which the difference between languages that have WH-scrambling and those that do not can be captured. According to Chomsky and Lasnik, deletion is a last resort operation that may be performed with the intent of deriving a legitimate object (from an otherwise illegitimate one) at the interface. Deletion of a link of a chain is therefore permissible if the chain is nonuniform and the deletion does not violate general principles of the recoverability of deletion. Applying this to the matter at hand, in languages with overt scrambling and covert WH-movement, the resultant chain at the LF interface will always be a nonuniform chain, as it will be a chain headed by an item in [Spec, CP] (= the covert part of the chain) with an intermediate link in an XP-adjoined position (= the overt part of the chain). It will therefore be a chain in which the deletion of the link in the adjoined position will always meet the last resort requirement on deletion. Assuming as given that the deletion of the XP-adjoined link does not violate principles constraining the recoverability of deletion, the link in the XP-adjoined position will delete, yielding a uniform chain. Thus, WH-scrambling in languages such as Japanese and Hindi-Urdu is perfectly licit.

The situation in languages such as German is different. Intuitively, the crucial distinction between it and languages such as Hindi-Urdu is that in German, WH-movement is an overt operation, i.e., is driven by the morphosyntactic imperative of checking a [strong] feature of $C^0$. WH-scrambling in simple questions will always fail convergence conditions at the PF interface, as movement to an XP-adjoined position will not serve Greed. The question of uniformity only arises in multiple WH-questions such as (23), where MS use the notion of a projective PUB to explain why the WH- in situ cannot scramble. As will be apparent, our reinterpretation of the PUB in terms of the Chain Uniformity Condition does not yield the same conclusions as those of MS, as WH-scrambling in this German context followed by covert raising to [Spec, CP] will yield a nonuniform chain in which deletion of the offending link should well be possible.

Although it is a standard assumption that the WH- in situ in overt WH-movement languages raise to [Spec, CP] at LF, Reinhart (1994) argues that minimalist assumptions indicate it to be a flawed one. She suggests that the evidence that was formerly taken to indicate that WH-movement at LF is immune to Subjacency must actually be construed to signify that WH- in situ in overt WH-movement languages do not in fact raise to [Spec, CP] at LF, and receive their scopal interpretations in situ. Stepping away from the debate on the syntactic mechanisms by which these interpretations accrue to the WH-phrase (unselective binding, absorption, raising the WH-determiner alone, etc.), consider only the disruptive effect that overt WH-scrambling will have on the configuration in which the in situ WH-phrase would normally be accorded its operator interpretation—as it will not be in situ, it will not be accorded the status of an operator, thereby violating Full Interpretation. WH-scrambling in an overt WH-movement language will then also create an illegitimate LF object, but the locus of the violation will be Full Interpretation rather than the Chain Uniformity Condition.

In conclusion, this section has argued that scrambling does not target [Spec, CP] because even as it does exhibit some properties typically associated with the position, the divergence in the properties of the two movement types suggests that scrambling targets a distinct landing site from WH-movement. In addition, it is obvious that both the optionality of the scrambling operation as well as its obligatory overtness require an analysis that distinguishes it from WH-movement. Then, if scrambling shares neither the properties of NP-movement nor those of WH-movement, the claim that it is best analyzed as XP-adjunction is strengthened but not yet made conclusive. A frequent observation in the literature is that scrambling is one of the information-packaging strategies available in discourse (Gambhir 1981), which induces topical and presuppositional readings of the scrambled XPs. It is therefore worth considering whether scrambling (to the sentence-initial position at least) is actually topicalization. The next section shows that despite the similar presuppositional interpretation accorded to topics and scrambled XPs, scrambling does not share the syntactic properties of topicalization.

## 2.3   Scrambling Is Not Topicalization

It is by now quite standard in linguistic theory to analyze topicalization as left-adjunction to IP (Baltin 1982, Culicover and Rochemont 1991, Lasnik and Saito 1992). If the thesis that scrambling is also adjunction to XP (where XP may well be IP) is also maintained, this indicates an overlap between scrambling and topicalization in both structural and functional terms. This is actually not the case, because scrambling and topicalization differ quite substantially in their syntactic properties.

First, although scrambling is iterable within a clause, topicalization may take place only once in the same domain. The Japanese examples in (27) and (28) demonstrate this fact:

(27)   naihu-de$_i$   Bill-o$_j$   John-ga     t$_j$  t$_i$  sasista
        knife-with   Bill-ACC   John-NOM              stabbed

    'John stabbed Bill with a knife.'

(28)   *naihu-wa   Bill-wa    John-ga    sasista
        knife-TOP   Bill-TOP   John-NOM   stabbed

    'John stabbed Bill with a knife.'

If both scrambling and topicalization involve adjunction to IP, there is no explanation for this asymmetry.

Second, as the English examples in (29) show, topicalization typically creates a 'topic island' effect for further topicalization and/or WH-movement out of the clause that contains the topic.

(29)   (a)   *What$_i$ do you think [$_{CP}$ t$_i$' that [$_{IP2}$ for Ben's car [$_{IP1}$ Mary will pay t$_i$]]]

        (b)   *That man$_i$ we know [$_{CP}$ t$_i$' that [$_{IP2}$ this book$_j$ [$_{IP1}$ Mary gave t$_j$ to t$_i$]]]

If scrambling were also adjunction to IP, it should also induce island effects for subsequent WH-movement/topicalization/scrambling. The very iterability of scrambling gives the lie to this prediction, as does the example in (30) from German, in which scrambling the DO does not affect the extractability of an adjunct by (long) WH-movement—and this in a language in which topicalization behaves exactly as in English in inducing topic island effects (MS 1993:481).

(30) Wie$_i$ meinst du [$_{CP}$ t$_i$′ daß dieser Frau$_j$      [$_{IP}$ der
     how think you      that this woman-ACC      the
     Ede t$_i$ t$_j$ geholfen hat]]
     Ede      helped has
     'How do you think that Ede helped this woman?'

Third, in the Germanic languages, topicalization but not scrambling is correlated with verb raising in a positive way as demonstrated by the German examples:

(31)   (a) Ich glaube [$_{CP}$ den Fritz$_i$      mogen$_j$ [$_{IP}$ viele t$_i$ t$_j$]]
       I believe    the Fritz-ACC like      many
       'I believe that many people like Fritz.'

    (b) *[$_{IP}$ den Fritz$_i$      mogen$_j$ [$_{IP}$ viele t$_i$ t$_j$]]
       the Fritz-ACC like      many
       'Many people like Fritz.'

Fourth, it is a widespread phenomenon that topicalization blocks clause-bound WH-movement. Scrambling, again, does not pattern with topicalization in this regard. Consider the German examples in (32):

(32)   (a) *Warum$_i$ den Fritz$_j$      hat diese Frau      t$_i$ t$_j$
       why      the Fritz-ACC has this woman
       geküßt?
       kissed
       'Why has this woman kissed Fritz?'

    (b) Was$_i$ hat dem Fritz$_j$      diese Frau      t$_j$ t$_i$
       What has the Fritz-DAT this woman
       geschenkt?
       given
       'What has this woman given Fritz?'

Fifth, topicalization appears to be more context-bound than scrambling. For example, consider the fact that embedded topicalization, in (33a), is prohibited in CP complements of nonbridge verbs (i.e., predicates that fail to L-mark their complements), but scrambling, in (33b), is possible in the very same contexts [MS 1993:483–84]):

(33)  (a) *Ich bedaure [CP den Fritzᵢ    mag [IP jeder    tᵢ]]
          I   regret      the Fritz-ACC likes     everyone

          'I regret that everyone likes Fritz.'

      (b) Ich bedaure [CP daß [IP dem Fritzᵢ      [IP diese
          I   regret      that   the Fritz-DAT        this
          Frau  tᵢ ein Buch gibt]]]
          woman   a  book gave

          'I regret that this woman gave Fritz a book.'

Sixth, scrambling appears to obey different locality constraints than those observed by topicalization. As the examples in (34) show, scrambling in German is clause-bound but topicalization is not:

(34)  (a) *daß niemand [VP Puddingᵢ sagt [CP daß sie tᵢ
          that nobody      pudding  says     that she
          mag]]
          likes

          'That nobody says that she likes pudding.'

      (b) Puddingᵢ glaube ich [CP daß sie tᵢ mogen wurde]
          pudding  believe I      that she    like  would

          'Pudding, I believe that she would like.'

Although I return to the matter shortly, let us assume that topicalization targets a substitution position [Spec, TopP], whereas scrambling is adjunction to XP. The differences between the two movements then follows from the PUB, as they target two distinct A-bar landing sites.[11]

In Hindi-Urdu as well, it can be argued that scrambling is distinct from topicalization, once it is recognized that Hindi-Urdu topics are morphologically marked by the particle *-to* and topicalization is a covert operation that targets [Spec, TopP]. The rest of this section is devoted to a description of Hindi-Urdu topicalization and a demonstration that in Hindi-Urdu as well, topicalization and scrambling exhibit radical asymmetries.

### 2.3.1  Hindi-Urdu *-to* Topicalization

#### The Distribution of *-to*

In terms of distribution, examples (35)–(37) show that the particle *-to* can attach to any maximal projection of a lexical category (DPs, PPs, VPs) but generally cannot be inserted 'inside' that maximal projection:[12, 13]

(35)  (a)  [$_{DP}$ meri   kɑli    kɪtɑb]-**to**   mɪl    gəyi
           my    black   book-TOP   found   went

      'My black book was found.'

      (b)  *[$_{DP}$ meri [$_{AP}$ kɑli-**to**] kɪtɑb]...

      (c)  ??[$_{DP}$ meri-**to** [$_{DP}$ kɑli kɪtɑb]]...

(36)  (a)  rɑm   [$_{VP}$ kɪtɑb   pəʈʰ-**to**]   rəhɑ    hɛ]
           Ram        book    read-TOP   PROG    is

      'Ram is reading a book.'

      (b)  *rɑm [$_{VP}$kɪtɑb pəʈʰ [$_{VP}$ rəhɑ-**to**] hɛ]

      (c)  ??rɑm [$_{VP}$kɪtɑb pəʈʰ rəhɑ hɛ]-**to**

(37)  (a)  sitɑ  [$_{PP}$  nur-ke-pɑs]-**to**       gəyɪ
           Sita        Noor-GEN-near-TOP     went

      'Sita went to Noor.'

      (b)  *sitɑ [$_{PP}$ [$_{DP}$nur-**to**-ke]] pɑs gəyɪ

      (c)  ??sitɑ [$_{PP}$ [$_{DP}$nur-ke-**to**]] pɑs gəyɪ

Following Bayer (1996) and Rothstein (1991), I will assume that particles such as *-to* are "minor" functional heads, which even as they subcategorize, do not have θ-grids or bind θ-positions or project category features. XP-*to* will then instantiate the configuration [$_{XP}$ XP PRT].

### The Semantics of *-to*

The most obvious interpretive consequence of marking an XP with *-to* is that it introduces the presupposition that the interlocutors in the discourse share in the knowledge of the referent of XP-*to*. Thus, in an example such as (38), *Ram-to* can be employed only when either the existence of Ram has already been mentioned in the discourse preceding the utterance of (38), or when the knowledge of the referent of *Ram* is assumed by the speaker to be shared by the hearer:

(38)  rɑm-to      ɑyegɑ
      Ram-TOP    will come

      'Ram will come.'

   Example (38) is particularly infelicitous as a discourse-initial utterance, or when the speaker cannot presume a shared knowledge of the referent of XP-*to*. In this sense, then, XP-*to* must be "old information," either aged discursively, or presumed old; in short, XP-*to* is interpreted as a topic.

The only potential problem with such a simple characterization of *-to* as a topic marker is that a sentence such as (38) is actually ambiguous out of context between a thematic and a contrastive reading in (39) and (40), respectively:

(39) ram-to    kəl       ayega
     Ram-TOP  tomorrow  will come
     'Ram will come tomorrow.'

(40) ram-to    ayega,   ɔr   koi   aye-na-aye
     Ram-TOP  will come  else  any  come-not-come
     'RAM will come, whether anybody else comes or not.'

Similar contrastive/thematic readings are available to PPs and VPs marked with *-to*. Consider the two readings available to each instance of PP-*to* and VP-*to* in (41) and (42), where the (a) examples instantiate the thematic reading and the (b) examples, the contrastive one:

(41)  (a) mina   nur-ke-pas-to        kəl      jayegi
           Meena  Noor-GEN-near-TOP  tomorrow  will go
           'Meena will go to Noor tomorrow.'

      (b) mina   nur-ke-pas-to        gəyɪ   pər  ʊske  sat$^h$  rɛh
           Meena  Noor-GEN-near-TOP  went,  but  her  with  stay
           nəhĩ  payɪ
           not    could
           'Meena did go to NOOR, but couldn't stay with her.'

(42)  (a) kyũ  naraz  ho  rəhe    ho,  nur   kɪtab  pəʈ$^h$-to
           why  angry  be  PROG  be,  Noor  book  read-TOP
           rəhi  hɛ
           PROG  is
           'Why are you getting angry? Noor IS reading a book.'

      (b) nur  kɪtabẽ  pəʈ$^h$ti-to    hɛ,  pər  səməj$^h$ti    nəhĩ  hɛ
           Noor  books  reads-TOP  is,  but  understands  not  is
           'Noor READS books but doesn't UNDERSTAND them.'

A consideration of the Japanese topic particle *-wa*, however, suggests that this semantic ambiguity could very well be characteristic of topic particles in general, because *-wa* also exhibits this variation between a thematic and contrastive use (Kuno 1973, Miyagawa 1987). Thematic *-wa* DPs or NPs must be either referential or generic, whereas contrastive DP/NP/PP-*wa* need not be. Hindi-Urdu *-to* topics also exhibit the same properties. Examples (43)–(46) from Japanese and Hindi-Urdu exemplify the close correspondence between the uses of the two particles:

(43)   (a) jon-wa        hon-o       yonda
           John-TOP    book-ACC    read

           'As for John, he read a book.' (*thematic*)

       (b) jɔn-to        kɪtab    pəɽʰta   hɛ
           John-TOP    book    reads    is

           'As for John, he reads books.' (*thematic*)

(44)   (a) kujira-wa       hongyu-doobutsu    desu
           whales-TOP    mammals              are

           'Whales are mammals.' (*thematic*)

       (b) kutte-to       wəfadar    hote       hɛ̃
           dogs-TOP     faithful    be-HAB    are

           'Dogs are faithful.' (*thematic*)

(45)   (a) ame-wa       futteimasu-ga,   yuki-wa        futteimasen
           rain-TOP    falling but       snow-TOP    not-falling

           'It's raining but it isn't snowing.' (*contrastive*)

       (b) barɪš-to     ho    rəhi     hɛ,    pər    ole          nəhĩ    pəɽ
           rain-TOP    be    PROG    is,    but    hail stones    not    fall
           rəhe    hɛ̃
           PROG   is

           'It's raining, but there's no hail.' (*contrastive*)

(46)   koi-to            aya
       someone-TOP    came

       '*As for someone, he came.' (*thematic*)

       'At least someone came.' (*contrastive*)

Examples (43), (44) and (45) show that topicalization is possible with referential and generic DPs. Example (46) demonstrates that -*to*-marked quantificational DPs cannot receive a thematic reading because they are not referential, and may be accorded only the contrastive interpretation.

Miyagawa (1987) suggests that a unified semantic analysis of the thematic and contrastive usage of the topic particle -*wa* (and by extension -*to*) is possible according to the view that these two distinct semantic usages spring from its property of *set-anaphoricity*. That is, -*wa* refers to the shared knowledge between the speaker and the hearer "of an identifiable set of individuals in the immediate conversational context" (Miyagawa 1987:188). A consequence of this property -*wa* has of referring to sets rather than individuals is that given a -*wa* phrase, every member of the shared set must somehow be exhaustively represented by it. If a referential/generic DP is *-wa/-to* marked, and if that NP exhaustively represents each member of the discursively determined shared set, the result is a thematic use of *DP-wa/-to*. On the other hand, if only a portion of the set is picked out referentially, "the only way for remaining member(s) of the set to 'become involved' is to have the one picked out contrasted (exhaustively) with every other member of the set. In other words, by picking out a portion of the set referentially, that portion gains the relation IS IN CONTRAST TO with every other set member, thereby making it possible for all the members to be exhaustively represented even though a subset is referentially picked out" (Miyagawa 1987:197).

As an example of how Miyagawa's semantic analysis works, consider once again example (38), which we have seen is ambiguous between the readings in (47a) and (47b):

(47)  (a)  As for Ram, he will come.

  (b)  At least Ram will come.

In Miyagawa's framework, the set that the topic marker *-to* in (40) refers to, on the thematic reading in (47a), is a single-membered set [*Ram*]. Now, *Ram-to* exhaustively represents each (in this case, the single) member of this contextually shared set, and because it is also a referential DP, the thematic reading is the most salient. In (47b), on the other hand, the contextually shared set contains at least one other member besides Ram [*Ram, person X*]. The topic particle only referentially picks out one member of the set, i.e., *Ram*, and because all members of a topic particle set require representation, the only way *person X* can be represented is by the establishment of the relation IS IN CONTRAST TO between members of the set and the DP referentially picked out by the topic particle. Hence, the contrastive reading is most salient in (47b).

**The Syntax of *-to***

If the availability of the contrastive reading of XP-*to* poses no problems for its analysis as a topic particle, then the simplest possible syntactic analysis is that *-to* topicalization is a covert analogue of the overt operation involved in German, English, and Japanese topicalization. Maintaining this analysis is not, however, a straightforward task, for not only do we have to garner empirical confirmation that XP-*to* topics share the syntactic properties of overtly moved topics, we also have to simultaneously identify the landing site that topicalization (overt or covert) targets.

The first task is readily accomplished. For example, topicalization in Hindi-Urdu takes place just once in a clause, as shown by (48b–c).[14, 15]

(48)  (a) ram-to       kɪtabẽ  pəʈʰta  hɛ
          Ram-TOP      books   reads   is
          'Ram, he reads books.'

     (b) *ram-to       kɪtabẽ-to     pəʈʰta  hɛ
          Ram-TOP      books-TOP     reads   is
          'Ram, books, he reads them.'

     (c) *ram-to       kɪtabẽ  pəʈʰta-to     hɛ
          Ram-TOP      books   reads-TOP     is
          'Ram, he does read books.'

Scrambling in Hindi-Urdu, on the other hand, is iterable, as (49) shows:

(49)  ye     kɪtabᵢ       ram-koⱼ     sita-ne     tⱼ  tᵢ  di
      this   book(DO)     Ram(IO)     Sita(SU)            gave
      'This book to Ram, Sita gave.'

   Second, the occurrence of a -to topic creates a topic island for LF WH-
movement in Hindi-Urdu, as shown by (50). In contrast, scrambling in (51)
does not affect the LF extraction of a WH-phrase or a -to topic.

(50)  *sita  [ənjum-ki-gaʈi-ke-liye-to]   kɪtna       pɛsa     degi
       Sita   Anjum-car-for-TOP           how much    money    will give
      'How much money [for Anjum's car] will Sita pay?'

(51)  [ənjum-ki-gaʈi-ke-liye]ᵢ      sita  tᵢ   kɪtna/pɛsa-to
      Anjum-GEN-car-GEN-for         Sita       how much/money-TOP
      degi
      will give
      'How much will Sita give for Anjum's car?'
      'Money, Sita will give for Anjum's car.'

   Third, as (52) shows, the occurrence of a -to topic blocks clause-bound
WH-movement in Hindi-Urdu:

(52)  *kɪsne  sita-ko     kɪtab-to     di
       who    Sita(IO)    book-TOP     gave
      'Who gave the book to Sita?'

In fact (53a) shows that, just as in German and English, WH-phrases can
never be topicalized in Hindi-Urdu, indicating that an analysis that accords
an identity of landing sites to WH-movement and topicalization is in order.
However, then the fact that both WH-phrases and topics may be scrambled, in (53b–c), runs counter to this analysis, as this data suggests that
scrambling is quite distinct from both topicalization and WH-movement.

(53) (a) *kɔn-to    ayega
         who-TOP   will come

         'Who will come?'

     (b) kitab-to$_i$      ram       t$_i$  layega
         book-TOP(DO)   Ram(SU)       will bring

         'The book, Ram will bring.'

     (c) kisko$_i$      ram       t$_i$  layega
         who(DO)     Ram(SU)       will bring

         '(lit.) Who, Ram will bring?'

Fourth, Hindi-Urdu embedded *-to* topicalization is only licensed by verbs
that L-mark their CP complements. As shown by (54), in contexts in which
this requirement is not met, topicalization is prohibited.

(54) (a) mina   janti   hε  [$_{CP}$ ki    sita-to    ayegi]
         Meena  knows   is        that  Sita-TOP   will come

         'Meena knows that Sita will come.'

     (b) *mina-ko    dʊkʰ   hε  [$_{CP}$ ki    sita-to    ayegi]
         Meena-DAT  sorrow  is       that  Sita-TOP   will come

         'Meena is sad that Sita will come.'

Again, Hindi-Urdu scrambling in (55) diverges sharply in this regard, as it
is completely insensitive to the nature of the embedding predicate.

(55) (a) mε̃  janti   hũ  [$_{CP}$ kitab$_i$    ram-ne    kɪse    t$_i$
         I    know   am        book(DO)  Ram(SU)   who(IO)

         di]
         gave

         'I know who Ram gave the book to.'

     (b) mʊjʰe   dʊkʰ   hε  [$_{CP}$ ki    kitab$_i$    ram-ne
         me-DAT  sorrow  is       that  book(DO)  Ram(SU)

         tumhε̃   t$_i$  nəhĩ  di]
         you-DAT       not   gave

         'I am sorry that Ram didn't give you this book.'

Let us then conclude that scrambling and topicalization in Hindi-Urdu also
target different landing sites. On the basis of the crosslinguistic evidence
presented in this section, it appears that it must be scrambling that targets
an XP-adjunction site—the facts that scrambling is iterable, unaffected by
embedding context, and does not trigger V-2 in Germanic are best explained

under an XP-adjunction account. Topicalization, on the other hand, appears to target a specifier position inside the CP projection, given the asymmetries between it and WH-movement. Conceptually such an analysis is very attractive because it would yield a simultaneous explanation for the asymmetries between topicalization and WH-movement on the one hand and topicalization and scrambling on the other. Such an analysis presents itself in the work of MS (1993), discussed in the next subsection.

### 2.3.2 Analyzing Topicalization: MS (1993)

The primary justification for a unified analysis of WH-movement and topicalization lies in the complementary distribution between the two movements and the fact that the two often respect the same locality constraints. The major empirical obstacle for an analysis that holds that both topicalization and WH-movement target the CP projection is the distribution of the topic phrase/WH-phrase vis-à-vis the complementizer: Topics must appear to the right of the complementizer, but WH-phrases can only surface to its left. MS (1993:485–86) overcome this problem by proposing that topicalization targets the specifier of its own *Topic Phrase* (TopP) and that this phrase is located within the CP projection. The structure of an English example such as (56a) would then be (56b):

(56)    (a) I know that in no case will he give up

       (b) I know [$_{CP}$ that [$_{TopP}$ [in no case]$_i$[$_{Top}$ will] [$_{IP}$ he give up t$_i$]]]

MS suggest that the reason why WH-phrases can never undergo topicalization in either Hindi-Urdu, English, or German is the fact that [Spec, TopP] counts as a distinct landing site for the PUB. In English and German, because the PUB is projective, it evaluates both the overt movement of the WH-phrase to [Spec, TopP] and its covert movement to [Spec, CP]. The chain thus formed will violate the PUB, because the head of the chain occupies an A-bar position ([Spec, CP]) distinct from the one its intermediate link is in ([Spec, TopP]). Similarly, we can explain why WH-phrases in Hindi-Urdu cannot be *-to* marked—because both WH-movement and topicalization are covert, the nonprojective PUB will be able to 'see' the impropriety of the raising of the WH-phrase from [Spec, TopP] to [Spec, CP]. The scrambling/topicalization asymmetries noted earlier then follow without stipulation. These differences now reduce to the fact that scrambling is a distinct movement operation (adjunction to XP) from topicalization (substitution into [Spec, TopP]); consequently, no identity of syntactic behavior between the two is expected.

As yet, however, we do not have an explanation for the asymmetry between topicalization and WH-movement. For, if there are not one but two

specifier positions within the CP projection, we do not expect topicalization
to block clause-bound WH-movement. In fact, we expect topicalization and
WH-movement to co-occur, in direct contravention of the empirical facts.
MS suggest that these problems can be overcome if we employ the concept
of *matching projections* proposed by Haider (1988) to characterize the CP
and TopP projections in a clause (MS 1993:487):

(57)  MATCHING
      Two functional projections match iff one immediately dominates the
      other, and at least one specifier position of these projections is
      empty.

The essential idea is that matching projections behave such as a single projection in some instances and as two distinct projections in others, each
functional projection functioning as a segment, in analogy with adjunction structures. For CP and TopP to qualify as matching projections, the
specifier position of one must be empty at the level at which matching is
determined, presumably LF. MS (1993:487–89) accomplish this by proposing that only one of the two heads $C^0$ or $Top^0$ can be active, or *designated*,
in a clause: If $Top^0$ is the designated head, topicalization will occur, if
it is not, then $C^0$ must be active, and WH-movement may occur. Designation is an overt phenomenon that is roughly equated with phonological
realization and a designated head must be visible as such by Spellout—so
$Top^0$ must be designated by overt verb raising, and $C^0$ by the presence of
a lexical complementizer.[16] Only the designated head may license an A-bar
specifier, which must agree in all features with the designated head.

The Hindi-Urdu facts require some modification to MS's proposals regarding designation, as their account relies quite heavily on overt verb-
raising phenomena to activate the $Top^0$ head. Not only are these assumptions problematic for such languages as Japanese and Hindi-Urdu, which do
not link designation to overt verb raising in any demonstrable way, it also
appears that at least in Hindi-Urdu designation need not necessarily be an
overt phenomenon. A solution within minimalism presents itself. First, let
us assume that the concept of 'designation' reduces to a morphosyntactic
feature of a lexical item that is represented on the functional item responsible for checking it. This is most obvious in such languages as Hindi-Urdu
and Japanese, where the presence of topic morphology designates the $Top^0$
head. Suppose that English and German topics can be incorporated into
the paradigm by assuming that they also bear such morphology, except that
it is null. Then, once a head is designated, it may bear [strong] or [weak]
features, with the obvious consequences. Languages such as Japanese that
force overt topicalization and covert WH-movement are languages in which
$Top^0$ is [strong] but $C^0$ is [weak], whereas languages such as English and

German are ones in which both $C^0$ as well as $Top^0$ are [strong]—hence they do not procrastinate either WH-movement or topicalization to LF. Hindi-Urdu is a language in which both $C^0$ and $Top^0$ are [weak]; hence both topicalization and WH-movement are covert.

To conclude, this section has argued that the similarities between the discourse functions of scrambling and topicalization notwithstanding, the divergence between the syntactic properties of the two suggests that the two are intrinsically quite distinct operations. I have followed MS (1993) in analyzing topicalization as substitution into [Spec, TopP], extending their proposals to analyze Hindi-Urdu *-to* topics as covert topicalization. The arguments in this and the earlier two sections thus advance our claim that scrambling is an XP-adjunction operation. The next question that we must then answer is how scrambling is to be distinguished from QR at LF, which has also been analyzed as an XP-adjunction operation. A number of questions need to be answered if both QR and scrambling are to be accounted for by the PUB as well as subsumed under a uniform theory of XP-adjunction. For one, we need to determine whether the XP-adjoined positions targeted by scrambling need to be distinguished from those targeted by QR, given that there are some instances in which scrambling has the interpretive consequences of an overt QR. The next section examines the issues involved in the characterization of scrambling as S-structure QR and concludes that the distinction between QR'd positions and scrambling positions need to be maintained in the grammar.

## 2.4    Scrambling Is Not QR

MS (1993:499–502) suggest that it is possible to maintain both scrambling and QR as XP-adjunction operations and still distinguish between the two operations. They argue that the crucial difference between the two operations is that whereas QR is universally clause-bound and exclusively an LF-phenomenon, scrambling is necessarily overt and may move XPs long distance. They propose that this distinction between QR and scrambling can be captured by a relativization of the notion of 'possible adjunction site' across levels of derivation, by which sites such CP and DP are rendered impossible adjunction sites for LF-movement. Therefore, QR, which involves LF-movement, is universally clause-bound, whereas scrambling is not subject to similar restrictions.

Furthermore, given that QR cannot use adjunction to CP as an escape-hatch for LF-movement, any derivation that involves QR across clause boundaries will always violate the PUB, because that movement will always necessitate the use of either [Spec, CP], [Spec, TopP] or adjunction to CP as an escape-hatch, all of which would result in an ambiguously bound

QP-trace at LF. Movement in one swoop, on the other hand, would result in ECP/Subjacency violations.

Thus XP-adjoined positions targeted by QR and scrambling are distinct in that QR can access only a subset of the positions available for XP-adjunction. Within the IP, our theory of movement allows in principle for QR *from* a scrambled position as well as QR *over* a scrambled XP, because both these movements will yield a uniform chain formed by movement from one XP-adjoined position to another. The question that therefore needs an answer is whether this situation does actually obtain, because it has been suggested that neither of the two situations can in fact occur. Reinhart (1994) argues that QR is such an expensive operation that UG will prefer that if an overt operation has already accomplished this LF-movement, no further QR will be required at LF. Kiss (1987) has suggested that this is exactly what happens in Hungarian and other free word order languages— such languages express scopal relations through overt, rather than covert, moment. Bayer and Kornfilt (1994:42) phrase her proposals in the way given in (58):

(58)  Scrambling bleeds LF-movement.

As I see it, there are at least two major problems for such a proposal. Consider first the issue of whether QR from an XP-adjoined position is needed in the grammar. The principle in (58) requires that (59a–b) should both receive the identical LF representation in (60) (assuming, of course, that scrambling is XP-adjunction):

(59)  (a)  *Uski$_i$  bɛhen-ne   hər   ləṛke$_i$-ko  dek$^h$a
            his       sister(SU)  each  boy(DO)      saw
            'His$_i$ sister saw every boy$_i$.'

      (b)  hər   ləṛke$_i$-ko  Uski$_i$  bɛhen-ne   t$_i$  dek$^h$a
            each  boy(DO)      his       sister(SU)        saw
            'His$_i$ sister saw every boy$_i$.'

(60)  [$_{IP}$ [hər ləṛke$_i$-ko]$_j$ [$_{IP}$ Uski$_i$ bɛhen-ne t$_j$ dek$^h$a]]

It is therefore expected that both (59a) and (59b) should yield the same interpretation of the pronominal in the subject DP, but as I have already indicated, QP-scrambling has the option of overriding WCO effects, an option not available to the default configuration. It would thus appear that in order to derive the judgment that in situ QPs are subject to WCO effects, we have to assume that scrambling is not an instance of overt QR. In our approach, this can be achieved only by assuming that scrambled QPs must undergo further raising at LF.[17]

Consider next the issue of whether QR is permissible over a scrambled XP. Recall that our analysis entails that QR is possible over scrambled QPs, but then we have to explain why this option is rarely, if ever, available.[18] To appreciate the problem consider (61) from Hindi-Urdu:[19]

(61) (a) hər  admi    kɪsi  ɔrət-ko     pyar  kərta  hɛ
         each man(SU) some  woman(DO)  love  does   is

         'Every man loves some woman.' (*unambiguous*)

     (b) kɪsi  ɔrət-ko$_i$  hər  admi     t$_i$  pyar  kərta  hɛ
         some  woman(DO)   each man(SU)        love  does   is

         'Some woman, every man loves.' (*unambiguous*)

Example (61) shows that Hindi-Urdu, like Chinese, encodes the relative scope of quantifiers in terms of their linear order. Example (61a) is thus unambiguous with the universal quantifier taking wide scope over the existential quantifier embedded in the DO. Surprisingly, scrambling in (61b) has the ability to alter the scopal interpretation, with the wide scope reading being accorded to the scrambled DO. This means that the QR of the subject QP is somehow blocked by the scrambled QP.

Note that this freezing effect cannot follow from the PUB. Nothing, in fact, should prevent QR of the subject from taking place over the scrambled QP, and the LF representation for (61b) in (62) must therefore be ruled out by some principle of the grammar other than the PUB.

(62) [IP [hər admi]$_i$ [IP [kɪsi ɔrət-ko]$_j$ [IP t$_i$ t$_j$ pyar kərta hɛ]]]

In (62), the variable left behind by QR is unambiguously bound in the sense of the PUB, as it is only bound by adjoined positions.

I propose that the impossibility of QR over a scrambled DP/QP derives from the *Minimal Binding Requirement* (MBR) on variables left by QR (Aoun and Li 1993:10) in (63):

(63) THE MINIMAL BINDING REQUIREMENT
     Variables must be bound by the most local potential A-bar binder.

(64) A qualifies as a potential A-bar binder for B iff A c-commands B,
     A is in an A-bar position, and the assignment of the index of A to B
     will not violate Principle C of the binding theory.[20]

As an example of how this proposal works, consider the LF representation of the examples in (61a–b) in (65a–b):

(65) (a) [IP [hər admi]$_j$ [IP t$_j$′ [VP [kɪsi ɔrət-ko]$_k$ [VP t$_j$ pyar kərta hɛ]]]]

     (b) [IP [hər admi]$_j$ [IP [kɪsi ɔrət-ko]$_k$ [IP t$_j$ t$_k$ pyar kərta hɛ]]]

In (65a), both the variables $t_j$ and $t_j{'}$ are bound by the closest potential A-bar binder (the QP c-commands the variable and is in an A-bar position and the coindexation of the variable and its antecedent does not lead to any Principle C violations). In (65b), on the other hand, the MBR is not satisfied: The closest potential A-bar binder for $t_j$ is the scrambled DO QP, but that does not bind it, viz., the difference in their indices. The derivation will therefore crash. The only convergent derivation is therefore the derivation that involves no QR over the scrambled QP.

To conclude, this section has argued that although both scrambling and QR target XP-adjoined positions, the differences in the interpretation of examples in which QPs stay in situ and those in which the QPs are scrambled suggest that a scrambled position does not count as an appropriate scope position for quantificational items. Our discussion thus indicates that positions that are created by overt scrambling do not in principle create adverse conditions for the application of QR, though conditions such as the MBR may conspire to eliminate interpretations that involve QR of an in situ QP over a scrambled QP.

## 2.5   Scrambling Is XP-Adjunction

This chapter has so far argued for the superiority of an XP-adjunction analysis of scrambling in Hindi-Urdu. Aside from the fact that such a description can capture the syntactic properties of the scrambling operation, it also indicates a fuller explanation of the apparent optionality, iterability, and semantic vacuity of the operation, for it locates scrambling in the class of constructions that exhibit such properties—constructions created by derived XP-adjunction.

It is possible to question the theoretical validity of the typology internal to the class of A-bar movements assumed here. As pointed out by an anonymous reviewer, a possible danger of the 'XP-adjunction is a third movement' approach is that I stipulate this third movement to have the properties it reflects and end up arguing for an enrichment of the theory on empirical, i.e., inherently weaker, grounds. This problem is exacerbated by minimalist assumptions about language design, where for XP-adjunction to qualify as a distinct movement type, the empirical facts that I collate in this chapter are simply insufficient, as XP-adjunction must be endowed with a morphosyntactic motivation as well. Because I argue scrambled constructions to be focus constructions in chapter 5, let us consider this latter problem as solved and concentrate on the former in this discussion.

In the discussion so far, the basic point has been that if the morphosyntactic motivation for a particular movement is its definitional property, UG allows for multiple distinctions between movement types, including at least WH-movement, NP-movement, XP-adjunction, QR, and topicalization. The resistance mentioned previously to this multiple typology of movement types has its roots in the hold the traditional A/A-bar distinction has on the study of movement types, even though the distinction is now actually largely irrelevant. A review of the role the typology has played in the grammar shows that it has in fact always maintained a distinction between XP-adjunction, topicalization, substitution into [Spec, CP], and substitution into Case and agreement checking positions. The apparently binary nature of the A/A-bar typology has never been intended to suppress these distinctions but, rather, to show how some properties end up as typical to more than one movement type.

In the understanding that originated from Chomsky (1981), the A/A-bar typology was used to distinguish between movements in terms of both their intrinsic and their correlational properties, though the primary focus of the typology was on the correlational properties of the movement type—the $\pm\theta$ nature of the target. Because at that stage in the theory, Cased positions were at the minimum 'potential' $\theta$-positions as well, a correlational property such as $\pm\theta$ could be used to unambiguously identify the intrinsic imperatives of the movement concerned as well. Yet the theory was careful to maintain the distinction between intrinsic and correlational properties of a movement, as A-movement was always driven by Case, rather than $\theta$-, motivations. The class of A-bar movement was a homogeneous one only insofar as the non-$\theta$- nature of its target was concerned; otherwise, various A-bar movements differed both in their intrinsic motivations (obligatory operations such as WH-movement vs. optional ones such as PP-preposing and topicalization) and in terms of the landing sites (substitution vs. $XP/X^0$-adjunction).

The typology of movement types in UG was thus born in a scenario in which Case and $\theta$-role were assigned in identical configurations. With the complete complementarity between $\theta$- and Cased positions enforced by the VP-internal subject hypothesis (Fukui and Speas 1986) and the association of (structural) Case with the AGR system (Chomsky 1989), the conditions for maintaining this typology no longer exist, as all movement is to a non-$\theta$- position. The necessity of maintaining this typology is in fact irrelevant for identifying the intrinsic properties of a movement, the last resort character ascribed to movement places the morphosyntactic imperative of a movement as its sole definitional property. Rather, the relevance of the A/A-bar typology is restricted to identifying the cluster of binding and reconstruction (correlational) properties typically associated with the landing sites targeted by each distinctly driven movement type.

Current approaches (Chomsky and Lasnik 1993) choose to explain the clustering of these correlational properties with the help of the *L-relatedness distinction*, by which the features of a lexical head come to be shared by the functional head(s) inherently associated with it and transitively by all the XPs in the projection of that functional head. Because [Spec, CP], [Spec, TopP], and an XP-adjoined position cannot be considered narrowly L-related to an inherent feature of a lexical head, they do not exhibit the binding and reconstruction properties of A-positions, but as Tns and AGR are heads that inherently associated with verbal categories, the specifiers of TP and AgrP will. The two sets of correlational properties that the L-/L-bar distinction (or the θ/non-θ distinction) yields are, however, merely the construct of an external typological parameter, as none of the properties isolated originate in any way from the typological parameter used to construct the classification. The ability of an L-related position (or a θ-position) to license reflexives, override the WCO filter, and resist reconstruction does not follow from its L-relatedness (or its θ-relatedness), except by definition. An approach such as mine, which holds that there are as many movements as there are morphosyntactic imperatives, can easily replicate the classifications of this typology by finding an appropriate typological parameter that will yield the required clustering of properties. In what follows, I use the L-relatedness distinction itself to show how [Spec, CP], though it is targeted for an imperative quite distinct from topicalization and XP-adjunction, actually ends up sharing the reconstruction properties of the latter two operations.

Notice that the L-relatedness distinction forces an internal differentiation between the type of positions that fail to meet the property of L-relatedness. Although [Spec, CP] is not narrowly L-related by virtue of its positioning as the specifier of a non–L-related head, XPs and $X^0$s adjoined to an L-related head are not narrowly L-related because they are not included in the category headed by the L-related head. Because they are also not excluded from that category, the theory accords them the status of broadly L-related positions. It is commonly assumed in the literature that broadly L-related positions share the correlational properties of non–L-related positions (Mahajan 1990, Chomsky 1992), which, I argue, reduces to just a single property—the amenability to reconstruction.

To see this, take an inventory of the properties that the three positions— [Spec, CP], [Spec, TopP], and adjoined-to-XP—are supposed to share. Clearly, the phrase-structure configurations of the three are different, as is the nature of the checking relationship each bears to the head of that projection of which it is a part. While the item in [Spec, CP] unambiguously checks an [operator] feature, items in XP-adjoined positions and in [Spec, TopP] do not. In the discussion in section 2.4, I argued that XP-adjoined items are not in appropriate scope positions at Spellout and are subject to QR (and raising to [Spec, CP]) at LF, thereby suggesting that positions created by overt XP-adjunction do not bind variables of the sort needed for semantic interpretation of the XP as an operator. The impossibility of QP topicalization in languages such as English also suggests that [Spec, TopP] shares this inability of XP-adjoined positions to qualify as scope positions. Finally, as we saw in sections 2.2 and 2.3, XP-adjoined positions and [Spec, CP] or even [Spec, CP] and [Spec, TopP] do not count as identical positions with respect to the PUB, and the movement involved in each obeys quite distinct locality constraints.

This leaves as members of the shared set the inability of items in XP-adjoined positions, [Spec, TopP], and [Spec, CP] to license reflexives in a position they did not c-command at some stage in the derivation, and the fact that they are subject both to reconstruction as well as the WCO Filter. Research has shown that at least the first two of these properties are related, in that the phenomenon of reconstruction exempts the XP-adjoined/[Spec, CP/TopP] item from acting as a legitimate binder. In chapter 4, I argue that the WCO effect also originates from a similar source, so for the moment assume as given that the set of properties shared by XP-adjoined positions and [Spec, CP/TopP] reduces to their amenability to reconstruction.

Chomsky (1992) suggests that reconstruction is the result of a conspiracy between movement as a copying and deletion operation and the preference principle for reconstruction, which forces the deletion of all nonoperator material from the [Spec, CP] position. The binding theory, applying to convergent derivations after copy-deletion has taken place, finds the conditions for its application met only in intermediate and terminal copies. Chains targeting Case checking positions do not invoke the preference principle and the binding theory will find relevant conditions satisfied by the copy at the head of the chain. This accounts for the absence of reconstruction effects in A-chains.

In such a framework, the only way in which XP-adjoined positions can be shown to be amenable to reconstruction is if they are shown to check a quantificational feature. The arguments in sections 2.2 and 2.4 show this conclusion to be imprudent. My view of reconstruction must therefore be slightly different, and I suggest that the process of reconstruction is actually best characterized as the (preference for the) deletion of all the nonquantificational material in a copy (see also Hornstein 1995), where quantificational items are those that check an instrinsic [+Q(uantificational)] lexical feature. The process of deletion is conditioned purely by the L-relatedness distinction, by which the deletion can apply only to copies in positions that are not narrowly L-related, i.e., L-bar positions. Defining reconstruction in this way has the advantage of providing for the broader contrasts between Case checking specifier positions versus [Spec, CP], [Spec, TopP], and XP-adjoined positions, as well as for a finer distinction between [Spec,

CP] and [Spec, TopP] and XP-adjoined positions. Because the specifiers of functional heads such as Tns and AGR-s will always be narrowly L-related, [–Q] material may never be deleted from the head of the chain. On the other hand, because [Spec, CP], [Spec, TopP], and XP-adjoined positions will never be narrowly L-related, [–Q] material may always delete. The difference between [Spec, CP] and XP-adjoined and [Spec, TopP] positions will emerge after such deletion; because [Spec, CP] is targeted in satisfaction of a [+Q] feature, it will always contain a quantificational item at LF. The LF outputs of constructions involving overt XP-adjunction or topicalization, on the other hand, may yield configurations in which only the foot copy of the chain is available for the binding theory—if the positions do not involve the checking of a [+Q] feature, successive copies down to the tail may be wholly deleted.

Chomsky's preference principle and my proposals actually share the same intuitive content, as they both emerge from a Full Interpretation perspective on the role of deletion. If Full Interpretation requires arguments to be interpreted in argument positions, then the deletion of argument material from a nonargument position must be one of the permitted options. My perspective, even though it derives the same results as his, then differs from Chomsky's, for whom reconstruction is a process driven to construct a legitimate operator–variable pair. This difference, in turn, derives from the way the term 'operator' is interpreted—although Chomsky takes an operator to be defined in terms of positioning in an L-bar position, my approach suggests that such positioning is only a sufficient condition for operatorhood—the item in question must also check a [+Q] feature in this L-bar position.

I would like to think that my proposals conform more strictly to the minimalist objective of a grammar driven by, and stated over, the formal/morphosyntactic properties of linguistic items, but even keeping that aside, this reading of "reconstruction" also allows for greater empirical coverage. Approaches such as of Chomsky (1995:325–26), which restrict the checking of Case-features to narrowly L-related positions, must dismiss Kayne's (1989) analysis of French participial agreement as involving checking from a position broadly L-related to AGR-o, but in my approach, there is no such proscription. XP-adjoined positions may also involve the checking of Case-features, but in such cases the item must undergo full reconstruction. In the next chapter, my investigation of the double-object construction across languages provides empirical confirmation of this claim, as I show that (dative-shifted) indirect objects check dative Case in an XP-adjoined position and always undergo reconstruction.

In conclusion, my claim is that a multiple classification of landing sites is not a novel contribution to the theory. The theory has always maintained an internal typology within A-bar movements in terms of their intrinsic properties as well as the structural configurations they occupy. Although I follow the earlier strategy of deriving the apparent binary clustering of correlational properties by employing an external typological parameter, my approach attempts to give content to this typology by invoking Full Interpretation. The fact that XP-adjunction, topicalization, and raising to [Spec, CP] exhibit an amenability to reconstruction follows from the requirement that arguments cannot occupy nonargument positions at LF.

## 2.6   Conclusion

I set out in this chapter to identify the syntactic properties of the scrambling operation, and to that end I examined the tenability of the hypotheses that scrambling can be uniformly characterized as either Case-driven NP-movement, WH-movement, topicalization, or S-structure QR. I show that neither of these analyses can actually be maintained as scrambling does not share the intrinsic motivation of either of these movements or the locality constraints typical to either of these movement types. Section 2.1 shows that an NP-movement analysis of scrambling receives no independent empirical corroboration; even the erroneous assumption of a strict identity between A-binding positions and Cased positions cannot explain the ability of scrambled XPs to override WCO effects and license possessive reflexives. Sections 2.2 and 2.3 show that scrambling, even as it does exhibit some properties and functions typically associated with WH-movement and topicalization, diverges quite sharply from them in both its locality constraints and intrinsic motivations. The discussion in these two sections also derives the differences internal to the class of scrambling languages. I show that the absence of WH-scrambling in an overt WH-movement language such as German follows from an observance of Full Interpretation. The fact that WH-phrases may scramble in languages such as Hindi-Urdu is traced to a combination of factors, the most significant of which is the role that deletion plays in allowing WH-scrambled configurations to surface. In section 2.3, I show that Hindi-Urdu differs from German in that in the latter, both scrambling and topicalization are overt operations. However, in Hindi-Urdu -*to* topicalization is a covert operation, whereas scrambling is overt.

Section 2.4 further distinguishes scrambling from QR, showing that although both operations target XP-adjoined positions, the differences in the interpretation of examples in which QPs stay in situ and those in which the QPs are scrambled suggest that a scrambled position does not count as an appropriate scope position for quantificational items. Our discussion thus indicates that positions that are created by overt scrambling do not in principle create adverse conditions for the application of QR, though conditions such as the MBR may conspire to eliminate interpretations that involve the QR of an in situ QP over a scrambled QP. Section 2.5 discusses the theoretical status of XP-adjunction in the grammar and the multiple classification of positions that the arguments entail. The essence of my claim is that such a multiple typology of landing sites is not a novel contribution to the theory, as the theory has always maintained an internal typology within A-bar movement.

The central claim of the discussion has been that scrambling is best analyzed as uniformly an XP-adjunction operation that undergoes full reconstruction. Although this does not provide an explanation for the anti-reconstruction effects exhibited in scrambled configurations that we saw in section 2.1, the proposal does indicate the areas from which an explanation of these effects could originate—the theory of binding and reconstruction in UG. I take this conclusion to constitute a mandate to develop a theory of binding and coreference in UG that can explain these effects. The next chapter sets the stage for this discussion, as it explores the core syntactic configurations of Hindi-Urdu and UG clause structure to which the discussion in the rest of the book makes crucial reference.

# Chapter 3

# The Structure of the UG Clause

Inquiry in recent years into the architecture of the UG clause has yielded quite fruitful results. Since Chomsky (1989), structural Case and verb agreement is considered to be a reflex of the configuring of an argument and the verb in a SPEC-head relationship, now assumed to be effected via a checking relation in the universal clause structure as presented in example (2) of chapter 2. This chapter investigates the validity of this UG clause structure and the attendant assumption that Case can only be checked from a position narrowly L-related to an L-related head. Specifically, I argue that considerations of data and theory require the relocation of the AGR-oP projection to a position internal to VP as in (1), and that indirect objects check structural dative Case from a position broadly L-related to this VP-internal AGR-o.

The chapter thus not only sets the scene for the discussion of the coreference effects in scrambled constructions in the next chapter but also carries forward the thesis that XP-adjunction is a morphosyntactically driven operation that can enter into many of the same relations that a specifier, a substitution position, does. Section 3.1 details the empirical advantages to the relocation of the AGR-oP projection to a VP-internal position. Section 3.2 examines the consequences this VP-internal AGR-oP has for a minimalist configuration for ditransitives, especially for languages such as Hindi-Urdu, which lack the dative alternation altogether. Section 3.3 concludes the chapter with a discussion of the implications of my proposals for Full Interpretation.

## 3.1  Locating the AGR-oP Projection

It is my claim in this section that the appropriate structure for the UG clause is as in (1).

(1)

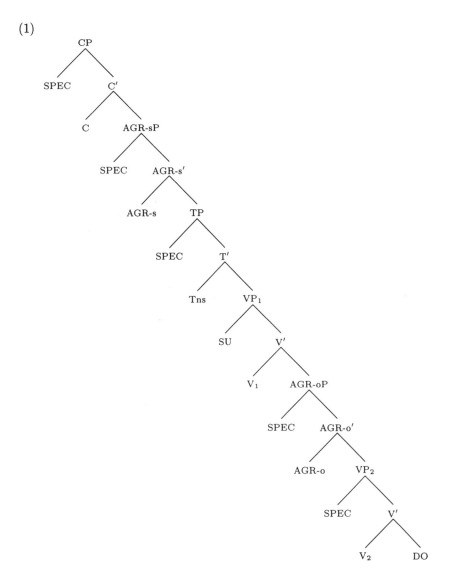

The major objections to this relocation of the AGR-oP to a VP-internal position are empirical rather than theoretical, as the theory of Case licensing in the minimalist program is actually insensitive to the VP-internal/VP-external positioning of the AGR-oP projection.[1]

As readers are aware, the minimalist program perceives the licensing of lexical elements to involve a checking relation between the licensing functional head and the linguistic item concerned. Steering clear of specific formulations and keeping to its intuitive content, checking involves the raising of a (fully inflected) linguistic item to enter into a checking relation with a functional head typically associated with licensing one of its properties, such as [Case], [+WH], etc. The checking relation is very local—the checking domain of a head includes an element adjoined to it (attracted there by its *V-features*) and the category in its specifier position (attracted there by its *D-features*). The stage at the derivation at which such checking may take place is constrained by the strength of the formal feature involved—if the feature is [strong], Greed forces checking to take place before Spellout; if the feature is [weak], Procrastinate proscribes overt raising. Covert raising is forced by the core assumption that features need to be checked for convergence.

The peculiarities of the derivation created in the checking of Case features suggest that movement for checking is a very local relation. Take the most complex case, in which the D-features of both the AGR-s and AGR-o heads are [strong]. In the course of subject and object raising to the specifier positions of AGR-s and AGR-oP, respectively, the DO actually crosses the trace of the subject in its movement to [Spec, AGR-oP], yet no relativized minimality violation obtains. Chomsky (1992:24) proposes that the crossing paths created in the course of checking can be exempted from relativized minimality violations, as the crossing involved in checking is in a very local domain. This intuition is formalized as the *Shortest Move Condition*:

(2)      If $\alpha$, $\beta$ are in the same minimal domain, they are equidistant from $\gamma$.

Shortest Move interacts with the intuition that the notion 'minimal domain of a chain'—the set of categories contained in the chain but excluding the links of the chain—is a relational one, defined as distinct at various points in the raising of a lexical item. While Shortest Move restricts movement to positions in the same minimal domain, the definition of minimal domain over chains allows for movement to proceed in short moves. Consider again the crossing path created by raising the DO to [Spec, AGR-oP] over the trace of the raised subject. Because the AGR heads are nondistinct collections of $\phi$-features that are given identity only by the head that adjoins to them, [Spec, Agr-oP] can be licensed as a target for object raising only after verb raising. Now, with this movement, the minimal domain of the chain ($[_{\text{AGR-o}}V\ [_{\text{VP}}\ldots t]]$) includes not only the specifier position of AGR-oP but also the specifier position of $VP_1$. By the definition in (2), movement to either specifier position will not violate Shortest Move. And because [Spec, VP] is occupied by the trace of the raised subject, the only landing site available for the object is [Spec, AGR-oP]. This is true for every further step in the derivation of Case-checking relations in the framework—verb raising and incorporation to the next higher functional head must necessarily precede the movement of various arguments to the specifier positions of these higher functional heads.

Notice that checking is sensitive only to the relative hierarchical positioning of the two AGR projections vis-à-vis each other and not to their positioning in the clause. Shortest Move requires that the AGR-sP projection dominate the AGR-oP projection and not vice versa, as in that configuration, derivations will never converge (Jonas and Bobaljik 1993). Relocating the AGR-oP projection to a VP-internal position does not affect either the relative hierachical positioning of the two AGR projections or the requirements imposed by Shortest Move. All that changes is that for subject raising to [Spec, TP], the lexical verb will have to raise to AGR-o, the [AGR-o–V] complex to $V_1$, and the [AGR-o–V–$V_1$] complex to Tns.

In fact, the major obstacles to locating the AGR-oP projection within the VP arise from data, as it is commonly assumed that the instances of object shift in Germanic (Vikner 1990) and object agreement in Hindi-Urdu (Mahajan 1990) target a VP-external AGR-oP. Arguments for this analysis make reference to two aspects of grammatical structure as corroborating evidence—linear order and semantic interpretation. The observation that shifted objects receive a specific interpretation at LF and tend to precede quantifiers floated from subjects and certain VP-level adverbs are taken to indicate their positioning in a VP-external AGR-oP projection. In the discussion that follows, I show that the evidence from Hindi-Urdu at least is far from conclusive in this regard.

Mahajan (1990, 1991, 1992) links the linear order of objects and the specificity effects observed with positioning in a VP-external AGR-oP projection. Mahajan (1990) makes the following assumptions: (1) objects can be structurally Case-marked either by V or by AGR-o; (2) nonspecific objects get structural Case from V within VP, while specific objects get Case-marked by AGR-o, where nonspecific objects are defined as the non-Case-marked objects of all predicates except perfective participles and psych-predicates.[2] In Mahajan's system, then, agreeing, scrambled, Case-marked, and/or specific DOs all target a VP-external AGR-oP projection. I return to a fuller discussion of specificity in chapter 5, concentrating here only on the claim that the AGR-oP projection that mediates DO licensing is VP-external.

Mahajan provides two types of evidence for the claim. First, because Mahajan assumes that the scrambling that creates binders is movement to a specifier position where Case is checked, an OSV order will necessarily require the DO to be situated in a VP-external AGR-oP projection. We have seen in chapter 2 that these observations cannot be correct, because they would predict that only agreeing/Case-marked/specific DOs can be scrambled and act as binders. Example (3) demonstrates that this is patently not the case. Here a nonagreeing nonspecific scrambled DO, which is not the object of either a perfective participle or a psych-predicate, may corefer with a pronominal embedded in the subject.

(3)  ek-do    ləṛkiyõ-ko$_i$  unki$_i$  maẽ      t$_i$  kuč$^h$  zyada-hi
     one-two  girls(DO)    their    mothers       some  more-EMPH
     ḍaṭtĩ  hẽ
     scold  are

     'One or two girls are scolded far too often by their mothers.'

The second set of evidence that Mahajan provides for the VP-external location of the AGR-oP projection comes from adverbial interpretation. These arguments are based on the examples in (4): The most salient reading for the adverb in (4a) is a event reading, but in (4b), it is the process one.

(4)  (a)  pulis-ne      jəldi-se   cor         pəkəṛ  liya
          police(FSG)  quickly   thief(MSG)  catch  took(MSG)

          'The police quickly arrested the thief.'

     (b)  pulis-ne      cor         jəldi-se  pəkəṛ  liya
          police(FSG)  thief(MSG)  quickly   catch  took(MSG)

          'The police arrested the thief quickly.'

Adopting Travis's (1988) suggestion that event adverbs are universally attached to an I-projection and process adverbs to a V-projection, Mahajan links the saliency of the process reading in (4b) to the syntactic position of the DO—because the adverb must be attached to the VP, the DO must be outside the VP. The DO concerned being an agreeing object of a perfective participle, this VP-external position must be [Spec, AGR-oP]. Mahajan claims that examples such as (5), where no object agreement obtains and adverbial interpretation is ambiguous, support this conjecture. The ambiguity of (5), he suggests, is due to the fact that because the DO does not move out of VP for Case, it is difficult to identify the attachment site of the adverb:

(5)  (a)  pulis         jəldi-se   cor         pəkəṛ  leti   hɛ
          police(FSG)  quickly   thief(MSG)  catch  takes  is(FSG)

          'The police quickly arrests the thief.'

     (b)  pulis         cor         jəldi-se  pəkəṛ  leti   hɛ
          police(FSG)  thief(MSG)  quickly   catch  takes  is(FSG)

          'The police arrests the thief quickly.'

This claim is, however, contradicted by the data in (6), where even as no object agreement prevails, no such ambiguity obtains either. The process reading of the adverb is clearly more salient in (6a) and the event reading in (6b). In addition, the scrambled DO receives a specific reading.

(6)  (a)  sita      jəldi-se  kʰana      xətəm  kəregi
         Sita(FSG)  quickly   food(MSG)  finish  will do(FSG)

      'Sita will quickly finish the food/eating.'

      (b)  sita      kʰana$_i$   jəldi-se  t$_i$  xətəm  kəregi
          Sita(FSG)  food(MSG)   quickly          finish  will do(FSG)

      'Sita will finish the food/??eating quickly.' [3, 4]

Even Mahajan's approach would characterize the DO in (6b) as adjoined to VP, because the verb in question is a structural Case-assigner and the DO therefore lacks the necessary Case motivation for movement to [Spec, AGR-oP]. The specific reading that it receives thus goes unpredicted—unless, of course, the configurational requirement on specificity effects is weakened to a VP-external positioning by Spellout. A closer look at the examples in (4) and (6) shows that in fact that is all these examples corroborate.

I am thus suggesting that the data supposed to corroborate the VP-external positioning of the AGR-oP projection is in actuality neutral to any such claim, because it makes no specific or exclusive reference to the AGR-oP projection at all. Decisions about the location of the AGR-oP projection have then to be made independent of these facts, and it turns out that there are a number of advantages to a VP-internal positioning of the AGR-oP projection. Besides the arguments in Koizumi (1993) and Travis (1991) for languages as disparate as English and Tagalog, Hindi-Urdu agreeing objects can also be claimed to necessitate this relocation. If specificity effects are a consequence of the Case checking in a VP-external AGR-oP projection, there is no explanation for the fact that there are contexts in which a DO that triggers overt verb agreement or bears an overt *-ko* Case does not receive a specific interpretation. Because we would expect the DO to be located in a VP-external AGR-oP projection in both these cases, data such as (7) is entirely unexpected:

(7)  (a)  sita-ne     ek . ləɽke-ko  pəsənd  kiya
         Sita-ERG    a   boy-DAT    liking  did

      'Sita liked a boy.'

      (b)  mujʰe    inam-mẽ    kitabẽ       mɪlī̃
          I(SG)    reward-in  books(FPL)   got

      'I was given books as a reward.'

Example (7a) shows that the overt specification of the DP as indefinite ensures that no specificity effects obtain, despite the fact that the DP *a boy* is a *-ko* marked object of a perfective participle. Example (7b) shows that a bare plural such as *books* is not given a specific interpretation despite the fact that it controls verb agreement and is the complement of a perfective participle.

Another advantage of this account is that it eliminates the improper analysis of Case checking in ditransitives, exemplified by (8):

(8)

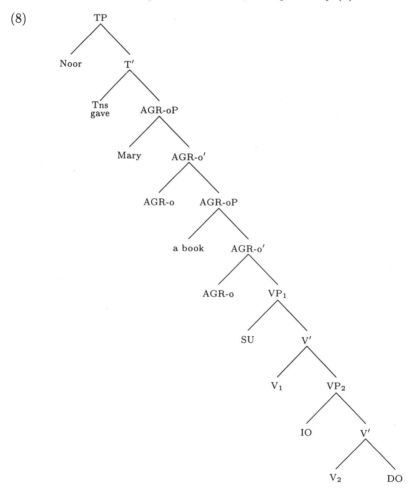

Such an analysis (e.g., Jayaseelan 1989/1995) assumes that dative shift involves overt checking of the IO Case-features in the higher AGR-oP and the DO Case-features in the lower one, as in (8).

Citing the work of Bures (1992), Collins and Thráinsson (1993) point out that (8) is not a legitimate LF object, because the movement of either one of the objects actually causes the other to fail Shortest Move: If the DO raises first, the IO must fail to make the shortest move because it will cross *two* intervening filled specifier positions—[Spec, $VP_1$] and [Spec, AGR-oP]—on its way to the higher AGR-oP. The derivation in which the IO moves to AGR-oP is equally illicit, because now it is the DO that does not make the shortest move, as two filled specifier positions [Spec, $VP_1$] and [Spec, $VP_2$] intervene between it and the specifier of the lower AGR-oP.

Collins and Thráinsson take these facts to suggest that Case checking in ditransitives actually involves both a VP-internal as well as a VP-external AGR-oP projection, but as I show in the next section, there is enough evidence that suggests that all that is involved is a single VP-internal AGR-oP projection, against which the DO checks it Case from the specifier position and the IO from a position adjoined to AGR-oP.

## 3.2 Ditransitives in the Minimalist Program

Languages differ in the realizations that a ditransitive predicate may receive. Whereas languages such as English allow certain ditransitives as *give, send, present*, etc., to have two distinct manifestations at Spellout, languages such as Hindi-Urdu and French allow only a single derivational output. The limits of the set of realizations are apparently expressed by the English paradigm, where these ditransitives may surface in either of the two forms of SU-V-IO-DO or SU-V-DO-IO (where in the latter, the IO is realized as a PP). Languages such as French and Hindi-Urdu apparently make a 'choice' between these two realizations, as Hindi-Urdu ditransitives can surface only in the former and French ditransitives only in the latter.

This section presents a minimalist appraisal of the universal configuration that enables this choice and argues that considerations of theory and crosslinguistic validity require a reanalysis of the structure of ditransitives in UG. I argue that both the structural realizations of a ditransitive are derived from a common base. The difference between languages is shown to follow from the variation in the means available to individual languages for the satisfaction of the Case requirements of arguments.

### 3.2.1 The Standard Analysis

Until Larson (1988), the two structural realizations of the two internal arguments of a ditransitive predicate in English (*I gave/presented him a book, I gave/presented a book to him*) were hypothesized to have the D-structures in (9) (based on Chomsky (1981), and ignoring external arguments):

(9)

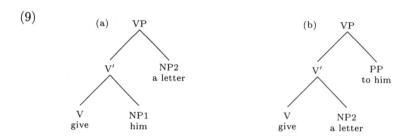

The assumption underlying the D-structure representations in (9) is that these two realizations of *give* are not derivationally related to each other. However, as Larson (1988) points out, when the very empirical adequacy of these representations is in question (Barss and Lasnik 1986), the rationale behind prohibiting any transformational relationship between the two becomes an immediate question as well. For example, in the structure referred to as the double object construction (DOC) in (9a), the fact that $NP_2$ asymmetrically c-commands $NP_1$ leads us to expect that $NP_2$ may license anaphors and bound variables and negative polarity items in $NP_1$. These predictions are, however, sharply contradicted by the empirical facts:

(10)   (a) *I showed herself$_i$ Mary$_i$

       (b) *Whose$_i$ pay did you send his$_i$ mother t$_i$

       (c) *I gave anyone nothing.

Because all the evidence actually points to a configuration in which the IO precedes as well as c-commands the DO, the D-structure representations in (9) clearly need to be revised. Larson (1988) proposes that such a revision would be significant only if it could be built on a recognition that the two realizations of *give* actually involve different permutations of an identical set of thematic relationships.[5] Then, on a strong thesis of the relation between thematic and categorial structure, expressible in terms of Baker's (1988) *Uniformity of θ-Assignment Hierarchy* (UTAH) in (11), a derivational link between the DOC and the construction in (9b) is virtually inevitable. The construction in (9b) shall henceforth be termed the prepositional dative construction (PDC).

(11)   UNIFORMITY OF θ-ASSIGNMENT HIERARCHY
       Identical thematic relationships are represented by identical
       structural relations between the items at the level of D-structure.

Larson proposes that the DOC is derived from the PDC by a rule of *VP-Passive*. Both constructions take the VP in (12) as the base configuration from which the D-structure representations of the DOC and the PDC in (13) are derived.

(12)

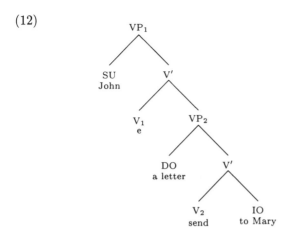

(13)

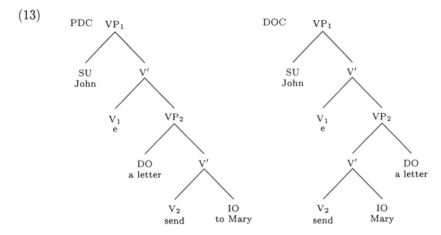

Concentrating on only the Case-assignment relations in the structure, the PDC is derived by head-to-head movement of the lexical verb, $V_2$, to the $V_1$ position, the movement being triggered to Case-assign the DO. The DOC is also derived from (12) by the rule of VP-Passive, which absorbs the structural Case-assigning property of $V_2$ and forces the demotion of the external argument to the status of an adjunct. Suggesting that the governed preposition *to* has the status of a Case marking, Larson proposes that its absorption is a natural consequence of VP-Passive. This renders the IO Caseless in its base position and it must therefore raise to a Cased position to satisfy the Case Filter. The vacant Cased position that this movement targets is [Spec, $VP_2$], the position vacated by the DO, as VP-Passive absorbs the DO θ-role. Case-assignment to the IO is then accomplished by verb raising to the $V_1$ position, whereas Case-assignment to the adjunct

DO takes place under a rule of V'-reanalysis, by which the V' $\longrightarrow$ [$_{V'}$ t$_V$, t$_{IO}$ ] is reanalyzed into a V that can Case-assign the adjunct DO. A rule of Argument Demotion, by which an undischarged θ-role of a predicate can be optionally assigned to an adjunct, facilitates the θ-assignment of the DO.

Although Larson's proposals intuitively have a universal appeal, they suffer from some empirical and theoretical inadequacies. For one, despite its efforts at providing a derivational relationship between the PDC and the DOC, Larson's analysis places this link at a presyntactic level, with the result that the PDC and the DOC result from different D-structures altogether. This invisible derivational link is therefore expected to be completely irrelevant for subsequent syntactic operations, with the specific result that we expect both the arguments in the DOC and the PDC to exhibit similar syntactic properties. The contrast (Iwakura 1987) in (14) and (15) then come as a complete surprise:

(14)  (a)  Who did Noor give the book to?

      (b)  The book was given to Mary.

(15)  (a)  *Who did Noor give the book?

      (b)  *The book was given Mary.

The DOC in English forbids WH-extraction of the IO and passivization of the DO. These facts are unaccounted for by the Larsonian analysis, which must consider these properties to be independent of the derivational link between the PDC and the DOC. However, there must be a connection between the two sets of data above; because (15) is derived from (14) by movement, it is quite likely that the ungrammatical examples in (15) can be accounted for within a general theory of movement from moved configurations. The problem with Larson's analysis is that it turns out to virtually *prohibit* the syntax from taking note of these facts.

In fact, it is crosslinguistically the case that the IO in the DOC does not exhibit prototypical argument properties. Müller (1992), Snyder (1992), and MS (1994b) provide evidence that suggests that dative-shifted IOs have the properties of adjuncts. For example, in German (MS 1994b:357–87, Müller 1992:204), English, and Hindi-Urdu, IOs that have undergone dative shift are adjunct islands. As the (b) examples from German, English and Hindi-Urdu in (17)–(18) respectively show, such IOs are resistant to WH-extraction, in direct contrast to DOs which, as the (a) examples show, display more normal argument properties:

(16)  (a)  Who$_i$ did you give them [a photo of t$_i$]?

      (b)  *Who$_i$ did you give [a friend of t$_i$] a present?

(17)   (a)   [uber   wen]$_i$   hat   der   Verleger   ihr   [ein   Buch         t$_i$]
             about   whom   has   the   publisher   her   a      book-ACC
       gegeben?
       given
       'About whom has the publisher given her a book?'

       (b)   *[uber   wen]$_i$   hat   der   Verleger   [einem   Buch         t$_i$]
             about   whom   has   the   publisher   a        book-DAT
       keine   Chance   gegeben?
       no      chance   given
       'The publisher gave no chance to a book about whom?'

(18)   (a)   [marksvad-pər]$_i$   ram-ne     Use     [t$_i$   ek   kitab]        di
             Marxism-on         Ram(SU)   her(IO)         a    book(DO)    gave
       'Ram gave her a book on Marxism.'

       (b)   *[marksvad-pər]$_i$   alocək-ne   [t$_i$   ek   kitab-ko]   bɔhɔt   bʊri
             Marxism-on         critic(SU)        one   book(IO)   very    bad
       ʈɪppəni   di
       review   gave
       'The critic gave a very bad review to the book on Marxism.'

This impossibility of extraction of IOs patterns with that noted in (15b).
If the IO here is indeed in a specifier position, i.e., a position from which
extraction could take place, it should display the same behavior as the DO.
The same point is also illustrated by the impossibility of IO passivization
in Dutch and Albanian, as shown by (19a–b), a fact inexplicable under an
analysis that accords both objects an identical configurational status:

(19)   (a)   *zij   werd   het   boek   gegeben
             She   was   this   book   given
       'She was given the book.'

       (b)   *baba   i   tij   iu   tregua   secilit   djala
             father   his   CL   show   each   boy
       'His father was shown each boy.'

   Finally, Larson's proposals can make no adequate predictions about either languages such as Hindi-Urdu and Albanian (Snyder 1992), which lack
the PDC altogether, or languages such as French, which do not exhibit
the DOC at all.[6] Though Larson (1988:351, n.18) does suggest that the
difference between languages may lie in which of the two configurations,
the PDC or the DOC, is taken to be the basic one, this suggestion does
not turn out to be of much help. Allowing variation of this sort at the

base, besides being theoretically problematic, also does not yield obvious empirical advantages. To see this, consider Dayal's (1993) description of the structure of the Hindi-Urdu ditransitive as having a 'basic' DOC-type form at D-structure, as in (20):

(20)

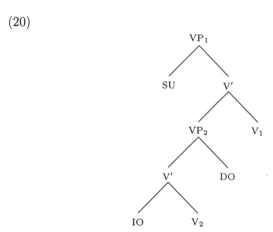

In (20), the DO asymmetrically c-commands the IO, but not vice versa. It is therefore expected that reflexives and pronominals embedded within the DO will not show Principle A or B effects. This is confirmed by (21), in which the reflexive in the DO obviates from the IO, and by (22), in which a possessive pronominal may be bound by the IO even as it obviates from the subject:

(21) nur$_i$-ne      vrInda$_j$-ko   əpni$_{i/*j}$  kitab       di
     Noor(SU)   Vrinda(IO)   self's      book(DO)   gave

     'Noor$_i$ gave Vrinda$_j$ her$_{i/*j}$ book.'

(22) nur$_i$-ne      vrInda$_j$-ko   Uski$_{*i/j}$  kitab       di
     Noor(SU)   Vrinda(IO)   her       book(DO)   gave

     'Noor$_i$ gave Vrinda$_j$ her$_{*i/j}$ book.'

The validity of the D-structure representation in (20) is, however, questioned by the facts in (23). As Dayal herself points out, contrary to the expectations generated by (20), the DO cannot license reflexives and bound pronominals in the IO:

(23)   (a) ram$_i$-ne    əpni$_{i/*j}$  mã-ko         bəcca$_j$      t$^h$əmaya
           Ram(SU)   self's    mother(IO)   child(DO)   handed

           'Ram$_i$ handed the child$_j$ to his$_{i/*j}$ mother.'

(b) ram$_i$-ne   Uski$_{*i/*j/k}$  mã-ko      bəccα$_j$    t$^h$əmaya
     Ram(SU)  his         mother(IO)  child(DO)  handed

'Ram$_i$ handed the child$_j$ to his$_{*i/*j/k}$ mother.'

Dayal holds the impossibility of binding in these contexts to call for a redefinition of the notion of binding itself, by which it comes to make reference to *linear precedence* as well as hierarchical dominance (see also Barss and Lasnik 1986, Jackendoff 1990). Then, in (23a–b), the fact that the putative DO antecedent for the reflexive/pronominal in the IO c-commands but does not precede its bindee explains the illegitimacy of these examples.[7] However, Reinhart (1986) and Larson (1990) question the theoretical desirability of such mixed definitions of binding domains on a number of counts. As Larson (1990:593–94) observes, such a redefinition yields a highly unrestrictive analysis as "a notion of domain involving both structure and order entails very few structural consequences, and is, in fact, compatible with all possible structurings of V-NP$_1$-NP$_2$." Considerations of economy thus suggest that a minimalist account of ditransitives must maintain the universal base hypothesis in its strongest form.

### 3.2.2   Ditransitives in UG: A Proposal

(24)

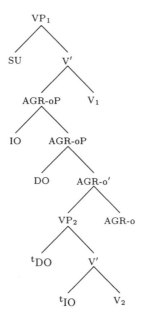

My proposal for the structure of ditransitives in UG is represented in (24). I will argue that this structure provides a better representation for some of Larson's own intuitions. Take first the case of UTAH. One of the prime motivations for Larson's proposals was the appeal it made to UTAH, but as Jackendoff (1990) points out, because Larson's PDC and DOC do not have *identical* structural representations, this objective is not actually achieved. In response, Larson (1990) suggests that it may be that all that is sought to be maintained is the same *relative* structural prominence between role-bearing elements. The requirements of this Relativized UTAH are satisfied in the DOC and PDC constructions, as in both, Theme arguments are always generated higher than Goals. Happily, (24) no longer requires this retreat into relativism, as the D-structure configuration from which both alternants, the DOC and the PDC, are derived is identical.

### Case Checking in (24)

Objective Case and agreement checking in the VP-internal AGR-oP proceeds as follows: The VP internal AGR-o head bears two Case features that must be checked by raising DPs into its checking domain. It is my contention that the IO checks its features in a broadly L-related position to AGR-o, as this explains why IOs crosslinguistically exhibit the properties of adjuncts rather than arguments. In the DOC, the DO raises to [Spec, AGR-oP] to check structural accusative Case, and the IO adjoins to AGR-oP to check structural dative Case. Since this raising is facilitated by verb-raising to AGR-o, neither movement yields a Shortest Move violation if we assume that *all* elements in the residue of the minimal domain of a head may enter into a checking relation with it. No actual redefinition of the notion of checking domain is required to accomplish this, because the exclusion of adjoined positions from checking domains is achieved only by stipulation in Chomsky (1992).

Although I maintain Larson's intuitions that the absorption of a Case-feature of the argument licensing head lies at the root of the dative alternation, I do not define the absorption in analogy to the sentential passive as he does and therefore do not need rules such as argument demotion to undo the effects of passivization on θ-structure. As the account maintains a strict separation between Case and θ-positions, the rule of VP-Passive affects only the AGR-o head, absorbing the Case feature of the IO. In my account, it is the PDC, and not the DOC, which is derived by a rule of VP-Passive, with the result that only the DO can raise to [Spec, AGR-oP] and the IO must remain in situ. Preposition insertion takes place at PF as a last resort to save the derivation.[8]

The proposal that IOs check Case in a position broadly L-related to

AGR-o provides a natural explanation for the contrasts between IOs and DOs noted in (15)–(19), properties that go unpredicted by either a Larsonian analysis or those based on it (Collins and Thráinsson 1993, Koizumi 1993). The impossibility of IO passivization in languages such as Albanian and Hindi-Urdu arises from the fact that these languages lack the IO Case-absorption mechanism that I continue to call VP-Passive, perhaps due to the unavailability of preposition/postposition insertion as a last-resort operation. Consequently, these languages will only exhibit the DOC configurations in ditransitives, the IO occupying a Cased adjoined position at Spellout. IO passivization, as it involves raising to [Spec, AGR-sP], will result in L- and L-bar interleaved chains, a clear violation of the Economy of Derivation (Collins 1994). DO passivization, on the other hand, proceeds without any problem, as sentential passive absorbs the Case feature of the DO on the AGR-o head, triggering DO raising to [Spec, AGR-sP].

The fact that English DOCs appear to allow passivization of the IO and *not* of the DO in (25) poses problems for this claim:

(25)　(a)　Mary was given a book

　　　(b)　*A book was given Mary

Notice, however, that only one IO and one DO passive form exists for both the DOC and the PDC in English. Though it is standardly held that the IO and DO passivization in (25) involve a DOC configuration, this assumption seems to derive more from tradition rather than from any empirical fact. For the account presented here, the compulsions actually point the other way, as the conditions allowing IO passivization simply do not obtain in the DOC. My suggestion, therefore, is that IO passivization in English uses the PDC as its basic configuration. Recall that the PDC is derived from (24) by a rule of VP-Passive that absorbs the IO Case feature of the VP-internal AGR-o. This ensures that the IO cannot move, and in active sentences, a preposition has to be inserted. However, when sentential passive is involved, the IO *can* move, as [Spec, VP₁] will not be licensed, given that the external argument θ-role is absorbed by passive morphology. Consequently, raising of the IO to [Spec, AGR-sP] will not violate the Shortest Move Condition.

I suggest the source of the illegitimacy of (25b) is actually the IO, which is a victim of the failure of preposition insertion. In my analysis, the derivation in (25b) proceeds from the PDC, to which the sentential passive applies, and the DO raises to the [Spec, AGRsP] position. The IO however, now has no place to move, because its Case checking position internal to the VP is not licensed. It must therefore stay in situ, and if preposition insertion takes place the derivation is saved, yielding the convergent derivation *a book was given to Mary*; otherwise, the derivation crashes.

The structure in (24) yields a rich typology of languages on the use of VP-Passive as a typological parameter. Languages that have the VP-Passive rule will exhibit the dative alternation, whereas languages that do not may have either the DOC or even the PDC, specially on the assumption that the PDC can be an output of the base configuration as well (where the IO will be a genuine PP). Presumably, French is one such language that derives its PDC from the structure projected at the base rather than from the rule of VP-Passive..

### Binding and reconstruction in (24)

The proposal that IOs occupy an adjoined position also explains a number of binding facts in DOCs. As I return to these facts in the next chapter, I do not dwell on the details of each example here. Recalling the characterization of reconstruction we have so far adopted, by which the XP-adjoined copy of a nonquantificational XP deletes prior to the application of the binding theory, it will be apparent that the binding theory will always make reference to the base, rather than the derived, position of the IO.

This hypothesis that the IO in the DOC undergoes 'full reconstruction' makes specific predictions regarding Principle A. Because the reconstructed position of the IO will be lower than that of the DO, we expect that although IOs can never bind reflexives in the DO, they will be able to antecede reflexives in more deeply embedded constituents. Both these predictions are, according to MS (1994b:360–61), confirmed for German in (26) and (27a). In Hindi-Urdu, as all DO reflexives are subject-oriented, the first of these effects does not obtain, but as (27b) shows, the second does:

(26) daß   der   Arzt   dem   Patienten$_i$   sich$_i$   im   Spiegel
      that   the   doctor   the   patient(IO)   self(DO)   in   mirror
      zeigt
      showed

      'That the doctor showed the patient$_i$ himself$_i$ in the mirror.'

(27)  (a) daß   Eva   ihr$_i$   die   Augen   [uber   sich$_i$]   offnete
          that   Eve   her(IO)   the   eyes   about   self   opened

          'Eve opened her$_i$ eyes about herself$_i$.'

      (b) nur-ne   əminɑ$_i$-ko   [apne$_i$   kəmre-mẽ]   bhɛj   diyɑ
          Noor   Ameena(IO)   self's   room-in   sent   gave

          'Noor sent Ameena to her room.'

With regard to pronominal binding, the fact that the IO reconstructs to its base position should facilitate pronominal coreference with a pronominal embedded in the DO, as the IO will not c-command the DO. As the Hindi-Urdu example in (28a) shows, this prediction is confirmed. We also now have an explanation for the illegitimacy of (28b), where the fact that the DO is a pronominal entails that, after reconstruction at LF, the DO *wo* binds the IO R-expression *Ram* in violation of Condition C.

(28) (a) mɛ-ne ram$_i$-ko  Uski$_i$ kitab      di
         I(SU)   Ram(IO)  his    book(DO)  gave
         'I gave Ram$_i$ his$_i$ book.'

     (b) *mɛ-ne ram$_i$-ko  wo$_i$      diya
         I(SU)   Ram(IO)  him(DO)  gave
         'I gave Ram$_i$ him$_j$.'

As far as quantificational IOs are concerned, for now assume that they too undergo reconstruction because they do not check a [+Q] feature in this position. Though I revise this analysis in the next chapter, this proposal explains the scope-freezing noted by Larson (1990:603–4) in the DOC. As the examples in (29) show, although the PDC gives rise to scope ambiguities, in the DOC, the IO quantifier always has wide scope:

(29) (a) we gave one problem to every student. (*ambiguous*)

     (b) we gave one student every problem. (*unambiguous*)

Aoun and Li's (1993) proposal of an MBR on variables left by QR explains these effects. Consider the LF representations of (29), where (29a) will have the representation in (30), and (29b) may choose between the representations in (31a) and (31b) :

(30) we gave [$_{VP1}$ [one problem]$_k$ [$_{AGR-oP}$ $t_k'$ [$_{VP2}$ [every student]$_z$ [$_{VP2}$ $t_k$ [to $t_z$]]]]]

(31) (a) we gave [$_{VP1}$ [every problem]$_k$ [$_{VP1}$ [one student]$_z$ [$_{AGR-oP}$ $t_k'$ [$_{AGR-oP}$ $t_z'$ [$_{VP2}$ $t_k$ $t_z$]]]]]

     (b) we gave [$_{VP1}$ [one student]$_z$ $_{AGR-oP}$ $t_z''$ [$_{AGR-oP}$ $t_z'$ [$_{AGR-oP}$ [every problem]$_k$ [$_{VP2}$ $t_k$ $t_z$]]]]

Consider first the LF representation of quantifier scope in the PDC in (30). The representation does not violate the MBR in any way. The variable, $t_k'$, of the DO quantifier in [Spec, AGR-oP] is bound by the closest L-bar binder *one problem*. Similarly, the variable, $t_z$, of the IO quantifier is also unambiguously bound by the closest potential L-bar binder, *every student*, adjoined to VP$_1$. The trace of the DO in the lower VP$_2$ does not count as a variable because it is not a Cased empty category. Thus (29a) is correctly predicted to be ambiguous.

Now consider QR in the DOC in (31a–b). Which of these two representations is the legitimate one at LF? Recall that in the DOC, both the IO and the DO occur in the checking domain of the VP-internal AGR-o. Example (31a) represents the derivation in which the DO quantifier *every problem* has QR'd over the AGR-oP-adjoined IO quantifier *one student*. Consider the variable, $t_k{}'$, left behind by this QR. Is it bound by the closest potential L-bar binder? No, because the closest potential L-bar binder is the IO quantifier *one student*, which does not bind it. Thus, the representation in (31a) violates the MBR.[9] Example (31b) then turns out to be the only licit LF representation for (29b), where the IO quantifier is the only one that can QR to get the wide scope reading. Scope-freezing is thus a result of the fact that the only convergent derivation of quantifier interaction in DOCs is the one that forbids the QR of the DO quantifier.

## (24) and the Overtness of XP-Adjunction

A property of my account is that it has made no appeal to the notion of feature strength, although it has been my tacit assumption that the features involved in the Case checking in ditransitives are always [strong]. Although, in principle, it is expected that languages may allow one or both the Case features of AGR-o to be [weak], it is also worth considering whether natural language is actually committed to realizing every logical option permitted by a typology. There is enough evidence to suggest that substitution positions are subject to the [strong]/[weak] distinction, but the question that we need to ask is whether covert feature-checking XP-adjunction has the same wealth of evidence bearing on it. Allowing covert XP-adjunction could, in principle, create havoc in the grammar (see also Jones 1994). Consider, for example, the difference between Hindi-Urdu and English vis-à-vis scrambling. The [strong]/[weak] distinction would suggest that the features that drive scrambling are [weak] in English, leading us to expect that English should also exhibit the interpretive judgments shown by Hindi-Urdu scrambled [+Q] elements. Not only that, but if XP-adjunction is allowed at LF and by definition overrides WCO effects, we could even expect English to show no WCO effects at all, because scrambling may act as an escape-hatch for all [+Q] elements.

It thus appears that the optimal result would be one that restricts derived XP-adjunction operations to the overt syntax. In chapter 5, I suggest that the overtness of the XP-adjunction operation involved in scrambling is forced by certain pragmatic requirements, but this is an account that does not easily motivate the overtness of the Case checking XP-adjunction operation. Although I am not in a position to make a firm proposal as to why this latter operation must necessarily be overt, the evidence presented below that that Case checking in adjoined positions constitutes a special environment for the rules of the PF-component may indicate that the overtness of Case checking XP-adjunction originates from a basic 'PF-orientation' of the operation.

According to Mohanan (1992), the fact that only the Hindi-Urdu IO may bear the dative/accusative Case-marker -*ko* (e.g., [21]) derives from a more general prohibition against the co-occurrence of DPs with phonologically identical Case formatives in adjacent constituents:

(32)  (a) ??ram-ko    bəccõ-ko      səmbʰalna pəṭa  
           Ram-DAT children-ACC  manage      fell  
           'Ram had to manage the children.'

      (b) *ram-ko    bəccõ-ko      kitabõ-ko  dena     hoga  
           Ram-DAT children-DAT books-ACC  to give will  
           'Ram will have to give the books to the children.'

Ignoring the fact that (32b) is much worse than (32a) for the moment, consider where this marginality comes from. Mohanan (1992:319) proposes that (32a) is a consequence of the Hindi version of Leben's (1973) *Obligatory Contour Principle* (OCP) in (33a), a principle which constrains the distribution of identical elements in adjacent units. The Hindi Case OCP in (33b) rules out the configurations in (32), because it interprets the OCP to apply across word boundaries to adjacent Case formatives of the participants of the same predicate:

(33)  (a) THE GENERALIZED OCP  
         Identical elements (melodic/formatives) are disallowed in  
         adjacent units.

      (b) HINDI-URDU CASE OCP  
         Identical element: Case formative.  
         Adjacent unit: Phonological word.  
         Environment: Participants of the same predicate.

The fact that DOs in Hindi-Urdu ditransitives can never appear with the -*ko* Case-marker (which they bear in simple transitives) is now explained by the Hindi-Urdu Case OCP, as the IO must necessarily be Case-marked, and a violation of the OCP results if the DO is Case-marked as well.

Although Mohanan (1992:221) believes that the Hindi-Urdu Case OCP cannot be stated without reference to order, semantic participation in a predicate, and phonological shape, I feel this conclusion to be a trifle hasty. The facts here are perfectly amenable to an account that considers the Hindi-Urdu Case OCP to apply to the purely syntactic output of overt movement, as in (34):

(34) SYNTACTIC ENVIRONMENT FOR THE HINDI-URDU CASE OCP
Items in (overt) Case checking positions (specifiers and XP-adjoined positions) of adjacent functional heads.

Recall that lexical items are inserted fully inflected into the derivation. Now, because any such item that has undergone overt checking must be phonologically identifiable as a 'word' and because checking in adjacent functional heads would involve only participants of the same semantic predicate, (34) adequately captures the essence of Mohanan's observations. The statement would also explain the difference in the OCP violations in (32a) and (32b): In (32a), the adjacent functional heads involved in checking the Case of the SU and the DO are Tns and AGR-o, respectively; in (32b), the Case checker for both the IO and the DO is the same functional head, a VP-internal AGR-o. The DO and the IO are strictly adjacent in (32b) but not in (32a), and therefore the strength of the Hindi-Urdu Case OCP violation.

This statement has the additional advantage of explaining why Hindi-Urdu Case OCP effects are significantly mitigated in scrambled configurations. Contrast (35a) with (35b):

(35)  (a) *ram  sita-ko    us    kitab-ko    dega
          Ram  Sita-DAT  that  book-ACC   will give
          'Ram will give Sita that book.'

      (b) ??us kitab-ko$_i$    ram    sita-ko    t$_i$  dega
          that  book-ACC   Ram   Sita-DAT        will give
          'Ram will give Sita that book.'

On the natural assumption that the Hindi-Urdu Case OCP applies after copy-deletion at PF, the scrambled DO is no longer in the appropriate environment for triggering the Case OCP effect.[10]

## 3.3   Conclusion

The objective of this chapter was to delineate the basic structural environment in which binding and coreference is to be determined in Hindi-Urdu. In addition, the claim that the AGR-oP projection is located VP-internally, by delinking the specific readings of scrambled noun phrases from their positioning in a particular Case checking position, sets the stage for an independent account for this phenomenon. In chapter 5, I extend the analysis of indefinites in Diesing (1992) to provide an analysis that links specificity effects to positioning in the linear hierarchical order.

Although the proposal that ditransitives are universally configured in the structure in (24) has many descriptive advantages, it is important to recognize that it does some damage to current conceptions of the economy of representation. Recall that Chomsky's (1989) Full Interpretation defines as legitimate only those argument chains in which each link is in an A-position in accordance with the Chain Condition. By my proposals in this chapter, the chain created by dative shift cannot thus ever be legitimate, as the adjoined-to-AGR-oP IO satisfies neither of the two criteria by which A-positions have come to be identified in the recent years—location in the specifier position of a Case checking functional head or in the specifier/complement position of a θ-marking lexical head.

Observe, however, that this definition of legitimate LF objects is grounded in the P&P understanding of the role of Case in making argument chains visible for θ-marking at LF. Minimalism, however, does not maintain this causal role accorded to Case, not only because θ-marking is considered a base property that is complementary to checking but also because checking is no longer a special property of Case alone—it is subsumed under a general interface condition that all morphosyntactic features must be checked for convergence. Minimalism thus asks us to consider Case and θ-role as two independent rather than related properties of arguments, and traces the fact that argument chains typically locate the Case checking position at the head and the θ-position at the tail to the economy principle of Greed—because only Case features are morphosyntactic, and because only morphosyntactic imperatives can trigger movement, movement will never be able to target a θ-position without a θ-Criterion violation.

It thus becomes necessary, quite independent of the issue of Case checking from XP-adjoined positions, to redefine how Full Interpretation recognizes an argument chain to be a legitimate LF object in minimalism. Because the two properties of θ-relatedness and a checked Case are now independent, all that Full Interpretation would require is that a legitimate argument (chain) bear a unique checked Case and a unique θ-role. Furthermore, given the Chain Uniformity Condition and the Economy of Derivation, it is also no longer required that Full Interpretation too evaluate argument chains for uniformity.[11] I return to the proper formulation of Full Interpretation in chapter 6.

# Chapter 4

# Binding and Coreference in UG

The claim that scrambling is uniformly an XP-adjunction operation meets its major empirical challenge from the instances of scrambling that override WCO effects and putatively license reflexives. These instances provide a mandate for a reappraisal of the theory of binding, coreference, and reconstruction in UG, rather than for a fracturing of the uniform analysis of scrambling as an XP-adjunction operation. This chapter initiates this exercise. Because the cases in which scrambling exhibits the binding properties of Case-driven NP-movement involve possessive reflexives and pronominals, I examine, in the first two sections of the chapter, the predictions a binding theory based on Chomsky (1986b) makes for these categories. The discussion here reveals that the configurations commonly held to be relevant for the application of Principles A and B of the standard binding theory cannot explain either the ability of Hindi-Urdu possessive reflexives to take long-distance subject antecedents or the anti-subject orientation of possessive pronominals.

Developing suggestions in the literature by Pica (1987), Cole, Hermon, and Sung (1990), Cole and Sung (1994), Hestvik (1992), and Avrutin (1994), I propose that the appropriate LF configuration for the evaluation of Principles A and B of the binding theory raising is achieved only after reflexives and pronominals have raised to the licensing domain of $T^0$ and $D^0$, respectively. Section 4.3 constitutes a minimalist execution of Reinhart's (1986, 1991) and Reinhart and Grodzinsky's (1993) insights by which coreference determined by the binding theory is the result of only a subset of the mechanisms available to determine the (co)referential use of expressions in UG. Making Reinhart's approach sensitive to movement as copying and deletion provides not only a binding-theoretic account of WCO and SCO effects but also an explanation for the possibility of pronominal coreference with positions created by overt XP-adjunction.

(1)   (a) The BINDING DOMAIN of an expression E is the minimal complete functional complex containing $\alpha$ and its governor.

   (b) A CFC is a domain in which all the grammatical functions compatible with its head are realized.

   (c) PRINCIPLE A: A reflexive must be bound in its binding domain.

   PRINCIPLE B: A pronominal must be free in its binding domain.

   PRINCIPLE C: An R-expression must be free.

   (d) BINDING: $\alpha$ binds $\beta$ iff $\alpha$ c-commands and is coindexed with $\beta$, where $\alpha$ c-commands $\beta$ iff the first branching node dominating $\alpha$ dominates $\beta$, and neither $\alpha$ nor $\beta$ dominate each other.

## 4.1   Principle A and Reflexive Binding

It is a historical accident that our understanding of the distribution of reflexive elements in natural language has been primarily based on languages that are relatively impoverished in reflexivization strategies. Reflexives in languages such as Chinese, Russian, Hindi-Urdu, Norwegian, etc., exhibit properties quite distinct from English, not the least in the fact that they employ more than one reflexive form. Such languages usually employ a monomorphemic 'self'-reflexive (which may also be used locally as a possessive reflexive) in addition to the morphologically more complex 'X-self' reflexive as attested in English, Hindi-Urdu *əpne-ap*, Chinese *ta ziji*, etc.[1] The monomorphemic self-reflexive exhibits properties that are quite distinct from those of the complex reflexive even in these languages. For one, monomorphemic reflexives may take (subject) antecedents quite a long distance away, but complex reflexives are typically local in character—witness the contrast between Chinese, Hindi-Urdu, and Russian monomorphemic reflexives in (2) and English and Hindi-Urdu complex reflexives in (3):

(2)   (a) Zhangsan$_i$  renwei  Lisi$_j$  zhidao  Wangwu$_k$  xihuan  ziji$_{i/j/k}$
       Zhangsan  think   Lisi    know    Wangwu     like     self

   'Zhangsan thinks Lisi knows Wangwu likes himself/herself.'

   (b) sita$_i$-ne  ram$_j$-ko  [PRO$_j$  əpni$_{i/j}$  kıtabẽ  pəʈʰne]  dĩ
       Sita      Ram                  self's    books   to-read  gave

   'Sita allowed Ram to read her/his books.'

   (c) professor$_i$  poprosil  assistenta$_j$  [PRO$_j$  citat'  svoj$_{i/j}$
       professor   asked     assistant               read    self's
       doklad]
       report

   'The professor asked the assistant to read self's$_{i/j}$ report.'

(3)    (a) Tom$_i$ thinks that Bill$_j$ likes himself$_{*i/j}$

        (b)
| sita$_i$-ne | ram$_j$-ko | [PRO$_j$ | əpne-ap$_{*i/j}$-ko | səmb${}^h$alne-ko] |
|---|---|---|---|---|
| Sita | Ram | | herself | to-control |

          kəha
          said

          'Sita told Ram to control himself.'

Second, unlike complex reflexives, these monomorphemic reflexives exhibit a very strong *subject-orientation*. As can be seen from the Norwegian and Hindi-Urdu examples in (4) and (5), DOs and IOs cannot antecede these reflexives, a behavior quite unlike that of English in (6):

(4)    (a)
| John$_i$ | fortalte | Per$_j$ | om | et | bilde | av | seg$_{i/*j}$ |
|---|---|---|---|---|---|---|---|
| John | told | Peter | about | a | picture | of | self |

          'John$_i$ told Peter$_j$ about a picture of himself$_{i/*j}$.'

        (b)
| John$_i$ | ga | Per$_j$ | [sin$_{i/*j}$ | jakke] |
|---|---|---|---|---|
| John | gave | Peter | self's | jacket |

          'John$_i$ gave Peter$_j$ his$_{i/*j}$ jacket.'

(5)    (a)
| nur$_i$-ne | sita$_j$-ko | əpne$_{i/*j}$ | bare-mẽ | kəhani | sunayi |
|---|---|---|---|---|---|
| Noor | Sita | self | about | story | recited |

          'Noor$_i$ told Sita$_j$ a story about herself$_{i/*j}$.'

        (b)
| sita$_i$-ne | nur$_j$-ko | [əpni$_{i/*j}$ | kitab] | di |
|---|---|---|---|---|
| Sita | Noor | self's | book(DO) | gave |

          'Sita$_i$ gave Noor$_j$ her$_{i/*j}$ book.'

(6)    John$_i$ showed Peter$_j$ a picture of himself$_{i/j}$

These properties of monomorphemic reflexives do not follow from the binding theory as stated earlier. In each of the cases in (2), (4), and (5), the standard binding theory would identify the binding domain of the reflexive as the IP that contains them, and Principle A would require that the reflexive be locally bound by a c-commanding antecedent in this local domain. This formulation of the binding domain then not only rules out the possibility of long-distance binding but also allows the option of nonsubject antecedents for the reflexive.

Pica (1987), developing suggestions in Chomsky (1986b) that reflexive interpretation is accomplished by raising it into the domain of its antecedent, suggests that the divergence in the properties of the two types of reflexives follows from a difference in their categorial status. He proposes that whereas monomorphemic reflexives are projections of an $X^0$-level category, complex reflexives are inherently XPs that lack any internal X-bar theoretic structure. Then, on a strong thesis of the X-bar compatibility of movement, it follows that XP-reflexives can either substitute into [Spec, XP] or adjoin to XP at LF, but $X^0$-reflexives can undergo successive cyclic $X^0$-movement at LF. The difference in the properties of the two types of reflexives follows directly—assuming that the $X^0$-reflexive moves successively cyclically to each $I^0$ in (2), it satisfies Principle A at each step. $X^0$-reflexives are thus only seemingly long distance, for at the point that Principle A applies, the relationship between the reflexive and its antecedent is covertly local in nature. The fact that such reflexives are necessarily subject-oriented then comes as no surprise, as the only possible candidate for antecedenthood will be the subject in [Spec, IP]. XP-reflexives, on the other hand, cannot move successively cyclically, and may therefore only adjoin to their containing XP.[2] They will therefore not be able to take long-distance antecedents but may be interpreted as coreferential with any c-commanding antecedent within the binding domain identified after such raising. By Pica's proposals then, (4a), (5b), and (6) will have the LF representations in (7):

(7)  (a) John $I^0$-seg$_i$ [fortalte Per [om et bilde av t$_i$]]

  (b) sita-ne $I^0$-əpni$_i$ nur-ko [t$_i$ kɪtɑb] di

  (c) John told Bill [$_{PP}$ himself$_i$ [$_{PP}$ about t$_i$]]

The only c-commanding antecedent for the Norwegian and Hindi-Urdu $X^0$-reflexive is the subject, but for the (English) XP-reflexive, there are two c-commanding antecedents, the subject and the DO.

The descriptive potential of the LF raising approach to reflexive-binding nothwithstanding, some questions still need to be answered before it can be employed in a minimalist binding theory. The next two sections explore some of the more complex issues in this regard, but the most obvious question regarding the morphosyntactic imperative for this LF raising can be settled with reference to Chomsky and Lasnik (1993). Chomsky and Lasnik suggest that it is necessary to regard reflexives as licensed under agreement with their antecedents, and because agreement is strictly a local phenomenon, the reflexive and its antecedent must be in the configuration where agreement relations are licensed. A derivation in which the reflexive does not occupy the SPEC-head configuration by LF will crash at that interface because of a Full Interpretation violation—the reflexive cannot be licensed in any other base or derived position.

### 4.1.1   Raising XP-Reflexives in Minimalism

As Chomsky and Lasnik (1993) analyze both XP- and $X^0$-reflexives (at least the part that raises) to have the categorial status of an $X^0$-category that cliticizes onto an inflectional head in order to agree with its specifier, their analysis must ignore Pica's observations regarding the distribution of the two types of reflexives. This appears to be a cost too dear to pay, for, if all reflexives raise to Tns/AGR-s at LF, then neither the fact that Chinese, English, and Norwegian XP-reflexives may take IO antecedents nor the fact that only $X^0$-reflexives take long-distance antecedents can receive an adequate explanation.

At the same time, it is equally clear that XP-reflexives are also licensed under agreement with an antecedent, viz., the contrast in (8), where the mismatch of φ-features between the XP-reflexive and the antecedent in (8b) results in ungrammaticality:

(8)     (a)  John$_i$ thinks himself$_i$ to be the best person for the job

        (b)  *John$_i$ thinks herself$_i$ to be the best person for the job

Holding onto Pica's original analysis of the difference between the two types of reflexive elements, I suggest that XP-reflexive licensing proceeds in a way which is in some sense the opposite of the way in which $X^0$-reflexives are licensed. Like $X^0$-reflexives, XP-reflexives too need to be in an agreement configuration with their antecedents, but my definition of this configuration is somewhat larger than Chomsky and Lasnik's. Given the proposal of Case checking from a position broadly L-related to AGR-o in the last chapter, we can allow licensing relations from a broadly L-related position as well. In this case, then, the XP-reflexive adjoins to the maximal projection that hosts the antecedent (or its copy) in its SPEC. Because the head of that functional projection bears the φ-features of the antecedent, if the φ-features on the functional head match those of the XP-reflexive, the derivation converges. The impossibility of long-distance uses of XP-reflexives follows as before, as does the explanation of the ability of XP-reflexives to take nonsubject antecedents.

### 4.1.2   Raising $X^0$-Reflexives in Minimalism

Turning now to the issue of the functional head targeted by $X^0$-reflexives, we find that with the resolution of $I^0$ into a number of functional projections, the choice reduces to one between AGR-s and Tns, given subject orientation. Although analyses vary in details, the choice of AGR-s as the relevant head is usually motivated to establish a correlation between inflectional morphology and the distribution of $X^0$-reflexives across languages.

For example, Cole and Sung (1994) necessarily associate $X^0$-reflexives with AGR-s primarily because they also trace the differences in the properties of Chinese and Italian $X^0$-reflexives to the the relative richness of verb agreement morphology in the two languages. Although I am also of the opinion that factors other than Tns have an effect on $X^0$-reflexive interpretation, it appears to me that the effects of these other factors are always felt in conspiracy with the properties of Tns. This section argues that universally $X^0$-reflexives cliticize onto Tns at LF, though languages may differ as to whether reflexive interpretation takes place before or after the [Tns-REFL] complex raises to AGR-s.

Consider first the ineligibility of AGR-s as the relevant head. Analyses such as those of Cole and Sung (1994) suggest that overt phenomena play a role in the properties of covert movement, but minimalism would require overt distinctions to make an *overt* difference. In addition, Hindi-Urdu provides evidence against the claim that $X^0$-reflexive raising has anything at all to do with agreement relations in AGR-s. Hindi-Urdu is a language with three major subsystems of verb agreement (see note 2 to chapter 2), but $X^0$-reflexives are always subject-oriented, irrespective of the (nominative/nonnominative) Case on the subject and whether or not it controls verb agreement. For example, in (5a) the subject is in the ergative case and does not control verb agreement, yet the $X^0$-reflexive must obligatorily be bound by it.

In fact in Hindi-Urdu, Tns seems to be the relevant head that licenses $X^0$-reflexives (Davison 1995). As (9) shows, only $X^0$-reflexives in nonfinite clauses can take long-distance antecedents:

(9)  (a) sita$_i$-ne   kəha  [$_{CP}$ ki    ram$_j$-ne   əpni$_{*i/j}$  kɪtab
         Sita(SU)  said       that  Ram(SU)   self's      book(DO)
         p$^h$ẽk  di]
         throw  gave
         'Sita$_i$ said that Ram$_j$ threw away self's$_{*i/j}$ book.'

     (b) sita$_i$-ne   ram$_j$-ko   [$_{CP}$ PRO$_j$ əpni$_{i/j}$  kɪtabẽ
         Sita(SU)  Ram(DO)        self's      books(DO)
         pəʈ$^h$ne]  di͂
         to-read  gave
         'Sita allowed Ram to read her/his books.'

In both examples, the subjects of both the matrix and embedded clause do not control verb agreement, and on the assumption that [Spec, AGR-sP] is the position occupied by agreeing subjects, all four subjects here are in [Spec, TP]. After $X^0$-reflexive raising to Tns, the simplified LF representations for (9a–b) would be as follows, assuming Dayal's (1997) analysis of

Hindi-Urdu finite complements as syntactic adjuncts:

(10)   (a)  sita-ne kəha [$_{CP}$ ki [$_{TP}$ ram-ne [$_{Tns}$ əpni$_j$-Tns] [$_{AGR-oP}$ [t$_j$ kɪtab] p$^h$ēk di]]]

     (b)  *[$_{CP}$ [$_{TP}$ sita-ne [$_{Tns}$ əpni$_j$-Tns] kəha]] [$_{CP}$ ki [$_{TP}$ ram-ne [t$_j$ kɪtab] [p$^h$ēk di]]]]

(11)   (a)  [$_{TP}$ sita-ne ram-ko [$_{CP}$ [$_{TP}$ PRO [$_{Tns}$ əpni$_j$-Tns] [$_{AGR-oP}$ [t$_j$ kɪtabē] pəʈ$^h$ne]]] dĩ]

     (b)  [$_{TP}$ sita-ne [$_{Tns}$ əpni$_j$-Tns] [$_{CP}$ [$_{TP}$ PRO [t$_j$ kɪtabē] pəʈ$^h$ne]] dĩ]

The nonconvergence of (10b) follows from the ECP, because as the finite CP is an adjunct and therefore not L-marked, $X^0$-reflexive raising out of the finite clause will cross the CP and the TP barrier. No such violations obtain in either (10a) as the movement is clause-bound, or in (11a–b) where the CP *is* L-marked.[3, 4]

This explanation appears to be adequate for describing the distribution of $X^0$-reflexives in Hindi-Urdu, but its crosslinguistic validity is questionable. Russian, an SVO language, exhibits a similar role of finite tense in blocking successive cyclic $X^0$-reflexive raising at LF. One could argue that these prohibitions in Russian are also derived by a similar intervention of language-specific factors, but this strategy of reducing what does not appear to be an isolated phenomenon to a matter of coincidence is surely undesirable. I therefore present some tentative speculations about how the similarity between Hindi-Urdu and Russian may be derived.

Consider the basic difference between the Hindi-Urdu types of languages and the Chinese types of languages to be whether they allow covert (intermediate) adjunction to $C^0$. If we suppose that the former do not but the latter do, then the Chinese facts follow at once, as now $X^0$-reflexive raising from a complement clause (irrespective of its tense specification) will always respect relativized minimality (Rizzi 1990). The Hindi-Urdu/Russian facts require some further tinkering, as we wish to block raising from finite CP complements. Watanabe's proposals about the way in which Tns/AGR-s interacts with the licensing of CP complements provide the relevant ammunition.

Watanabe (1993) suggests that CP complements are in general licensed by his proposal that Case-checking in AGR-sP creates a feature [F] that must be satisfied by the raising of AGR-s and its incorporated heads into the domain of a follow-up checker—$C^0$—that is capable of checking this [F] feature. The difference between the various CP complements (in terms of the kinds of subjects they allow) is a consequence of the kind of feature [F] that is created and the type of $C^0$ that is appropriate for checking this feature. "Depending on which Case is to be checked, different [F] features are created, and accordingly different COMP nodes have to exist to check off these features" (Watanabe 1993:90). Now, suppose we assume that the feature $[F_{NULL}]$ created by Null Case checking in Hindi-Urdu and Russian is such that the follow-up checking of $[F_{NULL}]$ in $C^0$ renders it transparent to intermediate adjunction, but the follow-up checking of $[F_{NOM}]$ lacks this property. Then, reflexive raising via $C^0$ is permitted only in non-finite clauses, because in finite clauses the feature $[F_{NOM}]$ does not license the transparency of $C^0$ to subsequent LF-adjunction in the required way. Presumably this transparency effect of the follow-up checking of $[F_{NULL}]$ is a universal phenomenon, except that in languages such as Chinese, which allow intermediate adjunction to $C^0$ anyway, these effects are invisible.

Languages that employ $X^0$-reflexives also exhibit some variation with respect to their subject orientation, a fact that is unpredicted by our analysis so far. While Hindi-Urdu possessive $X^0$-reflexives are uniformly subject-oriented, possessive $X^0$-reflexives in Italian, as (13) shows, are ambiguous in reference.

(12) ənjUm$_i$-ne    rɑhUl$_j$-ko    [əpne$_{i/*j}$  bɑre-mẽ  ek  məzmun]
     Anjum(SU)   Rahul(IO)   self       about-in  an  article(DO)
     diyɑ
     gave

     'Anjum gave Rahul an article about herself/*himself.'

(13) Gianni$_i$     ha    ricondotto  Maria$_j$     alla     propria$_{i/j}$
     Gianni(SU)  has   returned    Maria(DO)  to-the  self
     famiglia
     family

     'Gianni has brought back Maria to her own/his own-family.'

While Cole and Sung (1994) trace the Italian facts to an "additional language-specific requirement" by which Italian $X^0$-reflexives cannot raise to Tns at all, less stipulatory analyses are available. Note that both the examples in (12) and (13) involve ditransitives. Then, Hindi-Urdu and Chinese differ from Italian in a specific way—Hindi-Urdu and Chinese employ the DOC form of a ditransitive, Italian uses the PDC. Recall that this means that in Hindi-Urdu and Chinese, IOs are in a position adjoined to a VP-internal AGR-oP and the DO is in the specifier position of that VP-internal AGR-oP. Italian, on the other hand, forces the IO to remain in situ (where preposition-insertion Case-marks the IO) and raises the DO to [Spec, AGR-oP]. Thus at Spellout, the VPs in Hindi-Urdu and Italian will have the structure in (14):

(14)  (a)  ...$[_{VP1}$ $t_{SU}$ $[_{AGR\text{-}oP}$ rɑhUl-ko $[_{AGR\text{-}oP}$ [əpne$_{i/*j}$ bɑre-mẽ ek məzmun] AGR-o $[_{VP2}$ $t_{DO}$ $t_{IO}$ $t_V$]]] diyɑ]

(b)  ...$[_{VP1}$ $t_{SU}$ ricondotto $[_{AGR\text{-}oP}$ Maria AGR-o $[_{VP2}$ $t_{DO}$ $t_V$ $[_{PP}$ alla propria famiglia]]]]

So far I have maintained that all languages raise $X^0$-reflexives to Tns and that Principle A can evaluate derivations only when the reflexive reaches Tns. This is surely stipulatory, as Principle A should be able to apply wherever the conditions of its application are met. Thus, if any of the heads that the $X^0$-reflexive moves through hosts a DP in its specifier that can license the $X^0$-reflexive under agreement, Principle A should find the conditions for its application met. This is exactly what happens in Italian: In the course of $X^0$-reflexive raising to Tns via the $V_2$, AGR-o, and $V_1$ positions, the reflexive is in a position in which it can be licensed under agreement not once but *twice*, once by the DO in [Spec, AGR-oP] and once when it is in a SPEC-head configuration with the SU in [Spec, AGR-sP] (after the [Tns-REFL] complex incorporates into AGR-s). Principle A may thus be evaluated at two points in the derivation, and therefore the ambiguity of reference of the Italian reflexive in (14b).

Consider next the Hindi-Urdu example in (14a). The successive cyclic raising of the $X^0$-reflexive to Tns does not involve movement through the VP-internal AGR-o head, because the reflexive is embedded in a constituent in the specifier of that functional head. Consequently, any movement through AGR-o entails a lowering operation in violation of the ECP. As a result, the $X^0$-reflexive in the Hindi-Urdu (and the Chinese) ditransitive satisfies Principle A just *once*, when it is in a SPEC-head configuration with the subject in the specifier of AGR-sP/TP, and hence its subject orienta-tion. The correlation established here is thus quite simple: If a language has the PDC, $X^0$-reflexives in ditransitives will not be subject-oriented; if a language has the DOC, $X^0$-reflexive in ditransitives will necessarily be subject-oriented. In simple transitives, DO reflexives across languages are expected to exhibit a similar subject orientation.

To conclude, this section has suggested that reflexive interpretation is contingent upon the licensing conditions for reflexives. Adopting Chomsky and Lasnik's suggestion that reflexives are licensed under agreement, I have shown that the difference in categorial status between the monomorphemic reflexives and the complex reflexives proposed by Pica (1987) results in differences in the physical range of the interpretations accorded to the two. I have proposed that because complex reflexives are XPs, they are licensed in an agreeing XP-adjoined position to a functional head that bears the features of a licensing DP, and hence the locality of their antecedents. The monomorphemic reflexive, on the other hand, is an $X^0$ category that can undergo successive cyclic raising at LF. It therefore may be in more than one configuration that satisfies Principle A, and hence its ambiguity. In the next section, I argue that the range of interpretations of pronominals is similarly constrained by the configurations in which they are licensed. Following and adapting Hestvik (1990, 1992) and Avrutin (1992, 1994), I argue for a LF raising approach to pronominal reference as well.

## 4.2  Principle B and Pronominal Binding

Principle B in the standard binding theory in (1) imposes a condition of referential independence on pronominals in the binding domain defined as the CFC, but outside this domain pronominals may freely be used coreferentially. This formulation of Principle B captures the distribution of pronominals in a language such as English in (15), where pronominals embedded in PP and DP constituents allow a coreferential use with other referential expressions in a sentence but nonembedded ones do not.

(15)  (a)  John$_i$ likes his$_{i/j}$ car

     (b)  John$_i$ looked behind him$_{i/j}$

     (c)  John$_i$ saw him$_{*i/j}$

The standard binding theory identifies the binding domain for the pronominal in (15a–b) to be the containing DP and PP, respectively, so the pronominal may be used (co)referentially with the subject. In (15c), on the other hand, because the binding domain is identified as the IP, the pronominal must be referentially independent from all c-commanding antecedents.

Possessive and PP pronominals in languages such as Danish (Vikner 1985), Russian (Avrutin 1994), Norwegian (Hestvik 1990, 1992), and Hindi-Urdu (Dayal 1993, Davison 1995) then come as a surprise. In these languages, although nonembedded pronominals respect Principle B just as in English, possessive and PP pronominals must obligatorily obviate from the closest c-commanding subject antecedent, as shown by the examples from Norwegian (Hestvik 1992) and Hindi-Urdu in (16)–(17):

(16)  (a)  John$_i$   liker   hans$_{*i/j}$   bil
          John   likes   his     car

        'John$_i$ likes his$_{*i/j}$ car.'

     (b)  John$_i$   kikket   bak       ham$_{*i/j}$
          John   looked   behind   him

        'John$_i$ looked behind him$_{*i/j}$.'

(17)  (a)  sita$_i$   Uski$_{*i/j}$  gaṛi  layi
          Sita   her        car    brought
          'Sita brought her$_{*i/j}$ car.'

      (b)  sita$_i$-ne   Uske$_{*i/j}$  piᵡʰe   dekʰa
          Sita       her        behind  looked
          'Sita$_i$ looked behind her$_{*i/j}$.'

That it is the *closest subject* argument that counts as the relevant binder is
shown by the examples from Russian and Hindi-Urdu in (18)–(19), where
the embedded pronominal may be bound by either a higher c-commanding
object or a subject outside its containing clause:

(18)  (a)  každeja  devočka$_i$  pokazala  Ol'ge$_j$    ee$_{*i/j}$  komnatu
          every    girl(SU)    showed    Olga(IO)  her     room(DO)
          'Every girl$_i$ showed Olga$_j$ her$_{*i/j}$ room.'

      (b)  hər    ləṛki-ne$_i$  sita$_j$-ko  Uska$_{*i/j}$  kəmra    dɪkʰaya
          every  girl(SU)   Sita(İO)  her       room(DO)  showed
          'Every girl$_i$ showed Sita$_j$ her$_{*i/j}$ room.'

(19)  (a)  každyj  student$_i$  dumal   čto   Ivan$_j$  cital     ego$_{i/*j}$
          every   student    thought  that  Ivan   will read  his
          stat'ju
          article
          'Every student$_i$ thought Ivan$_j$ will read his$_{i*j}$ article.'

      (b)  hər    ləṛki$_i$  janti  hɛ  ki   nur$_j$   Uski$_{i/*j}$  kɪtab  pəṛʰegi
          each   girl    knows  is   that  Noor   her        book   will read
          'Each girl$_i$ knows that Noor$_j$ will read her$_{i/*j}$ book.'

    It is thus clear that a binding theory designed to capture the facts of
English alone cannot explain why Hindi-Urdu, Russian, and Norwegian
pattern together in this fashion. Although Manzini and Wexler (1987) suggest that the only way this phenomenon can be incorporated into UG is in
the form of a language-specific stipulation in the binding theory, Hestvik
(1992:558) takes issue with such ad hoc solutions, suggesting that a generalization of the reflexive raising approach to pronominals can instead provide a more principled explanation for these facts. Making the necessary
assumption that pronominals, like reflexives, divide universally into two
types—$X^0$ and XP—Hestvik suggests that $X^0$-pronominals must raise to
$I^0$ at LF, while XP-pronominals may stay in the specifier of their governor.
The difference between English–type and Hindi-Urdu–type languages then

is that in the former pronominals are XPs, while in the latter, they are $X^0$s. After $X^0$-pronominal raising to $I^0$ at LF, the only possible antecedent for it is the subject in [Spec, IP], from which it is to obviate if Principle B is to be satisfied.

Although Hestvik's approach is conceptually quite attractive, in that it locates the difference between Hindi–Urdu–type and English–type languages in a difference in the structural configuration in which Principle B is respected, the evidence for an $XP/X^0$ distinction in pronominals is at best quite slender. Because monomorphemicity obviously cannot be the criterion to be used—pronominals crosslinguistically tend to be monomorphemic—Hestvik (1992:569) argues the distinction to lie in the differential ability of pronominals to take restrictive modification: If restrictive modifiers involve $X^0$ or $X'$ level adjunction, then it is expected that only $X^0$-pronominals will be able to take such modifiers, because out of the two they are the only ones that possess X-bar theoretic internal structure. XP-pronominals, being inherent maximal projections, are not expected to take such modifiers. This prediction is apparently confirmed for Norwegian and English, as English lacks such restrictive modification of pronominals but Norwegian allows it:

(20)　(a)　han　som　gar　der
　　　　　　he　who　walks　there
　　　　　'He who walks there.'

　　　(b)　*He who is walking there is nice.

Similar evidence from other languages that exhibit the anti-subject orientation phenomenon is however hard to obtain.[5] More important, pronominals must surely differ from reflexives in their licensing requirements. Although the appeal to reflexive licensing by agreement as the trigger for their covert raising has intuitive content, the fact that pronominals can have a referential use and are fully specified for $\phi$-features in both types of languages, suggests that the crosslinguistic differences cannot originate in the categorial status of pronominals. Similarly problematic is the assumption that Tns is the relevant head at which pronominal licensing takes place, as although there is enough overt evidence for a relationship between Tns and reflexivization (e.g., reflexive predicates in Romance), such evidence is lacking with respect to pronominalization. Finally, languages do not appear to exhibit both $X^0$- and XP-pronominals in the way that they may have both $X^0$- and XP-reflexives.

Thus, an approach that seeks to maximally approximate pronominals to reflexives in order to motivate the covert raising of pronominals is bound to be unsuccessful. In the next subsection, I discuss and adapt Avrutin's (1994) proposals on how the LF raising of pronominals may be built into the theory of grammar.

### 4.2.1 Raising Pronominals in Minimalism

As there appears to be a deficiency of morphosyntactic motivation available to drive pronominal raising at LF, Avrutin (1994) suggests that the motivation is at least partly interpretive in nature. Avrutin proposes that any pronominal that is to be evaluated for its referential (in)dependence from a syntactically c-commanding antecedent must be in the following structural configuration at LF:

(21) THE STRUCTURAL POSITION OF BOUND VARIABLES

At LF, a pronominal interpreted as a bound variable must be in a functional projection.

where 'inclusion in a functional projection' is disjunctively defined as either adjunction to its head or substitution into its specifier position, and where the relevant functional heads are $I^0$ and/or $D^0$.

Avrutin restricts the LF raising of pronominals to instances in which pronominal interpretation is sought to be controlled by an element in the syntactic context, because "although an element interpreted as a bound variable may have (at least some) φ-features .... . These features are not used for establishing the reference for the element. Bound variables do not receive their reference independently: their value depends on the choice of value for the operator that binds them" (Avrutin 1994:711). Pronominals that are used referentially, such as the pronominal in *Noor$_i$ gave Sita$_j$ her$_k$ book* need not raise, as their referential interpretation accesses only the φ-features intrinsically specified on them. As (21) is to be interpreted as a "a wellformedness condition that applies at the interface level between syntax and the interpretive mechanism, ruling out those representations where pronominals (interpreted as bound variables) appear in a lexical projection" (Avrutin 1994:711), pronominals that receive a bound variable interpretation will raise at LF.

In Avrutin's approach, the difference between Hindi-Urdu– and English–type languages is that in the former, pronominals that are syntactically bound do *not* satisfy (21) at Spellout, but in the latter they do. Consider again the contrast between Russian/Hindi-Urdu and English:

(22)  (a)  každyj   student$_i$  citaet     ego$_{*i/j}$  knigu
             every    student  is reading  his     book
             'Every student$_i$ is reading his$_{*i/j}$ book.'

      (b)  hər     ləʈki$_i$  Uski$_{*i/j}$  kItab  pəʈ$^h$  rəhi    hɛ
             every  girl    her      book  read  PROG  is
             'Every girl$_i$ is reading her$_{*i/j}$ book.'

      (c)  Every girl$_i$ is reading her$_{i/j}$ book.

As the $i$ reading in (22) represents the bound variable reading for the pronominal, it must be included in the functional projection of $D^0$ or $I^0$ by LF. Avrutin argues that in English, because possessors raise to [Spec, DP] by Spellout, the pronominal satisfies this requirement without LF movement. By the definition of the CFC in (1), the DP containing the pronominal will be identified as its binding domain and because the pronominal respects Principle B in this domain, it may freely corefer with the subject. In Russian (and Hindi-Urdu), Avrutin argues, Spellout chains do not involve overt raising of the possessor to [Spec, DP]; rather, the configuration that reaches PF is $[_{DP} \text{D} [_{NP} \text{POSSESSOR} [_{N\prime} \text{POSSESSUM}]]$.[6] As a consequence, LF raising of the pronominal to $D^0$ or $I^0$ is necessitated. Because this LF raising voids the 'binding domainhood' of the DP that contains the possessive pronominal, the IP is the binding domain for the pronominal. The subject quantifier cannot therefore bind the pronominal because a Principle B violation will result.

Although Avrutin's proposals execute Hestvik's intuitions with some elegance, the fact of the matter is that they allow (covert) movement that is driven primarily by interpretive considerations. The quasi-morphosyntactic imperative suggested, by which the pronominal moves to inherit the φ-features of its antecedent, cannot be formalized as a licensing requirement on bound pronominals, as raising to $D^0$ does not locate the pronominal in an agreement configuration with the antecedent. Avrutin's proposals thus indicate that at least some instances of covert movement may be driven not by morphology but by concerns of interpretation, a failure to raise resulting in nonconvergence with respect to Full Interpretation at LF. On the understanding that the checking of an interpretive feature does not significantly undermine minimalist assumptions about movement—presumably, similar features force the QR of quantifiers and definites—I will assume that all possessive pronominals enter a checking relation with $D^0$.[7]

An adoption of the alternative suggestion that bound pronominals actually raise to Tns is beset with problems of a different kind. It is hard to explain why pronominals, if they may adjoin to $I^0$ just like $X^0$-reflexives, do not move successively cyclically like them at LF. Although Avrutin actually allows for pronominal raising targeting Tns, this option is actually irrelevant in most cases: The choice between pronominal raising to $D^0$ or $I^0$ has, in all cases but one, no real effect on the analysis, because in either case pronominal raising identifies the IP containing it as the binding domain. The only instance in which raising to $I^0$ cannot be substituted for by raising to $D^0$ is the DOC in (23). In the structure of ditransitives, $[_{VP} \text{V}$ DP DP], that Avrutin (1994:715) adopts, raising the pronominal to $D^0$ will not remove it from the c-command domain of the IO. In order to achieve this result, it is therefore necessary that the pronominal raise to $I^0$:

(23)    (a) Ol'ga$_j$ pokazala každyj devočka$_i$ ee$_{i/*j}$ komnatu

          Olga    showed    each    girl(IO)   her    room(DO)

          'Olga$_j$ showed each girl$_{i/*j}$ her room.'

    (b) nur$_j$-ne    hər    lərki$_i$-ko Uski$_{i/*j}$ kɪtɑb di

          Noor(SU) each   girl(IO)   her       book   gave

          'Noor$_j$ gave each girl$_i$ her$_{i/*j}$ book.'

The analysis of ditransitives in the previous chapter now removes the need for such construction–specific stipulations. Recall that in the proposed structure of the DOC, the IO occupies an XP-adjoined position at Spellout. At the stage that the binding theory applies, the head copy of the IO chain is rendered irrelevant (in a way made precise in the next section), so the IO will not constitute a c-commanding binder for the pronominal contained in the DO. Pronominal raising to $D^0$ will then adequately capture the antisubject orientation of the DO possessive pronominal.

To conclude, this section has argued that an extension of the LF raising approach to reflexive interpretation to pronominals explains the antisubject orientation of possessive and PP pronominals in languages such as Hindi-Urdu, Russian, and Norwegian. I have suggested, following Avrutin (1994), that pronominals that are to receive their interpretation via syntactic binding must be included in the functional projection of $D^0$ by LF. The difference in pronominal orientation in languages such as Hindi-Urdu and English is shown to follow from the fact that whereas English pronominals satisfy this structural requirement at Spellout, Hindi-Urdu pronominals do not and need to undergo LF raising. Because such LF raising always narrows down the range of antecedents available to the pronominal to the DP in [Spec, TP], Principle B forces the pronominal to obviate from it.

## 4.3   Binding and Coreference in Minimalism

The standard binding theory in (1) seeks to determine the legitimacy of every instance of a coreferential use of a referential element, by which anaphora are obligatorily coreferential, pronominals only optionally so, and R-expressions are obligatorily noncoreferential. For such an approach, the facts in (25) are inexplicable, as each of the examples involves a violation of either Principle B or C, but somehow this coreferential use is licit (examples from Reinhart and Grodzinsky 1993:78–79):

(24)    (a) Churchill$_i$ likes Churchill$_{*i}$

     (b) He$_i$ likes Oscar$_{*i}$

     (c) I$_i$ like me$_{*i}$

(25)  (a)  Only Churchill$_i$ remembers Churchill$_i$ giving the speech about
            blood, sweat and tears!

      (b)  Everyone has finally realized that Oscar is incompetent. Even
           he$_i$ has finally realized that Oscar$_i$ is incompetent!

      (c)  I dreamt that I was Brigitte Bardot and I kissed me!

Whereas an approach such as that of Chomsky (1981, 1986b) and Chomsky and Lasnik (1993) must find the means of explaining this coreferential use in apparent violation of the binding principles from within the binding theory, Reinhart (1986, 1991) and Reinhart and Grodzinsky (1993) suggest that this coreferential use actually springs from the computations of a different interpretive module altogether. Distinguishing between coreference determined by syntactic context and coreference determined by discourse context, speaker intentions, etc., Reinhart proposes that the binding theory be restricted to computing the legitimacy of bound variable anaphora, i.e., instances in which the referential element that is to be evaluated by the binding theory is coindexed with a c-commanding antecedent. Instances of coreference such as in (25), on the other hand, are the results of the computations by the rules in the coreference component.

One such rule in the coreference component is *Rule I* which, informally, allows the referential use of an expression only when the meaning that obtains from this use is semantically *distinct* from the meaning that obtains on the bound alternative:

(26)  RULE I: INTRASENTENTIAL COREFERENCE
      NP A cannot corefer with NP B if replacing A with C, C a variable
      L-bound by B, yields an indistinguishable representation.

Rule I works like this: An example such as (27) has the two possible semantic representations in (27a), the bound variable interpretation, and (27b), the coreferential one. The essential idea is that only if the coreferential use of the pronominal yields a meaning *different* from the one given by syntactic binding is coreference to be allowed:

(27)  Ram$_i$ loves him$_i$

      (a)  Ram $\lambda(x)$ (x loves x)

      (b)  Ram$_i$ $\lambda(x)$ (x loves him$_i$)

Example (27a) is ruled out by Principle B, as the pronominal is bound in its binding domain. The referential use in (27b) results in the same bound variable interpretation, and is thus forbidden. Recall however, that the constraints on coreference are extrasyntactic. Hence, context can play the most crucial role in determining the 'distinguishability' of coreferential semantic representations from bound variable ones. In the appropriate context, (28), the interpretation that roughly corresponds to 'Ram adores himself' is distinctly different from the meaning 'Ram adores him', and hence Rule I cannot prohibit coreference.

(28)   I know what Ram has in common with Sita and Laxman—Sita
        adores him, Laxman adores him, and RAM$_i$ adores him$_i$, too

Similar arguments (Reinhart and Grodzinsky 1993:81) show that in examples (25a–c) coreference is allowed precisely because it is motivated by the context, as only there can it yield a distinguishable semantic representation from that obtained on the bound alternative. For example, take (25c) in which the normally barred *I kissed me* is possible because here the interpretation of 'self-kissing' yielded by the bound variable reading is easily distinguishable from the referential use, in which 'kissed me' is interpreted as 'kissed Brigitte Bardot'.

An approach that seeks to restrict the binding theory to an evaluation of only bound variable anaphora needs to make some changes to the binding theory in (1). Consider first the status of R-expressions in such a theory. Principle C of the standard binding theory prevents R-expressions from receiving a bound variable interpretation, so a theory that first licenses them as bound variables and then rules the coindexation as illegitimate is redundant. Reinhart and Grodzinsky suggest that this redundancy can be eliminated by including a *translation definition* within the binding theory, by which expressions that have 'independent reference' may not be translated as bound variables.

On the assumption that interpretive crashes fall within the definition of nonconvergence, an expression that cannot be translated as a bound variable but is nevertheless coindexed with another expression will yield a nonconvergent derivation. Reflexives and pronominals, on the other hand, can be translated as bound variables if they are syntactically bound by an L-related specifier, and once so translated are evaluated by Principles A and B, respectively, which they might respect or violate. There are thus two types of violations of the binding theory: (1) coindexation in spite of the failure to be translated as a bound variable, and (2) a violation of the binding principles. I shall call the former a *coindexation violation* and the latter a *binding principle* violation.

In the discussion that follows I develop Reinhart and Grodzinsky's intuitions to formulate a minimalist theory of binding and coreference. Section 4.3.1 provides an initial formulation that incorporates within it the LF raising of pronominals and reflexives and accounts for what were formerly known as cases of A-binding. Section 4.3.2 discusses the issue of binding from L-bar positions, and shows that modifications to Chomsky's (1992) understanding of the relation between reconstruction and binding provides an account that not only obviates the need for filters to rule out WCO violations but also predicts the variation showed by various L-bar movement constructions with respect to WCO effects.

### 4.3.1 L-Binding

Although Reinhart and Grodzinsky's core proposals capture the basic outlines of L-binding phenomena, the LF raising approach to reflexives and pronominals that I have adopted adds another clause to the translation definition of the binding theory: Only those expressions included in a functional projection at LF and bound by a L-specifier may be translated as variables. In sections 4.1 and 4.2, we saw there were three configurations that reflexives and pronominals could occupy at LF—adjoined to a functional head, in the specifier of a functional head, and adjoined to the maximal projection of a functional head—i.e., reflexives and pronominals must occupy a position in the checking domain of their licensing functional head.[8] Suppose that this is the configuration to which the binding theory must make reference; then, to be translated as bound variables, it necessarily has to be the case that $X^0$-reflexives must be in the checking domain of Tns, XP-reflexives in the checking domain of either Tns or the AGR heads, and pronominals in the checking domain of $D^0$.

Consider how an initial formulation of the binding theory and the coreference rules in (29) and (30) will capture the judgments in the instances of L-binding from English in (31):

(29) THE BINDING THEORY

    (a) DEFINITION
        A node $\alpha$ is bound by a node $\beta$ iff $\alpha$ and $\beta$ are coindexed and $\beta$ c-commands $\alpha$.

    (b) TRANSLATION DEFINITION
        A DP is a variable iff

        (i) it lacks independent reference,

        (ii) it is in a checking relation with its licensing functional head, and

        (iii) it is syntactically L-bound.

        Other cases of DP coindexation are uninterpretable.

    (c) PRINCIPLES

        A: A reflexive must be bound in its binding domain.

B: A pronominal must be free in its binding domain.

(d) BINDING DOMAIN

(i) The binding domain for a reflexive is the smallest CFC where it could potentially be bound.

(ii) The binding domain for a pronominal is the smallest CFC where it could potentially be free.

(iii) A CFC is a domain in which all the grammatical functions compatible with its head are realized.

(30) COREFERENCE RULES

RULE I: NP A cannot corefer with NP B if replacing A with C, C a variable L-bound by B, yields an indistinguishable representation.

(31)  (a) Ameena$_i$ adores her$_j$

(b) Ameena$_i$ adores himself$_{*i}$ /herself$_j$

(c) Saif$_i$ likes Saif$_{*i}$

(d) A party without Ameena$_i$ annoys Ameena$_i$

(e) His$_i$ friends like Ram$_i$

Working through the examples one by one, we see that the example in (31a) is acceptable because the R-expression is used referentially. Because it is not syntactically bound, it is not input to the binding theory at all. Rule I would, without further contextualization, prohibit coreference between *Ameena* and *her*, as replacing *her* with a variable L-bound by *Ameena* will yield the same semantic representation as the referential usage of the expressions. In (31b), the lack of syntactic binding is responsible for the unacceptability of the example, as Principle A allows XP-reflexives to be licensed only as bound variables. On the disjoint indexing in (31b), the example is a binding theory (Principle A) violation; on the coindexed reading, the violation stems from a mismatch of the features of the antecedent and the reflexive. On the coindexed reading, then, (31b) is not a violation of the binding theory but of Full Interpretation.

Example (31c) illustrates how this binding theory captures standard Principle C effects—because the R-expression bears independent reference, it cannot be translated as a bound variable despite its being syntactically bound. The fact that it is coindexed with another expression in its CFC therefore results in a coindexation violation. As is obvious by now, this is fertile ground for extrasyntactic coreference, as the structure will not be an input to Rule I in the coreference module. Because no interpretable representation results from the binding theory, any interpretation given by extrasyntactic means will always be distinguished from the one given by the binding theory.

Finally, each use of the expressions in (31c) is a referential use, because in no case is a relationship of syntactic binding established between two coreferring elements. The examples are also not inputs to Rule I, because in each instance, the environment for the application of Rule I is not met—it is impossible in (31d–e) to replace *Ameena/Ram* with a variable that will be L-bound by the expressions with which they are coindexed.

Quite obviously, the account of L-binding in Hindi-Urdu proceeds as in English in all cases, except those involving reflexive raising to Tns and pronominal raising to $D^0$, where this raising must precede the translation of the expressions into bound variables. Consider the two examples in (32):

(32)  (a)  sita$_i$-ne    ram$_j$-ko    [PRO$_j$  əpni$_{i/j}$  kɪtabẽ      pət$^h$ne]
          Sita(SU)    Ram(DO)              self's    books(DO)   to-read
          dĩ
          gave

      'Sita allowed Ram to read her/his books.'

     (b)  sita$_i$        Uski$*_{i/j}$  gaṛi        layi
          Sita(SU)    her          car(DO)    brought

      'Sita brought her$*_{i/j}$ car.'

In (32a), the $X^0$-reflexive raises successively cyclically from the lower Tns to the higher Tns, each copy being judged as a bound variable. Principle A applies, and because the reflexive is locally L-bound at each instance, the derivation converges. In (32b), once the possessive pronominal has raised to $D^0$, it can be translated as a bound variable. In this configuration it does not satisfy Principle B. It is also not amenable to a coreferential use, because the semantic representation that results is indistinguishable from the one that obtains on the bound variable reading.

## 4.3.2   L-Bar Binding

In our discussion of the phenomenon of reconstruction in chapter 2, I characterized it as the preference for the deletion for the non-quantificational material in the head copy of a chain. Implicit in that discussion was my agreement with Chomsky (1992) that the binding theory applies *after* copy-deletion takes place, but if we are to capture the P&P understanding that empty categories left behind by movement must also be locally bound, this surely cannot be correct. Then, if the copies of both L- and L-bar movement need to be licensed as bound variables, all copies must survive until the interface, and in fact copy-deletion must take place *after* the binding theory has evaluated every copy of a chain.

If copies must be licensed as bound variables, two issues immediately present themselves. The first is the status of WH- and quantifier copies. The traditional understanding was that these copies are subject to Principle C, which this approach classifies as a failure of translation as a bound variable. Because this entails that copies coindexed with the raised WH-phrase/quantifier will always result in a coindexation violation, it is hardly the result we want. So let us assume that all copies are, by definition, translated as bound variables, to express the intuition that copies left by movement are c-commanded by and coindexed with a local antecedent. Then, given the fundamental assumption that all copies are identical, it is also necessary to ensure that only the *heads* of L chains count as binders for lexical reflexives and pronominals. Example (33) demonstrates that this restriction is clearly needed:

(33)    (a)  Ram appears to himself to be the best man for the job that we advertized.

      (b)  [$_{IP}$ Ram appears to himself [$_{IP}$ [$_{TR}$ Ram] to be the best man for the job that we advertized]]

Here (33b) is the LF representation of the example (33a). Now, if the binding theory were allowed to see the tail copy of the raised DP *Ram* as a binder, at least one judgment would consider the reflexive in the PP to be unbound—a clear violation of Principle A. Thus, at least in the case of L-movement (and I generalize this later), the result we want is that a copy that has itself been adjudicated a bound variable is prevented from acting as a binder. If we make the assumption that all copies that are adjudicated bound variables may undergo deletion at LF, then, a copy that is to be deleted can never count as a binder, given general constraints on the recoverability of deletion. Then, the fact that L-chains do not show reconstruction effects with respect to the binding theory follows without stipulation, as the only copy that will not be adjudicated a bound variable will be the head of the L-chain, and therefore only that copy may count as a binder.

Incorporating these modifications to the definition of binding and the translation definition yields (34):

(34)    (a)  DEFINITION
           A node α is bound by a node β iff β is not a variable, α and β are coindexed and β c-commands α.

      (b)  TRANSLATION DEFINITION:
           A DP is a variable iff either (i) or (ii) hold.

(i) It is a copy that is locally bound,

(ii) It is syntactically L-bound, lacks independent reference and is in a checking relation with its licensing functional head.

Other cases of DP coindexation are uninterpretable.

## Operators in the Binding Theory

Consider now the binding in WH-movement and quantifier constructions in (36), the LF representations of the examples in (35) (ignoring the copies in $\theta$-positions):

(35)  (a) Who$_j$ does Noor$_i$ love?

(b) Every boy$_i$ loves his$_i$ parents.

(36)  (a) [$_{CP}$ [who] does [$_{AGR-sP}$ Noor love [$_{AGR-oP}$ [$_{TR}$ who] [$_{VP}$ t$_{SU}$ t$_V$ t$_{DO}$]]]]

(b) [$_{AGR-sP}$ [every boy][$_{AGR-sP}$ [$_{TR}$ every boy] loves [$_{AGR-oP}$ his parents [$_{VP}$ t$_{SU}$ t$_V$ t$_{DO}$]]]]

In (36a), the copy WH-phrase is translated as a bound variable as it is locally L-bar bound. Assuming that WH-expressions are what traditional grammar classifies them as, i.e., pronominals, this pronominal satisfies Principle B, because it is not syntactically bound—it is c-commanded by *Noor* but not coindexed with it. In (36b) as well, the copy of the raised quantifier is by definition translated as a bound variable. Because English possessive pronominals do not need to raise at LF, the minimal CFC for the pronominal is its containing DP, where it satisfies Principle B.

More interesting for this discussion are the cases of SCO and WCO, as in the example from English in (37) and Hindi-Urdu in (38). By LF, both languages will have the simplified LF representations in (39):

(37)  (a) **Who$_i$ does he$_i$ love?

(b) *Who$_i$ does his$_i$ sister love?

(38)  (a) Us$_i$-ne   kisko*$_i$   pyɑr  kiyɑ?
       he(SU)  who(DO)  love  did
       'Who$_i$ did he*$_i$ love?'

(b) Uski$_i$  bɛhen      kisko*$_i$   pyɑr  kərti  hɛ?
       his   sister(SU)  who(DO)  love  does  is
       'Who$_i$ does his$_i$ sister love?'

(39)  (a) [$_{CP}$ [who] does [$_{AGR-sP}$ he love [$_{AGR-oP}$ [$_{TR}$ who ]]]]...

(b) [$_{CP}$ [who] does [$_{AGR\text{-}sP}$ his mother love [$_{AGR\text{-}oP}$ [$_{TR}$ who ]]]]...

In the SCO case in (39a), the copy is L-bound in its binding domain, and on the assumption that WH-pronominals are subject to Principle B, (39a) represents a binding principle violation.[9] In addition, there is a coindexation violation as well, as the pronominal in the subject position is syntactically bound by the raised WH-phrase. Because this pronominal is neither part of a copy nor L-bound, it cannot be translated as a bound variable. Then, the interpretation on which the subject pronominal is interpreted as coreferential with the raised WH-phrase cannot accrue, as the binding theory rules this reading uninterpretable. WCO effects in (39b) differ from SCO effects in the absence of the Principle B violation. As the WH-pronominal in the copy satisfies Principle B, it is only the coindexation violation that causes its unacceptability. Here, too, the possessive pronominal is neither a copy nor L-bound, so an interpretation of it as coreferential with an L-bar element will be uninterpretable.

The common source of WCO and SCO effects is that they both involve coindexations that are uninterpretable, with SCO being worse than WCO because it involves a Principle B violation as well. This binding-theoretic characterization of WCO and SCO not only removes the need for linear statements on binding such as the WCO Filter, the Leftness Condition, etc., it also allows for finer distinctions between the two. Recall our observations concerning (1) in chapter 2, where we saw that WCO effects may be overriden in contexts such as parasitic gap constructions, topicalization, and appositive relatives. We can now trace this effect to the fact that the WCO configuration never meets the environment for the application of Rule I, as a consequence of which possessive pronominals may be used (co)referentially. SCO effects, on the other hand, can never be overriden, because they will always instantiate a Rule I configuration.[10]

To see this, reconsider the derivations in (39a) and (39b). In (39a), a referential use of the copy is strictly forbidden. Because the pronominal in the copy is c-commanded by its antecedent, a representation distinguishable from the bound alternative can never result. On the other hand, the referential use of the WH-pronominal in (39b) cannot be blocked, because the conditions for the application of Rule I are never met—it is impossible to replace [$_{TR}$ who] with a variable L-bound by *his*. Hence, the referential use of *who* in (39b) is allowed if it is sufficiently contextualized. Postal (1993:549) provides data that, I claim, acts as contextual specifications to distinguish the semantic representation provided by coreference from the bound variable. The net result is a mitigation of WCO violations:

(40)   (a) *Which lawyer$_i$ did his$_i$ clients hate?

   (b) ??Which lawyer$_i$ did only his$_i$ older clients hate?

    (c) ?Which lawyer$_i$ did even his$_i$ clients hate?

    (d) ??Which lawyer$_i$ did his$_i$ own clients hate?

The focusing particles *even, only,* and *own* provide the right syntactic-semantic context for a coreferential use of the WH-pronominals, as they differ from simple declaratives in truth conditions. Rule I cannot apply in any case, because the subject pronominal does not c-command the foot copy of the WH-pronominal. Coreference is therefore possible. The fact that the representation still contains a coindexation violation (the subject pronominal is an L-bar bound noncopy) is rendered marginal for many speakers. Other speakers who persist with the WCO violation clearly do not allow coindexation violations to be mitigated by a coreferential use of the expression in question. The difference between the two types of judgments, then, involves the strength either dialect accords to the coindexation violation by the subject pronominal.[11]

For speakers who allow the judgments in (40), the referential use of the WH-pronominal then lies at the root of the ameliorative effects. It is therefore predicted that where the referential use of WH-pronominals is forbidden, the contexts provided by the focusing particles will not succeed in reproducing the same effects. This is confirmed by the data in (41).

(41)    (a) *Which lawyer$_i$ did only he$_i$ hate?

       (b) *Which lawyer$_i$ did even he$_i$ hate?

Because the examples in (41) are configurations that are inputs to Rule I, a referential use of the WH-pronominal cannot yield a distinct representation from the one in which it is L-bound. Because the WH-pronominal in the copy violates Principle B, even speakers who allow coindexation violations to be rendered irrelevant by context will not allow SCO effects to be similarly mitigated.

SCO and WCO effects with quantifiers receive an identical analysis. Keeping in mind that Hindi-Urdu evinces the same pattern as in the English examples in (42), consider the LF representations in (43):

(42)    (a) **They$_i$ love everyone$_i$

       (b) *His$_i$ mother loves every boy$_i$

(43)    (a) [$_{IP}$ everyone [$_{IP}$ they love [$_{TR}$ everyone]]]

       (b) [$_{IP}$ every boy [$_{IP}$ his mother loves [$_{TR}$ every boy]]]

In both these cases, the subject pronominal is illicitly bound. Assuming that what is bound in the quantifier is the restrictor of the quantification, then, because *one* in (43a) is a pronominal, it must respect Principle B, which it does not. Example (43a) is thus both a coindexation and a binding principle violation, and therefore much worse than (43b), in which only a coindexation violation obtains.

### Topics in the Binding Theory

The proposed binding theory cannot as yet handle topicalization data, as it predicts that WCO and SCO effects should obtain with topicalization as well. As the English and Hindi-Urdu examples in (44)–(45) demonstrate, topicalization is actually immune to both WCO and SCO:

(44)   (a) Himself$_i$, he$_i$ likes t$_i$

       (b) Him$_i$, his$_i$ sister likes t$_i$

(45)   (a) vo$_i$      [əpne-ap$_i$-ko]-to      pəsənd   kərtɑ   hɛ
           He(SU)   himself-TOP(DO)   like      does    is
           'Himself$_i$, he$_i$ likes.'

       (b) Uski$_i$   bɛhen       Use$_i$-to       pəsənd   kərti   hɛ
           his      sister(SU)   him-TOP(DO)   like      does    is
           'Him$_i$, his$_i$ sister likes.'

Recalling the claim that the basic difference between English and Hindi-Urdu is that topicalization is a covert operation in the latter, both (44) and (45) can be considered to have the following (simplified) form at LF:

(46)   (a) [$_{TopP}$ himself [$_{IP}$ he likes [$_{TR}$ himself]]]

       (b) [$_{TopP}$ him [$_{IP}$ his sister likes [$_{TR}$ him]]]

Examples (46a–b) are judged unacceptable because the subject pronominal yields a coindexation violation, as L-bar bound pronominals cannot be given an interpretable coindexation. The copies of the moved elements, however, satisfy the binding theory in every way. The coindexation violations should then yield judgments of marginality, if not nonconvergence, but in fact both examples are perfectly fine. The problem, then, is how topicalization is to be distinguished from WH-movement and QR with respect to WCO (and SCO) violations. The solution lies in recognizing that WCO and SCO effects are properties of [+Q] elements rather than referential elements, a distinction that harks back to my proposal that defines operators as elements that check a [+Q] feature in the course of the derivation. That is, any element in an L-bar position is not automatically an operator unless it has the lexical properties of a quantifier (lexical quantifiers and WH-operators). The simplest possible solution to the problem is to build this intuition into the definition of syntactic binding:

(47) DEFINITION

A node $\alpha$ is bound by a node $\beta$ iff $\beta$ is not a variable, $\alpha$ and $\beta$ are coindexed and $\beta$ c-commands $\alpha$, where

(i) if $\beta$ is an L-bar position, $\beta$ must involve the checking of a [+Q] feature, or

(ii) if $\beta$ is an L-position, $\beta$ must involve the checking of a [Case] feature.

That this modification has the desired result can be seen by a reconsideration of (46). By the new definition of syntactic binding, the topic does not bind the subject pronominal because topics are not [+Q] elements. The subject pronominal can thus be used referentially, and no WCO or SCO effects obtain. Note that the account of WCO effects in (39b), is unaffected: As the WH-phrase checks a [+Q] feature, it counts as a binder for the subject pronominal, and because this pronominal cannot be translated as a variable, a coindexation violation obtains.

The facts noted by Postal (1994:542) in (48), in which the topicalization of quantified DPs yields WCO violations, now receive a straightforward explanation:

(48) *[$_{TopP}$ [everybody else] [$_{AGR-sP}$ we told his wife [$_{CP}$ that we had called [$_{AGR-oP}$ [$_{TR}$ everybody else]]]]]

Example (48) will presumably also be ruled out if [Spec, TopP] does not identify an appropriate scope domain for quantifiers, but even on the assumption that it is a scope-taking position, the fact that the quantifier syntactically binds the subject pronominal yields a coindexation violation.

The restriction of L-bar binding to [+Q] elements can also explain why WCO effects are not exhibited in nonrestrictive relatives and clefts, as in (49a–b), because these involve the extraction of a [–Q] element.

(49) (a) Gerald$_i$ who his$_i$ mother loves t$_i$ is a nice guy.

(b) It was John$_i$ who$_i$ his mother was talking about t$_i$

(c) Who$_i$ did [his$_i$ mother's stories about $pg_i$] amuse t$_i$?

This analysis predicts that parasitic gap constructions will exhibit WCO effects, and therefore the apparent absence of these effects in (49c) is problematic. Because the subject pronominal is syntactically bound by a [+Q] element, and leads to a coindexation violation, the analysis would classify these as mitigated WCO violations rather than ones in which no coindexation violations take place. I account for the weakness of the WCO effects here as a consequence of the Coreference component—for example, Rule I does not prohibit coreference in (49c) between *his* and [$_{TR}$ *who*].

## XP-Adjoined Positions in the Binding Theory

In the discussion of the DOC in the previous chapter, the major arguments for the proposal that IOs occupy XP-adjoined positions at Spellout came from the binding theory. There, I suggested that because IOs never check a [+Q] feature in a position broadly L-related to AGR-o, copy-deletion at the head of the chain entails that only the tail copy of the IO would survive at the point at which the binding theory applies. Consequently, IOs can never serve as binders for the purposes of the binding theory. Under the revised approach presented in this chapter, where the binding theory applies prior to copy-deletion, this analysis no longer holds. The account given for topicalization, however, carries over straightforwardly.

Consider first quantificational IOs. The two cases that need discussion are provided in (50):

(50)  (a) nur$_j$-ne      hər    ləʈki$_i$-ko   Uski$_i$   kɪtab      di
         Noor(SU)   each   girl(IO)   her    book(DO)   gave

      'Noor$_j$ gave each girl$_i$ her$_{i/*j}$book.'

      (b) nur$_j$-ne      hər    ləʈki$_i$-ko   Us-se$_{*i/*j}$   mɪlaya
         Noor(SU)   each   girl(IO)   her(DO)      introduced

      'Noor$_j$ introduced each girl$_i$ to her$_{*i/*j}$.'

The examples in (50) exhibit an asymmetry that we have as yet to encounter in the discussion: The adjoined IO exhibits SCO effects but is apparently exempt from WCO effects. Consider the LF representations of (50a–b) in (51a–b) below, assuming LF QR of the IO quantifier to adjoin to VP$_1$:

(51)  (a) [$_{TP}$ nur-ne [$_{VP1}$ [hər ləʈki-ko] [$_{VP1}$ t$_{SU}$ [$_{AGR-oP}$ [$_{TR}$ hər
         ləʈki-ko] [$_{AGR-oP}$ Uski kɪtab [$_{VP2}$ t$_{DO}$ [$_{TR}$ hər ləʈki-ko] t$_V$ [$_{Tns}$
         di]]]]]]]

      (b) [$_{TP}$ nur-ne [$_{VP1}$ [hər ləʈki$_i$-ko] [$_{VP1}$ t$_{SU}$ [$_{AGR-oP}$ [$_{TR}$ hər
         ləʈki-ko] [$_{AGR-oP}$ Us-se [$_{VP2}$ t$_{DO}$ [$_{TR}$ hər ləʈki-ko] t$_V$ [$_{Tns}$
         mɪlaya]]]]]]]

In the analysis proposed so far, both (51a–b) should be ruled out, because the IP-adjoined IO operator syntactically binds the DO pronominal, yielding a coindexation violation. But, (51a) is certainly not unacceptable. Notice first that there is one crucial difference between the representations in (51) and the ones used to represent the WCO and SCO effects in simple transitives—the representations in (51) involve not one, but *two*, chains of L-bar movement. The first chain involves the raising of the IO from its base position to the AGR-oP-adjoined position at Spellout; the second involves the QR of that AGR-oP-adjoined IO to a scope-taking VP$_1$-adjoined position. Now recalling the earlier proposal that any copy that has been adjudicated a variable cannot count as a binder, consider first the representation in (51a). Assuming that each chain is evaluated separately, the net result after all copies have been evaluated is that the foot copy of the QR chain in the position broadly L-related to AGR-o is a variable, as is the foot copy of the Spellout chain, as they are both locally bound by their L-bar antecedents.

Now consider the relationship between the AGR-oP-adjoined IO copy and the possessive pronominal in the DO. Can this copy count as an L-bar binder for the pronominal? This approach suggests not, as that copy has already been adjudicated a variable. The DO pronominal is therefore not syntactically bound and can be used referentially; hence the lack of WCO effects. The same arguments extend to the DO pronominal in (51b), the unacceptability of the example stemming instead from the fact that the R-expression in the quantifier copy at the foot of the Spellout chain is L-bound by the DO pronominal.

The account of relative quantifier scope too undergoes revision, in such a way that obviates the need for a statement of the MBR as an independent principle of the grammar. Recall that quantifiers exhibit scope-freezing effects in the DOC where the IO quantifier always has wide scope:

(52)  (a)  we gave one student every problem. (*unambiguous*)

   (b)  *we gave [$_{VP1}$ [every problem] [$_{VP1}$ [one student] [$_{AGR-oP}$ [$_{TR}$ one student] [$_{AGR-oP}$ [$_{TR}$ every problem] [$_{VP2}$ [$_{TR}$ every problem] [$_{TR}$ one student]]]]]]

   (c)  [$_{IP}$ we gave [$_{VP1}$ [one student] [$_{AGR-oP}$ [$_{TR}$ one student] [$_{AGR-oP}$ [$_{TR}$ every problem] [$_{VP2}$ [$_{TR}$ every problem] [$_{TR}$ one student]]]]]]

Example (52b) represents the impossible reading of (52a). Recall that to be adjudicated a bound variable, a copy must be locally (L-bar) bound. Now let us extend that definition to incorporate the MBR, by which to be adjudicated as a bound variable, a copy must be locally bound by the closest minimally c-commanding binder.

Considering first the copies of the VP-adjoined IO quantifier *one student*, we find that both the copy in the lower VP and the AGR-oP adjoined copy can be adjudicated as bound variables, as they are both locally L-bar bound. The copy of the DO quantifier *every problem* in [Spec, AGR-oP] is, however, not so bound, because even though the AGR-oP adjoined copy of *one student* does not count as a potential L-bar binder for it (because it has been adjudicated a variable), the VP-adjoined IO quantifier *one student* does. Hence the copy of *every problem* in [Spec, AGR-oP] will not be translated as a bound variable and, by earlier assumptions, will not delete at LF. This derivation will then violate Full Interpretation at LF because it will fail to yield an operator–variable pair.

Similar arguments will rule out derivations in which the DO QRs and the IO stays in situ, as well as those in which one quantifier QRs to TP and the other to VP, as in each case (at least) the copy of the IO in [Spec, AGR-oP] will fail to be licensed as a bound variable. It is therefore the case that the representation in (52c) is the only licit one, where only the IO QRs (or stays in situ).

Consider nonquantificational IOs next. Example (53) reflects pronominal coindexation with IOs:

(53)  (a)  mẽ-ne  ram$_i$-ko    uski$_i$  kɪtab       di
          I       Ram(IO)  his     book(DO)  gave

          'I gave Ram$_i$ /his$_i$ book.'

      (b)  mẽ-ne  us$_i$-ko     ram$_{*i}$-ki-kɪtab        di
          I       him(IO)  Ram-GEN-book(DO)  gave

          'I gave him$_i$ Ram$_i$ 's book.'

The two examples in (53) present conflicting data for our binding theory, for although we do have an explanation for pronominal coreference in (53a), we do not have one for (53b). Let us consider each example a little more closely in their LF representations in (54):

(54)  (a)  [$_{TP}$ mẽ-ne [$_{VP1}$ t$_{SU}$ [$_{AGR-oP}$ [ram-ko] [$_{AGR-oP}$ uski kɪtab [$_{VP2}$ t$_{DO}$ [$_{TR}$ ram-ko] [$_{Tns}$di]]]]]]]

      (b)  [$_{TP}$ mẽ-ne [$_{VP1}$ t$_{SU}$ [$_{AGR-oP}$ [usko] [$_{AGR-oP}$ ram-ki-kɪtab [$_{VP2}$ t$_{DO}$ [$_{TR}$ usko] [$_{Tns}$di]]]]]]]

First, taking (54a), the binding theory adjudicates the copy of the raised IO as a bound variable. The R-expression in this copy is not syntactically bound by the pronominal in the DO because it does not c-command the copy. Thus [$_{TR}$ *ram-ko*] can be used referentially, as Rule I does not prohibit coreference here. No coindexation violation with the DO pronominal obtains either, because the adjoined IO is not a [+Q] element. Example (54b) should receive an identical analysis, with the result that a referential use of the IO pronominal should be licit, but as the acceptability judgments on (54b) show, this is unconfirmed. Following Dayal (1993), I suggest that the impossibility of coreference in (54b) does not follow from the binder status of IOs, but from a rule in the coreference component, by which an R-expression may not be coreferential with a pronominal that precedes it in the linear order.

(55) RULE II

DP A cannot corefer with DP B iff A is a R-expression and B is a pronominal, and B immediately precedes A.

Rule II can apparently be overridden in discourse, as when the R-expression is given a discourse topic status in (56) (English and Hindi-Urdu being identical with respect to (53), I present the context in English):

(56) ??Sita gives only one present to everybody: She gave Noor Ram's book, she gave Ramesh Ram's book, and in fact, she even gave HIM$_i$ Ram's$_i$ book.

Turning finally to reflexive binding by IOs, my approach predicts that IOs should not be able to license reflexives. As noted earlier, there appears to be a general prohibition against DO XP-reflexives in Hindi-Urdu, but if the examples are allowed, speakers prefer coindexation with the subject rather than the IO in an example such as (57):

(57) *?ram$_i$-ne  sita$_j$-ko  əpne-ap$_{i/*j}$-ko  dɪkʰaya
     Ram(SU)  Sita(IO)  self(DO)  showed

'Ram showed Sita himself/herself.'

These examples are quite straightforwardly ruled out. Since the binding theory will apply to the copy of the IO, which does not syntactically bind the DO, the reflexive will not be able to take the IO as an antecedent at LF. The only syntactic binder available to it is then the subject and therefore the XP-reflexive will necessarily be subject-oriented.[12, 13]

## 4.4  Conclusion

This chapter began with the premise that because the syntactic evidence for an analysis of scrambling as XP-adjunction is overwhelming, what is required is a reappraisal of the theories of binding and coreference in UG. Because the cases in which scrambling exhibits the properties of Case-driven movement involve possessive reflexives and pronominals, sections 4.1 and 4.2 examined the properties of these two categories and showed them to have properties quite distinct from the same categories in English. Section 4.3 incorporates the LF raising approach to reflexive and pronominal interpretation into a novel theory of binding and coreference that is sensitive to movement as a copying and deletion process. The execution of Reinhart's proposals about restricting the theory of binding to bound variable anaphora and a separate coreference module not only provides an account of WCO effects that obviates the need for filters and linearity conditions to exclude them but also explains why WCO effects can be mitigated in constructions involving XP-adjunction. Although this chapter implements these facts only for IOs, the same analysis extends quite naturally to XP-adjunction operations such as scrambling, as the next chapter demonstrates.

The binding theory developed in this chapter eviscerates the notion of L-bar binding altogether. In fact, because the account locates WCO and SCO effects in instances of L-bar binding, derivations can only converge iff they contain no variables that are locally L-bar bound by the closest potential L-bar binder.[14] This is clearly quite different from the approach to reconstruction and binding in Chomsky (1992). It appears to me that the choice between the two approaches is both theoretical and empirical. As far as the empirical facts go, pronominal coreference in configurations involving L-bar movement is problematic for an account that retains L-bar binding. Theoretically, a possible shortcoming of Chomsky's approach is that it must necessarily posit an ordering relation between reconstruction (= copy-deletion) and the application of the binding theory to derive the result that the binding theory applies to copies in the base and intermediate positions. Aside from the fact that extrinsic orderings of this sort do not meet the guidelines of "virtual conceptual necessity", Chomsky's proposals also do not go the full distance in actually motivating this extrinsic ordering. Presumably, the proof of this hypothesis should show that instances in which the binding theory applies before copy-deletion takes place will necessarily result in non-convergence at the LF interface, but there is little in Chomsky's analysis that actually achieves this. An approach like the one developed in this chapter, on the other hand, need make no stipulations about the ordering of the copy-deletion and the binding theory—if, as I suggest, the binding theory that determines which copy qualifies for the deletion operation, then derivations in which copy-deletion precedes the binding theory will not converge.

This perspective on copy-deletion also asks us to reconsider the role of the L-/L-bar distinction in forcing such deletion. It will be recalled from chapter 2 that my initial proposals were similar to those of Chomsky's insofar as the deletion of argument material at the head of the chain was a property of L-bar chains. The revised system, however, looks quite different, as my proposals now allow arguments to occupy L-bar positions after copy-deletion. This difference is, however, not as significant as it may seem, because the effects that Chomsky seeks to capture are all taken care of. Recall that Chomsky needs copy-deletion at the head of the chain to ensure that the binding theory applies only to the arguments in the tail and intermediate copies, and because such binding is a property only of L-bar chains, he suggests that this deletion is driven by Full Interpretation conditions on what counts as an operator. In my approach, none of these properties are derived from copy-deletion. Because I define an operator as an element that checks a [+Q] feature, copy-deletion is no longer required to construct the operator–variable pair. Moreover, as I trace the difference between the binding properties in L- and L-bar chains to a general prohibition that forbids bound variables from counting as binders, it is no longer necessary to make reference to the L-/L-bar distinction with regard to copy-deletion.

In fact, my approach needs copy-deletion to construct the *variable* part of the operator–variable pair. Because most times the relationship between operator and variable is one to many in the system, the requirements of Full Interpretation as well as concerns of semantic compositionality require the deletion of at least intermediate copies. I return to whether such deletion targets the Case or the θ-copy in chapter 6, but it must already be obvious that the approach abandons the notion that variables are necessarily copies in Cased positions. This requirement was formulated to exclude PRO from the class of variables, but after the assimilation of PRO into the structural Case system (Chomsky and Lasnik 1991), the requirement has no *a priori* validity. In fact, given the complete separation between Case and θ-positions and the status of the θ-Criterion as a convergence condition at LF, it is the lexical link of the chain that must survive the copy-deletion operation.

# Chapter 5

# Scrambling, Focus, and Specificity

The theories of binding and coreference developed in the previous chapter suggest a way in which the binding–theoretic challenges to an analysis of scrambling as XP-adjunction may be tackled. Although this is an obvious step forward in the study of the phenomenon, it still remains to be shown why scrambling takes place at all and why it must necessarily be an overt phenomenon. If standard approaches to the phenomenon are to be believed, then scrambling is both an entirely optional and a semantically vacuous operation, but such a characterization of the phenomenon is simply inadequate from the perspective of minimalism.

Happily, there is evidence, discussed in section 5.1, that suggests that in fact the scrambling operation has distinct semantic/pragmatic effects and is only apparently optional. I suggest that scrambling in Hindi-Urdu is a focality-driven XP-adjunction operation, triggered with the objective of activating the preverbal focus position. Section 5.2 demonstrates how the theories of binding and coreference developed in the previous chapter explain coreference effects in scrambled configurations. Section 5.3 discusses the presuppositional interpretations that scrambled XPs receive and shows that an analysis of scrambling as XP-adjunction in conjunction with Diesing's (1992) proposals provides an adequate account of these effects.

## 5.1   Scrambling and Positional Focus

The assumption (often unstated) underlying most studies of the phenomenon is that scrambling has few logico-semantic effects in terms of truth conditions, its chief contribution being at the level of discourse. Scrambled configurations have prototypical information-packaging properties in that the scrambled constituent usually receives a strongly presuppositional reading, and a part of the information in such configurations is necessarily interpreted as asserted or *focused*. Scrambling thus shares the discourse properties of such stylistic constructions as topicalization and Directional/Locative Inversion (DLI) in English:

(1)  (a) Into the room walked John

    (b) The book, I gave John

    (c) kɪtabē     mē    laya    hũ
       books(DO)   I(SU)  brought  am
       'The books, I brought.'

These three examples presuppose discourse and a shared knowledge of the preposed constituent, and consequently none of the examples can be acceptable responses to the corresponding questions in (2):

(2)  (a) Where did John go?

    (b) What did you give John?

    (c) What do you want to bring?

Like topicalization and DLI, scrambling too does not affect truth conditions but rather serves the general principles of communicative ordering that require the (re)organization of the information structure of the clause in such a way as to present 'theme' before 'rheme', 'topic' before 'comment', and/or 'given' before 'new' information.

In preminimalist approaches to the scrambling operation, these properties of the scrambling operation could be considered incidental effects, interpretations that the operations of discourse grammar gave to configurations that involved XP-adjunction, but minimalism no longer has this luxury. For, if all the LF and PF effects of the scrambling operation are, at best, correlational properties of the movement, then scrambling lacks a distinct morphosyntactic imperative, a conclusion that makes its distinct interpretive effects difficult to derive. The task therefore is to derive the trigger for scrambling from the consequences it has for discourse and pragmatic felicity, i.e., to foreground what was earlier considered to be a correlational property of derived XP-adjunction as its intrinsic property. In the discussion that follows, my appeal is therefore to those generative traditions (Rochemont 1986, Culicover and Rochemont 1991) that consider 'stylistic' interpretations to be syntactically derived. On this view, the C-I system is the locus of both discursive/pragmatic and logico-semantic interpretation, and both types of interpretations must be licensed by derivations in the syntactic component. In other words, at least some discursive/pragmatic effects are accorded the status of convergence conditions at the LF interface. Presumably, topicalization and focalization are syntactic operations that are driven by two such discursive/pragmatic convergence conditions.

A closer look at scrambled configurations demonstrates that they also share the focalization properties of DLI in English, where the preposed constituent in (3a) can never be prosodically prominent, the formal encoding of focus in the language. Rather, prosodic prominence must be to the right of the preposed constituent, and attendant on this prosodic prominence is greater pragmatic salience—*John* is interpreted as the narrow focus of the utterance, where, following Erteschik-Shir (1998), I define focus pragmatically as in (4):

(3)    (a)  *INTO THE ROOM walked John

       (b)  Into the room walked JOHN

(4)    The focus of a sentence S is (the intension of) a constituent c of S, which the speaker intends to direct the attention of his/her hearer(s) to, by uttering S.[1]

Hindi-Urdu is a syllable-timed language, so focusing does not have the prosodic correlates that it does in English, rather, focus is marked by position—in (5), the immediately preverbal element is necessarily interpreted as the pragmatic indexical assertion of the utterance:

(5)    kɪtabẽ  kəl     **mɛ̃**  laya    tʰa
        books   yesterday  I     brought  was

    (a) 'It is I who brought the books yesterday.'

    (b) ##'It is yesterday that I brought the books.'

The infelicitous reading in (5b) demonstrates that focusing is usually indicated by preverbal position. Hindi-Urdu can thus be considered a member of the class of languages such as Malayalam (Jayaseelan 1989/1995), Hungarian (Horvath 1981), Turkish, Mongolian, Tibetan Sherpa (Kim 1988), Western Bade, Tangale (Tuller 1992), Aghem (Rochemont 1986), etc., which mark focus by position relative to the verb. Like these languages, Hindi-Urdu also locates (non-discourse-initial)[2] WH-questions in preverbally. Given discourse, (6a) is strongly preferred over (6b) (see also Laxmibai 1994):

(6)    (a) kɪtab     **kɔn**     layega
           book(DO)  who(SU)  will bring

           'The book, who will bring?'

    (b) **#kɔn**    kɪtab    layega
          who(SU)  book(DO)  will bring

          'Who will bring the book?'

Note that all the examples considered here require scrambling to license preverbal focusing. Interestingly, without scrambling, the preverbal focus position does not appear to exist, i.e., an example in the default SOV order does not unambiguously involve narrow focus of the DO. Scrambling is thus the causal link for focalization in the preverbal focus position, and it is in this role that I trace the morphosyntactic motivation for the scrambling operation in Hindi-Urdu.[3] I base my proposals in this regard on the structure in (7) (following Jayaseelan 1989/1995), in which the licensing of positional focus involves the checking of a morphosyntactic feature [FOCUS] in a *Focus Phrase* base-generated immediately dominating VP.[4]

(7)

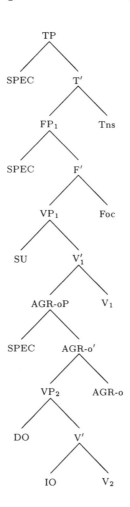

### 5.1.1   Raising Focused XPs

Consider first the configuration in the FP projection. Initially, let us assume that both the D- and V-features of $F^0$ are [strong] in Hindi-Urdu. Now, in an order such as DO–SU–V (in which the subject is focused), the DO is in a TP-adjoined position (ignoring for the moment how it got there), the subject in [Spec, FP], and the verb adjoined to $F^0$. The examples in (8) involving preverbal focusing of WH-phrases and focusing wrought by scrambling thus receive the identical analysis in (9) (ignoring irrelevant projections):

(8)   (a)   kɪtɑb        **kɪs-ne**      pəʈʰi?
             book(DO)   who(SU)   read
             'Who read the book?'

       (b)   kɪtɑb        **rɑm-ne**     pəʈʰi
             book(DO)   Ram(SU)   read
             'Ram read the book.'

(9)   [$_{TP}$ kɪtɑb$_m$ [$_{TP}$ [kɪsne/rɑm-ne]$_z$ [$_{FP}$ t$_z$ [$_{VP1}$′ t$_z$ [$_{AGR-oP}$ t$_m$′ [$_{VP2}$ t$_m$ t$_V$ [$_{AGR-o}$ t$_V$ [$_{Tns}$ di]]]]]]]]

Each step of the movement in (9) satisfies Shortest Move, because subject raising to [Spec, TP] via [Spec, FP] never skips more than one SPEC. As Hindi-Urdu has rich verb agreement, the strength of the V-features of Tns and AGR-s should force overt verb raising, with the result that the specifiers this subject raising targets will be equidistant from one another. Similarly, DO or IO raising to [Spec, FP] also will not violate Shortest Move.

Depending on how the feature [FOCUS] is characterized, other economy conditions may, however, prove difficult to satisfy. If [FOCUS] is a [+Q] feature (following Chomsky 1971), [Spec, FP] will have to be classified as an L-bar position. Then, subject raising to [Spec, AGR-sP] via [Spec, FP] will yield an L- and L-bar interleaved chain, in clear violation of the Economy of Derivation of Collins (1994). Note, however, that positional focus languages do not replicate the kind of binding-theoretic evidence, shown in (10), on the basis of which Chomsky (1971) makes his claims about the quantificational nature of focus. Chomsky suggests that the impossibility of coreference between the R-expression in (10b) with a pronominal embedded in the subject DP can only be explained by this assumption. As all [+Q] elements QR at LF, the raising of the R-expression establishes a relation of binding between it and the embedded pronominal, in clear violation of SCO.

(10)   (a)   The woman he$_i$ loved betrayed John$_i$

        (b)   The woman he$_i$ loved betrayed JOHN$_{*i}$

The Hindi-Urdu [Spec, FP] does not, however, exhibit the properties of an operator position. Although the test illustrated in (10) is inappropriate given the anti-subject orientation of Hindi-Urdu pronominals, the evidence from XP-reflexive binding by foci in (11) quite clearly demonstrates this.

(11) [əpne-ap$_i$-ko]$_z$  ram$_i$-ne  $t_z$ dek$^h$a
     himself(DO)     Ram(SU)        saw
     'Ram saw himself.'

Recalling that XP-reflexives cannot be bound from operator positions, if the subject in [Spec, FP] occupies a position that is equivalent to the QR position of an English focused phrase, XP-reflexive binding should be prohibited. As this is clearly not the case, [FOCUS] is not a [+Q] feature in Hindi-Urdu (and other positional focus languages), and [Spec, FP] is not an L-bar position.

The claim in Horvath (1981), Tuller (1992) that [FOCUS] is a Case-like feature also does not appear to be correct. As this claim identifies [Spec, FP] to be an L-position, it ends up barring the focusing of dative-shifted IOs, as the raising from a position broadly L-related to AGR-o to [Spec, FP] will violate the Economy of Derivation of Collins (1994).

Furthermore, there is little direct evidence to suggest that [FOCUS] is actually a feature like Case, as these approaches draw the analogy between [FOCUS] and Case with the sole purpose of motivating overt checking. Not only is this stipulation no longer required under checking theory, the implication that pragmatic features like focus and morphosyntactic properties like Case have an identical status in the grammar obscures the inherent difference between the two types of features: While the selection and licensing of a morphosyntactic feature like Case is determined exclusively by reference to the lexical and parametric choices made by the language, the selection and licensing of a pragmatic feature like [FOCUS] is ultimately dependent on embedding context provided by the discourse.

Moreover, although the licensing of [FOCUS] does draw on some parametric choices that a particular language makes (e.g., positional vs. prosodic focusing), the kind of correlation displayed between Case and other inflectional features like Tense is simply not evident with [FOCUS]. To consider such pragmatic features as at par with inflectional features is to obscure the distinction between discourse and core grammar.

[Spec, FP] thus appears to be *neutral* to the L-relatedness distinction. This neutrality, I suggest, is a special property of functional categories licensed primarily by discursive/pragmatic legibility conditions at the C-I interface, as such features do not enter the computation as morphosyntactic features that are either intrinsically or optionally related to a lexical head. Rather, the role that these pragmatic features play in the computation is almost entirely driven by the positioning of the whole sentence in the larger unit of discourse.

### 5.1.2   Licensing Focused XPs

One of the key assumptions made in the preceding discussion was that the D-features of $F^0$ are [strong] in Hindi-Urdu. The problem with this proposal is that it predicts that preverbal focusing is possible in the absence of scrambling, and obligatory for both ±WH- elements. Neither prediction is entirely correct, as positional focus in Hindi-Urdu usually requires scrambling, and WH-focusing is generally more obligatory than that of non-WH XPs. The proposals I now make regarding *head activation* offer a solution to both problems. First, let us exploit the observation that focus positions surface in noncanonical orderings in Hindi-Urdu to suggest that although $F^0$ is universally available, it is not necessarily *active*, i.e., it does not license D-features. Let us call such heads *dormant* heads, defining dormancy as in (12). These heads are not, however, totally inert, and can in fact be *activated* in the overt syntax under appropriate structural conditions.

(12)   DORMANCY
       A functional head is dormant iff its D-feature is not licensed in the numeration.

In order to derive the claim that that the left-scrambled XP is this appropriate licenser, let us pause now to consider the implications of imparting a pragmatic feature like [FOCUS] a computational status. If focusing is largely a pragmatic act, it must be a feature that marks the whole construction (just as politeness, informativeness, etc.), rather than an individual XP. Thus, even though [FOCUS] ultimately appears to be the property of an XP in [Spec, FP], this is merely a superficial consequence of the fact that the whole derivation has been marked as a focus construction. Languages like Aghem (Rochemont 1986), in which the focus and the predicate involved both bear morphological markers of [FOCUS], constitute evidence in support of this claim.

In languages that lack such overt focus specification on the predication, the only other candidate as a marker of the derivation as a focus construction appears to be the apparent adjacency requirement between the focused XP and the verb. Although the effects of this adjacency requirement are basically lost in FP analyses of positional focus, where preverbal positioning is effected by the hierarchical positioning of FP itself (rather than the linear position of the verb, which may well have moved to a higher projection), this relation can, in fact, be given a 'deeper' explanation. I suggest that the adjacency effects between foci and the predicator constitute a signal that the derivation is licensed as a focus construction, and analyze this licensing as the transmission of [FOCUS] to the predicational 'head' of the sentence—for concreteness, Tns (Abney 1987). In the discussion that follows, I will distinguish the feature [FOCUS] on XP-foci from predicational focus by referring to the latter as [PFOCUS] solely for descriptive clarity, as the feature content of the two is actually identical.

Now, in the numeration, crosslinguistically this [PFOCUS] feature is not intrinsically related to any lexical head. As free-floating features of this type cannot be checked, the numeration must contain an operation that merges [PFOCUS] with a host, formalized as in (13):

(13) NUMERATION: MERGER OF FREE FEATURES
A free feature must be merged with a host for convergence, where $\alpha$ is a free feature if it is not intrinsically related to any lexical category.

In languages such as Aghem, [PFOCUS] is merged with the verb in the numeration, and the raising of this complex to Tns via $F^0$, etc., accomplishes the activation of $F^0$. Hindi-Urdu–type languages, however, lack this option of merging [PFOCUS] with the predicator directly, so instead, [PFOCUS] is merged with any XP in the numeration, piedpiping that category along on its quest to serve Greed. As what is piedpiped is an XP, $XP_{[PFOCUS]}$ will only target broadly L-related positions. In the course of its raising to a TP/AGR-sP adjoined position this predicational feature must *activate* the focus position—a proposal that expresses the intuition that focusing of individual XPs is derivative of the focus-marking of the whole predication. This activation takes place from an adjoined position because the dormancy of FP does not allow the licensing of [Spec, FP] and involves the *transmission* of the [FOCUS] feature to $F^0$ by means of dynamic agreement (Rizzi 1996).

Rizzi's proposal plays on the fact that the desired outcome of checking theory is that the head and its specifier bear the same feature specifications. In standard practice, this is effected through SPEC-Head agreement, where the specifier matches its features against those on the functional head, but Rizzi observes that an identical result would obtain if the head inherited the feature specifications of its specifier. If we extend this proposal to include dynamic agreement from broadly L-related positions as well, the result will be that $XP_{[PFOCUS]}$ will transmit its [FOCUS] feature to the head of FP. The mechanism of head activation can then be described by (14):

(14) HEAD ACTIVATION
A dormant head $\alpha$ may be activated by feature transmission.

(15) FEATURE TRANSMISSION

    A feature $f$ may be transmitted to a functional head *FH* if $f$ is in the checking domain of *FH*.

Notice that the imperative for the XP-adjunction of $XP_{[PFOCUS]}$ to FP comes from a broad interpretation of the self-serving last resort character of movement—given that preverbal focusing is dependent on an activated FP, such intermediate XP-adjunction is forced for convergence. The activation of FP is, however, not sufficient for licensing the derivation as a focus construction, as FP is not the predicational head of the sentence. $XP_{[PFOCUS]}$ must thus raise to an adjoined-to-TP/AGR-sP position, where, by dynamic agreement, [FOCUS] is transmitted to Tns. The overt chain of $XP_{[PFOCUS]}$ raising thus involves a two-step XP-adjunction process, once to FP and then to TP/AGR-sP (although the second step of the process may be postponed until LF, as in the Hindi-Urdu order SU-DO-IO-V).

    Once the head of FP acquires a [FOCUS] feature, it licenses a specifier, to which [±WH] XPs may raise (in the overt syntax). On this account, then, the observation that positional focusing is crosslinguistically 'more obligatory' for [+WH] elements has no special status. If making this distinction is indeed descriptively relevant, it is then necessary to strengthen the licensing requirements on [+WH] elements to account for this difference. In the speculations that follow, I develop Probal Dasgupta's (personal communication) suggestion that obligatory positional focusing of WH-phrases may derive from Chomsky's (1992) contention that [+WH] is universally [strong]. Notice first that a key distinction between non-WH and [+WH] elements is that the latter are usually considered to be inherently focused elements (Rochemont 1986)—i.e., while the [FOCUS] feature of non-WH elements is discursive/pragmatic in nature, the [FOCUS] of [+WH] elements is a lexically specified morphosyntactic property. On the assumption that intrinsic morphosyntactic features must be checked in [Spec, FP] for convergence, WH-phrases in positional focus languages will always occupy [Spec, FP] by Spellout.

    A potential problem with the postulation of [FOCUS] as a morphosyntactic property of [+WH] elements is that it appears to predict that, crosslinguistically, the licensing of [+WH] implicates overt checking in an FP projection. As this is clearly not the case, we need to relax the requirement somewhat. Suppose first that WH-phrases are subject to not one but *two* licensing conditions at LF: A WH-phrase must be legitimized both by an appropriate [+WH] $C^0$ and a [FOCUS] feature. Assume next that a distinct $F^0$ is not necessarily implicated in the checking of this latter feature—intrinsic [FOCUS] may also be generated as a feature on another functional head like $C^0$. These LF licensing conditions on WH-elements are, however, relaxed at PF, where the satisfaction of even *one* of these requirements allows the derivation to converge at PF. In English, PF-convergence is assured by the fact that not only does $C^0$ have [strong] D-features, it is also the checker of intrinsic [FOCUS]. In Malayalam and Hindi-Urdu, on the other hand, only intrinsic [FOCUS] is checked overtly, the other licensing requirement on WH-phrases being met only after covert WH-raising to [Spec, CP].

The derivation in (16) summarises my proposals for deriving the causal link between scrambling and focus, where (16a) represents the structure at the base. In (16b), the process of head activation is shown, where the $DO_{[PFOCUS]}$, after checking its Case and agreement features in [Spec, AGR-oP] raises to adjoin to FP. By dynamic agreement, the feature [FOCUS] is transmitted to the head of FP. This activates the D-feature of $F^0$ which then can host a DP in its SPEC. Derivation (16c) shows the adjunction of $DO_{[PFOCUS]}$ to TP and the transmission of the [FOCUS] feature to Tns.[5]

(16)　(a)　THE STRUCTURE AT THE BASE

$[_{TP} [_{FP}$ *dormant* $[_{VP1}$ SU $[_{AGR\text{-}oP} [_{VP2}$ $DO_{[PFOCUS]}$ $V^0$ $]]]]]$

　　　(b)　HEAD ACTIVATION

$[_{TP} [_{FP}$ $DO_{[PFOCUS]}$ $[_{FP} [_{Foc}$ [FOCUS] $[_{VP1}...]]]]]$

　　　(c)　SU-RAISING TO $F^0$ AND $DO_{[PFOCUS]}$TO TP

$[_{TP}$ $DO_{[PFOCUS]}$k $[_{TP} [_{Tns}$ [FOCUS] $[_{FP}$ $t_k$ $[_{FP}$ $SU_{[FOCUS]}$ $[_{Foc}$ [FOCUS] [V+AGR-o] $[_{VP1}$ ... $]]]]]]]$

These proposals render the scrambling operation compatible with what are now conceived as prototypical properties of movement. As the mechanisms proposed give a morphosyntactic motivation to scrambling, scrambling can no longer be considered optional—just as there can be no raising to [Spec, CP] if there is appropriate $C^0$ and a WH-phrase, scrambling also cannot take place when there is no [PFOCUS] in the numeration. The presence or absence of a scrambling [PFOCUS] thus provides a simple parameter along which languages can be arranged, in that languages that do not have scrambling will have to lack the free feature [PFOCUS].

The crosslinguistic variation internal to the class of scrambling languages is also predicted: The absence of WH-scrambling follows from the nature of $C^0$—the strength of $C^0$ in Germanic bars WH-scrambling, whereas its weakness allows it. Languages such as Hungarian that allow multiple foci, presumably involve an $F^0$ that licenses multiple [strong] D-features. Furthermore, languages may also perhaps vary with regard to the categorial status of the elements [PFOCUS] may piedpipe—while I examine only XPs in Hindi-Urdu, it may be that [PFOCUS] also piedpipes $X^0$ categories such as verbs and determiners.

It appears to me that the theoretically permitted option of a [weak] [PFO-CUS] is not exercised by languages, as intuitively, focusing must necessarily be an overt phenomenon. In languages in which focus is given a distinct morphosyntactic and/or prosodic realization, the necessity of forcing this is obvious, but even in languages that do not have these consequences, the pragmatics of focus suggests the very same assumption. If focusing is largely a pragmatic act, a vehicle of speaker intentions, and an assertion that is of profound importance for the construction of the discourse (Erteschik-Shir 1998), then its overtness is expected.

## 5.2   Coreference with Adjoined Positions

This section examines how the theories of binding and coreference developed in the last chapter, and summarized in (17) and (18), derive the coreferential interpretations of pronominals and monomorphemic reflexives with leftward scrambled arguments.

(17)  THE BINDING THEORY

    (a)  DEFINITION
        A node $\alpha$ is bound by a node $\beta$ iff $\beta$ is not a variable, $\alpha$ and $\beta$ are coindexed and $\beta$ c-commands $\alpha$, where

        (i)  if $\beta$ is an L-bar position, $\beta$ must involve the checking of a [+Q] feature, or

        (ii)  if $\beta$ is an L-position, $\beta$ must involve the checking of a Case feature.

    (b)  TRANSLATION DEFINITION:
        A DP is a variable iff either (i) or (ii) hold.

        (i)  It is a copy that is locally bound by the closest minimally c-commanding copy.

        (ii)  It is locally L-bound, lacks independent reference and is in a checking relation with its licensing functional head.

        Other cases of DP-coindexation are uninterpretable.

    (c)  PRINCIPLES

        A:  A reflexive must be bound in its binding domain.

        B:  A pronominal must be free in its binding domain.

    (d)  BINDING DOMAIN

        (i)  The binding domain for a reflexive is the smallest CFC where it could potentially be bound.

> (ii) The binding domain for a pronominal is the smallest CFC
> where it could potentially be free.

> (iii) A CFC is a domain in which all the grammatical functions
> compatible with its head are realized.

(18) COREFERENCE RULES

Rule I: NP A cannot corefer with NP B if replacing A with C,
C a variable L-bound by B, yields an indistinguishable
representation.

Rule II: DP A cannot corefer with DP B iff A is an R-expression and
B is a pronominal, and DP B immediately precedes A.

The approach to coreference advocated here is that coreference in the
absence of syntactic binding is allowed if and only if it is motivated. It is
my claim that the kind of discourse-bound presupposition–assertion interpretations that scrambling creates provide fertile ground for coreferential
uses of elements subject to Principle B. As scrambled XPs receive a presuppositional, frequently topical, interpretation, considerations of discourse
cohesion encourage speakers to tolerate referential dependencies with such
XPs (Erteschik-Shir 1998). Coreference effects in scrambled configurations
are thus a consequence of basic principles of discourse organization.

## 5.2.1 Scrambling and Pronominal Coreference

In most cases, scrambling does not alter the potential of a coreferential
use of pronominals available in the base configuration. If the pronominal
involved is a possessive, then the option of a coreferential use with a [–Q] expression is always available. Nonpossessive pronominals, however, can never
be used coreferentially with [–Q] expressions at the base, so scrambling can
never motivate coreference in such cases. Only two cases thus stand out as
ones in which scrambling results in judgments that were not available in
the base configuration—the case of possessive pronominal coreference with
scrambled [+Q] elements, and the case of IO R-expression noncoreference
with a possessive pronominal in a scrambled DO.

Consider first (20), the simplified LF representation of (19). The absence
of a WCO violation in this example follows from the theory of coreference,
because XP-adjunction removes the conditions for the coindexation violation. As the revised binding theory forbids any expression that is translated as a bound variable from counting as a binder, the TP-adjoined copy
of the raised [kisko$_{\text{[PFOCUS]}}$] cannot count as a local binder for the subject
pronominal. The copy in [Spec, TP] is similarly ineligible, because it is not

a minimally c-commanding L-bar binder. Therefore a coreferential use of the subject pronominal is licit.

(19)    ??[$_{TP}$ [kɪsko$_i$]$_z$    [$_{TP}$ Uski$_i$   bɛhen-ne    t$_z$   dek$^h$a]]]
          who(DO)    his       sister(SU)      saw

     'Who$_i$ did his$_i$ sister see?'

(20)

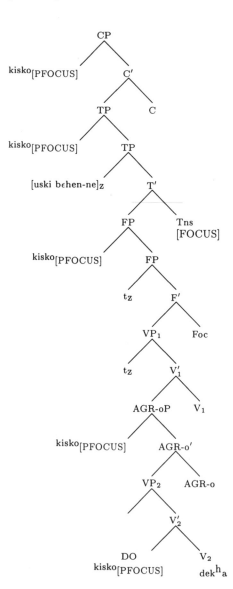

The conclusion that (19) is totally acceptable is, however, a little unexpected, because the actual judgments report some marginality. I suggest that this partial acceptability is due to the fact that WH-scrambling is not at all the preferred way of asking questions in Hindi-Urdu. The preverbal positioning of the WH-phrase appears to be necessary for discourse cohesion, as WH-phrases are inherently focused elements that must occupy [Spec, FP] by PF. The fact that QP scrambling in (21), which illustrates an identical mitigation of WCO effects, is generally held by native speakers to be more acceptable, is thus expected, as QPs are not similarly inherently focused, and may therefore scramble more freely.

(21) [$_{\text{TP}}$ [hər ləɽke$_i$-ko]$_z$ [$_{\text{TP}}$ Uski$_i$ bɛhen-ne t$_z$ dek$^h$a]]
       each boy(DO)      his  sister(SU)    saw
    'Each boy$_i$ was seen by his$_i$ sister.'

Recall that I have argued that scrambled QPs further QR at LF. The first TP-adjoined copy cannot induce a coindexation violation on the subject possessive pronominal, because this copy is adjudicated a bound variable. A coreferential use with the R-expression in the QP is then possible. The account of the mitigation of WCO violations with scrambled topics in (22) also follows the same pattern—covert raising from the adjoined-to-TP position in [Spec, TopP] removes the conditions for the coindexation violation by the subject possessive pronominal.

(22) [$_{\text{TP}}$ [hər ləɽke$_i$-ko]-to]$_z$ [$_{\text{TP}}$ Uski$_i$ bɛhen-ne t$_z$ dek$^h$a]]
       each boy-TOP(DO) his       sister(SU)    saw
    'Each boy$_i$ was seen by his$_i$ sister.'

Consider now the other case in which scrambling effects pronominal non-coreference in (23), in which DO left-scrambling out of the domain of an IO antecedent removes the possibility of coreference between the two:

(23)  (a)  mɛ̃-ne ram$_i$-ko  Uski$_i$ kɪtab     di
           I(SU)  Ram(IO)  his    book(DO)  gave
          'I gave Ram$_i$ his book.'

      (b)  mɛ̃-ne [$_{\text{VP}}$ [Uski$_{*?i/j}$ kɪtab]$_z$  [$_{\text{VP}}$ ram$_i$-ko  t$_z$ di]]
           I(SU)       his      book(DO)      Ram(IO)    gave
          'I gave his$_{*?i/j}$ book to Ram$_i$.'

By the binding theory developed here, this lack of coreference cannot follow from either a coindexation or a binding principle violation. Since the binding theory makes reference to the copy of the IO that is assymmetrically c-commanded by the DO, the possessive pronominal in the DO will not

syntactically bind the IO R-expression. As the configuration does not meet
the conditions for the application of Rule I, coreference between the two
is then an available option—but this is hardly the conclusion we want.
Notice, however, that this configuration closely resembles the environment
of Rule II, as this structure and the one in (25a), both share in the fact
that the DP containing the pronominal occupies an L-bar position, and the
R-expression, an L-position. Suppose then that we reformulate Rule II to
make reference to this configuration (after copy-deletion):

(24)  RULE II
      DP A cannot corefer with DP B iff DP A is an R-expression
      and DP B contains a pronominal, if DP B occupies an L-bar
      position, and immediately precedes DP A.

This formulation of Rule II allows scrambling to override Rule II effects in
(25b) because copy-deletion will yield a structure in which the R-expression
comes to precede the pronominal DP.

(25)  (a) *mɛ̃-ne   use$_i$      [ram$_i$-ki    kɪtab]        di
          I(SU)     him(IO)     Ram-GEN     book(DO)     gave
          'I gave him Ram's book.'

      (b) mɛ̃-ne  [ram$_i$-ki    kɪtab$_j$]     use$_i$     t$_j$  di
          I(SU)    Ram-GEN     book(DO)     him(IO)             gave
          'I gave Ram's book to him.'

## 5.2.2  Scrambling and Reflexive Binding

The binding theory I have formulated does not lead us to expect that
scrambling will affect the interpretation of reflexives available to the base
configuration. So the difference in the judgments in (26a–b) come as a
distinct surprise, as the only difference between these two examples is that
(26b) involves the left-scrambling of the DO:

(26)  (a) *əpne$_i$   bəccõ-ne       mohən-ko$_i$   g$^h$ər-se       nɪkal   diya
          self's     children(SU)   Mohan(DO)    house-from    threw   gave
          (lit.) 'Self's$_i$ children threw Mohan$_i$ out of the house.'

      (b) ?mohən-ko$_i$   əpne$_i$   bəccõ-ne t$_{DO}$   g$^h$ər-se       nɪkal   diya
          Mohan(DO)    self's     children(SU)      house-from    threw   gave
          (lit.) 'Self's$_i$ children threw Mohan$_i$ out of the house'

I suggest that what is happening here is not binding but a kind of coreference that draws upon special properties of the Hindi-Urdu X$^0$-reflexive
for a referential use. This use is acceptable even in default configurations,

as (27) shows, provided the subject-contained reflexive is focused (in this case, marked by the emphatic particle -*hi*):

(27) ??jəb  əpne$_i$-hi      bəccõ-ne      mohən-ko$_i$  Is    bət-pər
    when  self's-EMPH  children(SU)  Mohan(DO)  this  topic-on

    mara, to    ram-ko kya   doš   dena?
    hit   then  Ram    what  blame to-give

    'When even his *own* children hit Mohan for this deed why blame Ram (for doing so as well)?'

Additional evidence for this referential use comes from the fact that the possessive reflexive may also be contraindexed with *Mohan*, where it is then interpreted as referring to the speaker–hearer combine:

(28) jəb   əpne$_i$-hi      bəcce      mohən$_j$-ko  mərte hɛ̃,  to
    when  self-EMPH  children  Mohan       hit   are  then

    dusrõ-ke bəre-mẽ kya   kɛhna?
    others   about   what  to say

    'When *our* children hit Mohan how can we say anything about the others?'

Finally, the fact that these possessive $X^0$-reflexives in Hindi-Urdu may also regularly be used in an 'inclusive' pronominal sense, shown in (29), lends further support to the hypothesis that these pronominal-reflexives are subject to Principle B, rather than Principle A, of the binding theory:

(29) əpni   cizẽ    gəɽi-se      Utar  lao
    self's things  train-from  down  bring

    'Bring down *our* things from the train.'

None of these uses, as (30) and (31) show, are available to XP-reflexives, as these complex reflexives are uniformly subject to Principle A:

(30) *jəb  əpne-əp$_i$-ne-hi  mohən-ko$_i$  is    bət-pər  mara, to
    when  self-EMPH(SU)     Mohan(DO)    this  topic-on hit    then

    ram-ko kya   doš   dena?
    Ram    what  blame to-give

    (lit.) 'When Mohan hit *himself* for this deed, then why blame Ram as well?'

(31) *əpne-əp-ko dek$^h$o
    self-to      look

    'Look at *ourselves*.'

The distinction between XP and $X^0$-reflexives with respect to coreference is now predicted. Consider the LF representations in (32) and (33):

(32)  $[_{TP}$ [mohən$_i$-ko] $[_{TP}$ əpne$_i$ bəccõ-ne $[_{AGR-oP}$ $[_{TR}$ mohən$_i$-ko] $[_{Tns}$ marə]]]]

(33)  $[_{TP}$ [mohən$_i$-ko] $[_{TP}$ əpne$_i$-(əp)-ne $[_{AGR-oP}$ $[_{TR}$ mohən$_i$-ko] $[_{Tns}$ marə]]]]

In both (32) and (33), the TP-adjoined DO does not count as a binder for the subject reflexive because it is a [–Q] element. Both foot copies are adjudicated bound variables, but are accorded distinct rulings by the binding theory. The R-expression in the copy in (32) does not violate any principle of the grammar because it is not syntactically bound, but the one in (33) does, because an L-bound R-expression yields a coindexation violation. Now consider the reflexives in the subject position—because they are not syntactically bound, they are illegitimate on a reflexive interpretation. However, because the possessive $X^0$-reflexive in (32) can also be used as a pronominal, the fact that it is free does not yield an uninterpretable coindexation. Coreference between this pronominal-reflexive and the DO is then allowed. As XP-reflexives lack such a use, the example is ruled as a violation of Principle A.

## 5.3   Scrambling and Specificity

Chapter 1 showed scrambling to share the presuppositional interpretation accorded to topicalized XPs. In the literature on scrambling, this presuppositional interpretation has been identified primarily as a *specific* interpretation as in (34b), but as (35b) indicates, this must be extended to include a *partitive* interpretation as well:

(34)  (a)  mɛ̃-ne     rɑm-ko      fɪlm        dɪk$^h$ɑyi
           I(SU)     Ram(IO)     film(DO)    showed

           'I showed Ram a/the film.'

      (b)  mɛ̃-ne     fɪlm$_i$       rɑm-ko       t$_i$  dɪk$^h$ɑyi
           I(SU)     film(DO)     Ram(IO)            showed

           'I showed Ram the/*a film.'

(35)  (a)  rɑm-ne      kəyi      kɪtɑbẽ       xəridĩ
           Ram(SU)     many      books(DO)    bought

           'Ram bought many books.'

(b) kəyi kıtabẽ<sub>i</sub> ram-ne t<sub>i</sub> xəridĩ
many books(DO) Ram(SU) bought

'Ram bought many (of the) books.'

Following Diesing (1992), I subsume these interpretations under an over-arching notion of *presuppositionality*, in that both DOs are necessarily assumed to have a previously identified discourse referent, although I will continue to distinguish the two readings in description. In the discussion that follows, I argue that this presuppositional reading of scrambled DOs derives from their XP-adjoined status at LF, in direct contradiction to analyses such as those of Mahajan (1990, 1991, 1992) that link specificity to Case-marking and/or control of verb agreement.

Mahajan suggests that the link between linear order and the specific readings of the DOs in (34b) and (35b) is at best only superficial, because specificity effects are manifested by all agreeing and (*-ko*) Case-marked DPs, and are a consequence of positioning in a VP-external [Spec, AGR-oP]. The examples in (35a–b) are, under this analysis, accounted for by Case theory. Because the predicate is a perfective participle, accusative Case (realized overtly as *-ko*) can only be licensed in [Spec, AGR-oP], which is by definition a specific Case. The fact that the DO appears sentence-initially in (35a) but not in (35b) has nothing to do with the specific reading. Mahajan's analysis thus unifies specificity effects in scrambled constructions with those effected by Case-marking by *-ko* in (36b):[6]

(36) (a) ram kıtab laya
Ram(SU) book(DO) brought

'Ram brought a/the book.'

(b) ram kıtab-ko laya
Ram book(DO)-ACC brought

'Ram brought *a/the book.'

The costs of this unification of specificity effects in scrambled and default configurations turn out, however, to be quite high. For one, there is no explanation for the ambiguity of the in situ DOs in (34a) and (36a). As the two DOs control verb agreement, they must be in [Spec, AGR-oP] by Spellout to satisfy Mahajan's S-structure Visibility Condition. We thus expect these DOs to receive only a specific interpretation, and not to actually be ambiguous between specific and indefinite readings as they are.

Furthermore, as (37) shows, it is simply not the case that every Hindi-Urdu DP that either triggers verb agreement or is Case-marked is necessarily accorded a specific interpretation:

(37)  (a)  sita-ko      ek  ləɽka      pəsənd  hɛ
           Sita(FSG)    a   boy(MSG)   liking  is(MSG)

           'Sita likes a boy.'

      (b)  mUjʰe   inam-mẽ  kɪtabẽ      mɪlĩ   tʰĩ
           I(SG)   reward-in  books(FPL)  found  was(FPL)

           'I was given books as a reward.'

      (c)  sita          ek  ləɽke-ko   pəsənd  kərti  hɛ
           Sita(FSG)     a   boy(MSG)   liking  does   is(FSG)

           'Sita likes a boy.'

The examples in (37a) and (37c) show that the overt specification of the DP
as indefinite ensures that no specificity effects obtain, despite the fact that
the DPs in question are agreeing and -*ko* marked objects, respectively. Examples (37b) shows that bare plurals are not given a specific interpretation
either, despite the fact that they trigger agreement and are complements
of a perfective participle.

The fact that scrambling in these very examples can effect a specific
reading of the scrambled XPs suggests that, contrary to Mahajan, linear
order does play quite a significant role in determining the availability of
this presuppositional interpretation. In each of the examples in (38), the
scrambled indefinite gets a partitive reading.

(38)  (a)  ek  ləɽka    sita-ko     pəsənd  hɛ  ɔr  ek   mUjʰe
           a   boy(DO)  Sita(SU)    liking  is  and one  me

           'Sita likes one of the boys, and I another.'

      (b)  ek  ləɽke-ko$_i$  sita          t$_i$  pəsənd  kərti  hɛ  ɔr  ek-ko
           a   boy(DO)        Sita(SU)            liking  does   is  and one
           mẽ
           me

           'Sita likes one of the boys, and I another.'

      (c)  kɪtabẽ$_i$     mUjʰe   inam-mẽ   t$_i$  mɪlĩ  pər  baki  səb
           books(DO)      I(SU)   reward-in        got   but  rest  all
           cizẽ     xəridni  pəɽĩ
           things   to buy   fell

           'The books, I got as a prize, but the remainder I had to buy.'

In fact, as (39) and (40) show, this reading is available to *all* indefinites
and bare plurals, irrespective of whether they are agreeing objects or not:

(39)  (a) mẽ      us     dUkan-se   kUc$^h$  saman
          I(FSG)  that   shop-from  some    things(MSG)
          xəridũngi
          will buy(FSG)
          'I will buy some things from that shop.'

      (b) kUc$^h$ saman$_i$      mẽ       us      dUkan-se   t$_i$
          some  things(MSG)    I(FSG)   that    shop-from
          xəridũngi      ɔr    kUc$^h$  Is-se
          will buy(FSG) and    some    this-from
          'I will buy some things from that shop, and some, from this.'

(40)  (a) mẽ       kItabẽ      la       səkta       hũ
          I(MSG)   books(FSG)  bring    able(MSG)   am
          'I can bring books.'

      (b) kItabẽ$_i$      mẽ        t$_i$ la      səkta      hũ
          books(FSG)    I(MSG)          bring   able(MSG)  am
          'I can bring the books, but not the other things.'

These observations, taken together with the other problems with Mahajan's approach, suggest that there is no robust evidence that argues for an
analysis of specificity in terms of positioning in a Case-checking position.

   In addition, Mahajan appears to conflate the two distinct notions of
definiteness and specificity in his discussion. Unlike Mahajan, and following
Bhattacharya and Dasgupta (1996), I consider Case-markers and deictic
pronouns to be markers of definiteness rather than specificity. Bare DPs
are usually interpreted as indefinite, as are DPs that are marked by the
indefinite quantifiers, including the numeral *one*. As (41) shows, when a DP
is so specified, the definiteness effects of the Case-marker are obliterated:

(41)  (a) sɛf   kItab-ko    gusse-mẽ   aakər  p$^h$aʈ  ḍalega
          Saif  book-ACC    anger-in   came   tear    put-will
          'Saif will tear up the book in a fit of anger.'

      (b) sɛf   ek   kItab-ko   gusse-mẽ   aakər  p$^h$aʈ  ḍalega
          Saif  a    book-ACC   anger-in   came   tear    put-will
          'Saif will tear up a/*the book in a fit of anger.'

In (41a), the accusative Case-marker quite clearly induces the definite reading of the in situ DO, but in (41b), the presence of the indefinite quantifier
*ek* overrides the definiteness effects of the Case-marker.

   Since all definites are interpreted as specific, it is difficult to see the
distinction between the two concepts in anything but the scrambling of
bare DPs and overtly specified indefinites, as in (42):

(42)  (a) kɪtab$_i$      sɛher        t$_i$  pəʈ$^h$ rəhi    hɛ   ɔr   kɔmɪk
          book(DO)  Sehar(SU)          read  PROG  is   and  comic
          rɑm
          Ram

      'Sehar is reading the book, and Ram, the comic.'

      (b) ek  kɪtab(-ko)$_i$  rɑm        t$_i$  pəʈ$^h$egɑ  ɔr   ek(-ko)  sɛf
          a   book(DO)    Ram(SU)         will read  and  one      Saif

      'One book Ram will read and the other, Saif.'

      (c) kəyi   kɪtabẽ$_i$     sɛf-ne     t$_i$  rəkk$^h$ĩ  ɔr   kəyĩ   phẽkĩ
          many  books(DO)   Saif(SU)        kept      and  many   threw

      'Saif kept many of the books and he threw away many.'

In each of these examples, the scrambled DO receives a partitive reading
quite distinct from the one that it was accorded in its base position. These
effects are clearly a consequence of the linear positioning of the indefinite
DO. Thus, whereas definite readings of Hindi-Urdu DPs are the result of
a complex set of factors, the presuppositional interpretation of scrambled
XPs is a consequence of the fact that scrambling changes the hierarchical
and linear position of the indefinite. Diesing's (1992) proposals about the
interpretation of indefinites provide a straightforward explanation for the
presuppositional interpretations accorded to scrambled XPs in Hindi-Urdu.

The essence of Diesing's proposals is that presuppositional interpretations of noun phrases are necessarily associated with restrictive clause formation, while indefinite interpretations are associated with the domain of
existential quantification, the nuclear scope. Because the chief objective of
Diesing's work is to arrive at the syntactic representations that feed these
ultimate logical representations, her proposals introduce a tree-splitting
algorithm by which LF trees are partitioned into a nuclear scope, corresponding to the VP level, and a restrictive clause, corresponding to the TP
level. The hypothesis is that after tree-splitting at LF, indefinites within
the VP are mapped onto an existential interpretation, whereas those that
are at the TP level are mapped onto a presuppositional one.

The identification of material within TP versus that within VP makes
crucial reference to the segment–category distinction in Chomsky (1986a),
in which only those nodes of the tree that are dominated by each and every one of the segments of a category are considered to be dominated, or
'included', by the category in question. It then follows that any XP that
has been adjoined to VP or any functional projection above it can never be
accorded an existential interpretation. Now, from my argument that scrambling is an XP-adjunction operation, the fact that scrambled XPs receive
a strongly presuppositional reading follows at once—because XPs adjoined

to either VP or TP will never be included in the VP, adjunction to VP, FP, or TP necessarily entails restrictive clause formation. The interpretive similarity between scrambling and topicalization is also derived, as material from [Spec, TopP] will be included in the restrictive clause. All that appears to be required in order to make Diesing's proposals fully compatible with minimalism is the assumption that only the highest copy of a (scrambling) chain is visible to this process—that is, the mapping to semantic representation makes reference only to nonbound variable copies.[7, 8]

This analysis then provides an explanation for the problematic facts for Mahajan's analysis. Because I execute accusative and dative Case checking in a VP-internal AGR-oP position, the facts that nonagreeing objects may be interpreted as specific and that not all agreeing objects are specific follow straightforwardly—as Case and agreement checking are no longer implicated in deriving the specific interpretation, no connection between the two is actually expected. Presuppositional interpretation in now solely the consequence of the exclusion from VP in the derivation that exits LF.

## 5.4 Conclusion

I had raised a number of questions in chapter 1 that a study of the scrambling operation must address. This chapter constitutes answers to the major questions. I have shown that a uniform analysis of the leftward scrambling operation is indeed possible, once it is recognized that the coreferential use of elements subject to Principle B of the binding theory with scrambled XPs is not an instance of binding but discourse-motivated coreference. I have defined the morphosyntactic trigger for the scrambling operation as positional focusing in a [Spec, FP] projection immediately dominating VP and have suggested that the reason why scrambling is necessarily an overt phenomenon is because focus positions must necessarily be licensed in the overt syntax. Finally, I have shown that the presuppositional interpretation that scrambled XPs receive can be derived straightforwardly from the proposals of Diesing (1992) regarding the quantificational force of indefinites. By my proposals, scrambled constructions are focus constructions, which suggests that the proper study of scrambling across languages should locate it within the focalization strategies in natural language.

In conclusion, consider whether other argument scramblings can also be unified under an XP-adjunction account. Although research is unanimous on an analysis of long-distance scrambling as derived XP-adjunction, the claim that it cannot override WCO effects (Mahajan 1990) is unexpected. Actually, the data is rather more nuanced here, as speakers usually exercise severe normative judgments about scrambling across clause boundaries and will tolerate coreferential uses of possessive pronominals with adjoined el-

ements only if there is sufficient contextualization. Judgments such as the
one Mahajan reports in (43a) may well coexist with the one in (43b):

(43)　(a)　*[kɪsko$_i$ [Uski$_i$ bɛhen-ne kəha [ki　[ram-ne t$_i$ dekʰa]]]]
　　　　 who　 his　 sister　 said that Ram　　 seen
　　　　 'Who$_i$ did his$_i$ sister say Ram had seen?'

　　　 (b)　??[hər bhai$_i$-ko　　 [Uski$_i$ bɛhen socti hɛ [Uski biwi
　　　　 each　 brother(EDO) his　 sister thinks is　 his　 wife
　　　　 [tʰik tərɛh-se　 t$_i$ kʰana nəhĩ kʰɪlati]]]]
　　　　 proper way-ABL　　 feed　 not make eat
　　　　 'Every brother's sister thinks that his wife doesn't feed him
　　　　 properly.'

In a similar fashion, contextualization can also weaken Mahajan's claim that
though long-distance scrambling can license parasitic gaps, the scrambled
element must be noncoreferential with a subject pronominal in the matrix
subject. For example, consider (44), which crucially assumes the context
of marriages of convenience in the Indian subcontinent:

(44)　??[kɪsko$_i$ [Uski$_i$ mangetər [bɪna　　 PRO $pg_i$ dekʰe-hi]　　 t$_i$
　　　 who　 his　 fiance　 without　　 seeing-EMPH
　　　 pyar kərne ləgi]]
　　　 love to do began
　　　 'Who$_i$ did his$_i$ fiance start loving even before she saw him?

This variation is not unexpected in my approach. For coreference to be
motivated, the scrambled XP must receive a presuppositional reading. Although it is generally difficult to accord a presuppositional interpretation
to quantificational elements, the examples I provide show that this is not
an impossible task. In both examples, the use of kinship terms and predicates that are canonically associated with kinship relations as well as the
choice of habitual aspect contribute to a presuppositional reading of the
scrambled XP. Hence, coreference is tolerated in these contexts.

　　Argument scrambling to the right of the verb does not exhibit any of the
properties exhibited by leftward scrambling, except that it may marginally
license parasitic gap constructions. As the examples in (45)–(49) show,
right-of-V elements do not override WCO effects, do not corefer with reflexives, do not instantiate positional focus, and are not accorded presuppositional interpretations, even though they do pattern with left-of-V elements
in licensing parasitic gaps:

(45)　*Uski bɛ̃hen$_i$　　 t$_i$ pyar kərti hɛ kɪsko$_i$?
　　　 his　 sister(SU)　　 love does is　 who(DO)
　　　 'Who$_i$ does his$_i$ sister love?'

(46) *əpne$_i$ bəccõ-ne        g$^h$ər-se     t$_i$ nɪkəl diya mohan-ko$_i$
     self's   children(SU) home-from        threw gave  Mohan(DO)
     'Self's children threw Mohan out of the house.'

(47) *mẽ-ne **ram-ko**   t$_i$ di     t$^h$i  kɪtab$_i$
     I(SU)    Ram(IO)      gave was   book(DO)
     'I gave the book to RAM.'

(48) *nur-ne     aaj    t$_i$ k$^h$aya seb$_i$
     Noor(SU) today     ate     apple(DO)
     'Noor ate a/*the apple today.'

(49) ??mohən janta  hɛ [ki   ram  [bɪna      PRO$_i$ *pg*$_i$ pər$^h$e
     Mohan  thinks  is  that Ram  without                   reading
     t$_i$ p$^h$ẽk  dega]      kɔn-si  kɪtab$_i$]]
        throw will give which book(DO)
     'Which book does Mohan think that Ram will throw away without
     reading *pg*?'

Because these right-of-V elements exhibit none of the major properties
of the scrambling operation investigated in this book, I suggest that these
examples do not involve syntactic movement, and that all rightward scrambling configurations are base-generated. Parasitic gap licensing in such
configurations pose no significant problem, as they can be explained by
Cinque's (1990) analysis of parasitic gaps, by which that gap is a pronominal variable, i.e., a *pro* rather than a pure variable, L-bar-bound by the
WH-phrase base-generated as a right adjunct to VP.

# Chapter 6

# XP-Adjunction in UG

I suggested, in chapter 1, that a description of the syntactic properties of the scrambling operation would provide valuable insights not only into the theoretical status of XP-adjunction but also into the architecture of Universal Grammar. In this the concluding chapter, I discuss the implications of my proposals for the theory of grammar.

## 6.1   XP-Adjunction and Global Economy

My chief proposal has been that the derived XP-adjunction operation is just as morphosyntactically driven as the substitution operation and like it, has distinct LF and PF effects. Although this proposal assimilates XP-adjunction into the general theory of movement in the grammar, the special properties of the XP-adjunction operation, in terms of its obligatory overtness and the types of checking relations it enters into, suggest that derived XP-adjunction has a special status in the grammar.

With the morphosyntactic imperative in place, all the major XP-adjunction operations discussed in this book—scrambling (adjunction to FP and TP), IO Case checking in DOCs, QR, and XP-reflexive licensing—can now be held to be constrained by the economy principle of Greed, although I must allow subtle differences in the way in which each instance of XP-adjunction converges with respect to this requirement. In my analysis, only IO raising to adjoin to AGR-oP actually instantiates the canonical checking relation envisaged by Chomsky (1992)— a matching of the morphosyntactic features of $\alpha$ with identical ones on a functional head. Even though scrambling and XP-reflexive raising fulfil the basic objective of effecting an agreement configuration between a functional head and the XP-adjoined element, the two instances of checking have quite different properties. XP-reflexive raising to an adjoined position to, say, AGR-sP, places it in a configuration in which it can share the agreement features (of the subject argument) on the AGR-s head. In feature transmission, on the other hand, the agreement configuration is effected by dynamic agreement from a broadly L-related position to a functional head, by which the features of the adjoined XP come to be shared by the head. Finally, the XP-adjunction account of QR that I provide makes no reference to checking domains at all.

The difference in the nature of the checking relation that each XP-adjunction operation enters into necessarily assumes a broader definition of Greed than that in Chomsky (1992). Take, for example, the mechanism of feature transmission that I have held to be necessary for the activation of a dormant FP and the identification of the derivation as a focus construction. Strictly speaking, this mechanism cannot be considered to involve a checking relation because no morphosyntactic property of the raised element itself is checked. It is therefore an open question whether this adjunction to FP/TP can actually be considered self-serving last resort movement. I have suggested that the Greed construal of such XP-adjunction operations is possible only if we see Greed as an injunction to the grammar to ensure that all morphosyntactic/pragmatic features on $\alpha$ in the numeration are checked. In this conception of Greed, then, any movement that is necessary for the ultimate satisfaction of a morphosyntactic/pragmatic feature of $\alpha$ satisfies economy always.

Notice that this definition of Greed runs counter to Chomsky's (1995) characterization of movement as the *attraction* of a linguistic expression to the checking domain of a functional head. Attendant on this reformulation of the checking relation is the proviso that checking must involve features of both the head and the raised linguistic expression. None of the mechanisms that involve dynamic agreement from broadly L-related positions (feature transmission and XP-reflexive licensing) are comfortable in this Attract/Move account of movement. At the same time, this resistance is not a general characteristic of XP-adjunction, as a statement of IO Case checking in an adjoined-to-AGR-oP position in terms of Attract/Move is perfectly plausible.

This difference in amenability to an Attract/Move account, to me, appears to reduce to the split in the kind of features that are licensed: Where the objective is to license features that are mainly interpretive in nature, movement is recalcitrant to a more selfish definition of Greed, but where the licensing of features that are purely morphosyntactic (and low in interpretive content) is involved, more stringent definitions of Greed are applicable. In fact, this broader definition of Greed appears to be needed by interpretive movements in general, as pronominal raising to $D^0$ and QR cannot also be conceived of in terms of Attract/Move.

In terms of the distinction in Chomsky (1995), only the movement driven by features that are uninterpretable at the interface are subject to the most selfish definition of Greed. The proposals here also suggest an internal differentiation in the class of interpretable features, in that interpretable logico-semantic features differ quite substantially from interpretable discursive/pragmatic ones: While the latter type of features are not features of individual lexical items but of the construction as a whole, and their licensing implicates a version of the checking relation, the former are features of lexical items that do not need to be checked for convergence.

The behavior of derived XP-adjunction operations with respect to the economy principle of Procrastinate is equally intriguing. Aside from QR which, as it does not involve checking, always respects Procrastinate, most other instances of derived XP-adjunction are necessarily overt. The generalization appears to be that only the derived XP-adjunction driven by quasi-interpretive considerations may be covert; other instances of XP-adjunction are necessarily a pre-Spellout phenomenon. The approach I have adopted explains this preference for overtness as a function of the way natural language selects from the theoretically permitted options—though in principle covert scrambling and covert IO adjunction to AGR-oP are possible, natural language only selects the overt options of these operations. Similarly, although we will also have to allow the possibility of overt XP-reflexive (and $X^0$-reflexive) raising and QR, natural language prefers the option of covert movement. The (c)overtness of XP-adjunction operations thus find its origins (in uncharted areas) of 'natural language preferences' of the theoretically permitted options, and not from the conspiracy of feature strength with Greed and Procrastinate.

Derived XP-adjunction thus has special properties with respect to the economy principles and the theory of checking. The issue is not so much whether the modifications to economy principles and checking theory that it asks for are possible but rather whether such redefinition will bring us closer to an understanding of the status of XP-adjunction in UG. Recent research (e.g., Chomsky 1995) seeks to investigate the properties of movement in two broad areas of inquiry: (1) the difference in the properties of overt and covert movement, and (2) the differences in the class of overt movement itself, where such movement either takes place in the overt syntax or in the PF component. Accepting these as the parameters on which the discussion of the special properties of derived XP-adjunction must be based radically alters the perspective with which the analysis of derived XP-adjunction in this book is to be viewed. Because QR and XP-reflexive raising are instances of covert movement, the proper discussion of their validity with respect to Greed and Procrastinate is within the debate of the tenability of the [strong]/[weak] distinction with regard to movements that are interpretive in nature. My claim that both QR and XP-reflexive raising are necessarily covert operations then contributes to this debate the understanding that covert XP-adjunction is not driven by the [strong]/[weak] distinction, being a movement whose covertness is determined only by Procrastinate.

Similarly, the fact that some XP-adjunction operations must necessarily be overt can be placed within the debate about whether all overt movement is necessarily syntactic. Chomsky (1995:324–26) suggests that XP-adjunction is not a last resort operation and is best analyzed as a post-Spellout PF-movement. It will therefore necessarily be overt but irrelevant for interpretation at LF. My analysis of the XP-adjunction operation here is, at first sight, apparently firmly committed against Chomsky's. The fact that I ascribe distinct interpretive consequences as well as a morphosyntactic motivation to XP-adjunction operations like scrambling and dative shift suggests that the operation must target the interface with the C-I system. This conclusion is strengthened by my analysis of the way scrambling overrides WCO effects, as I make crucial use of the preservation of the XP-adjoined link to motivate coreferential interpretations. The proposals regarding dative-shifted IOs also make the same point—if it is only the XP-adjunction analysis that can explain the fact that dative-shifted IOs behave more like adjuncts than arguments, then XP-adjunction must be a syntactic operation.

On the first appraisal, then, the proposals in this book suggest that it is incorrect to exile XP-adjunction from the syntactic component. However, given the fact that maintaining XP-adjunction as syntactic movement not only entails a redefinition of checking procedures and some economy principles but also some rather hazy appeals to 'properties of natural language' to motivate the overtness of the operation, Chomsky's proposals may turn out to have some validity. On a sufficiently developed theory of PF-movement, its intrinsic properties, and its interpretive consequences (Aoun and Choueri 1996, Kidwai 1998, 1999, Zubizarreta 1998), the uniform analysis of scrambling as XP-adjunction that I provide may allow a wholesale relocation of it to the PF-component. In my system, coreference with XP-adjoined elements is the result of the computations of the coreference component and never the result of syntactic binding. The binding theory, an LF interface condition, thus has little role in determining these interpretive effects of the scrambling operation, and an alternative analysis could be constructed in which coreference is determined with primary reference to derivations at PF. Similarly, the fact that I locate scrambled constructions within the class of so-called stylistic (focus) constructions in natural language could also be adduced as evidence for Chomsky's claim, because it is these stylistic rules that he seeks to relocate to the PF component. Although in the discussion that follows I shall continue to assume that all XP-adjunction is syntactic movement, it appears that at least some aspects of my analysis of scrambling can actually be garnered as support for the PF-movement analysis of scrambling.

## 6.2   The Economy of Representation

Much current minimalist work assumes there to be not one, but two, mechanisms that delete copies, the first being the deletion that constructs the operator-variable pair, and the second, the option of last-resort deletion to allow chains to converge with respect to the Chain Uniformity Condition. A major feature of the system I have proposed is that copy-deletion is required only to construct the *variable* part of the pair. This section develops this proposal and demonstrates that it eliminates the option of deletion as a last-resort option to construct uniform chains.

My proposal for the deletion of copies in (1) necessarily assumes that because deletion is subject to general principles of recoverability, deletion of a nonbound variable copy will always result in nonconvergence.

(1)   DELETION OF COPIES
      Delete every bound variable copy of $\alpha$ in which a feature of $\alpha$ is checked (where checking includes dynamic agreement).

Thus, in chains involving WH-scrambling in Hindi-Urdu or raising in English, only the head copy and the tail copy will survive to the interface:

(2)    (a)  [$_{CP}$ kɪsko [$_{TP}$ [k̶ɪ̶s̶k̶o̶] [$_{TP}$ ʊs-ne [$_{VP1}$ [AGR-oP [k̶ɪ̶s̶k̶o̶] [$_{VP2}$
            [ʊ̶s̶-̶n̶e̶] [kɪsko]]]] dekʰa]]]

       (b)  [$_{TP}$ John seems [$_{TP}$ [J̶o̶h̶n̶] to be [$_{VP}$ [John] reading]]]

The derivation in (2a) makes the assumption that the computation treats [PFOCUS] as a morphosyntactic feature of $\alpha$, by virtue of the fact that this feature comes to be associated with $\alpha$ in the numeration itself (Chomsky 1995:277–78). Thus, the sharing of the [FOCUS] from the TP-adjoined WH-copy with Tns will count as the checking of a feature of the WH-phrase itself. The TP-adjoined copy and the copy in which accusative Case is checked will therefore delete. In the English raising construction in (2b), the categorial feature of the raised DP *John* is involved in a checking relation with the EPP-feature of the embedded Tns (Chomsky 1995:280) in the embedded [Spec, TP] position, so that copy will delete. In both these derivations, however, the copies in the $\theta$-position will survive to the interface because, by assumption, $\theta$-role is not a morphosyntactic feature of the XP in question (Chomsky 1995:312).

This conclusion that legitimate LF chains must preserve both the head and tail copies entails that the variable of an operator-chain will never be in a Case position. This is not, I believe, a shortcoming, as this latter requirement is a residue of the P&P framework that actually has little role to play in minimalism (see also Hornstein 1995, Safir 1996). This requirement first originated in a model of grammar that distinguished NP-trace and WH-trace from PRO in terms of Case, and sought to limit the phenomenon of reconstruction to Cased positions. In the current approach, where PRO has been assimilated into the structural Case system by the theory of null Case (Chomsky and Lasnik 1993), and where the phenomenon of reconstruction has been dispensed with altogether, this requirement is of little consequence. In addition, maintaining that Cased copies are preserved also entails substantial problems for semantic interpretation. As the theory completely separates Case and $\theta$-positions and excludes $\theta$-roles from the checking relation, the only way that the C-I system can access $\theta$-roles is if the copy which bears the $\theta$-role is, to borrow a familiar metaphor, *visible* at the interface. If at most one copy of the chain is allowed to survive after copy-deletion, then preserving a bound variable Cased copy simultaneously ensures the deletion of the $\theta$-copy. Minimalist considerations thus force the deletion of the bound variable in the Case position.

Chains in which more than one bound variable copy is preserved will violate Full Interpretation. Although this follows trivially from the bi-uniqueness relation for operators and variables assumed by Full Interpretation, nothing in the theory actually requires copy-deletion for L-chains. As maintaining a distinction between L- and L-bar chains purely by stipulation is hardly desirable, the optimal result would be to derive a unique copy-deletion mechanism that applies to both types of chains.

Notice that checking theory undermines this distinction in any case because it treats a [Case] feature at par with a [+Q] feature in terms of the checking domain and mechanisms involved. Then, Full Interpretation can no longer accord a special status to the operator-variable construction, with the result that there can be only one Full Interpretation definition of a legitimate object at the LF interface, the one in (3). The copy-deletion mechanism in (1) serves to ensure convergence with respect to it:

(3)  FULL INTERPRETATION: LEGITIMATE CHAINS AT LF
     $(\alpha_1, \alpha_2)$, where $\alpha_2$ must be in a $\theta$-position.

The principles in (1) and (3) have serious implications for Chomsky and Lasnik's Chain Uniformity Condition discussed in chapter 2, in that the deletion of copies is no longer an option for the construction of uniform chains—deletion of either of the two surviving copies in a chain will be unrecoverable and hence not permitted. As a consequence, however, not only is it impossible to maintain the analysis (in chapter 2) of the difference between languages with respect to WH-scrambling, we also no longer have an explanation for the argument-adjunct asymmetry with respect to extraction from a syntactic island that the Chain Uniformity Condition in conjunction with last-resort deletion was intended to capture:

(4)     (a) ??Which car did John leave New York [CP before t* [he fixed t]]?

        (b) *How did John leave New York [CP before t* [he fixed the car t]]?

Chomsky and Lasnik (1993) suggest that the difference in acceptability between (4a) and (4b) lies in the fact that because the chain created by adjunct movement in (4b) yields a uniform (L-bar) chain, deletion cannot target any of its copies. The copy in the adjunct [Spec, CP] will then yield an ECP violation. In argument extraction, on the other hand, the chain created is nonuniform, and after the deletion of the intermediate copy, all that (4a) violates is Subjacency. It will be obvious that this account is no longer available under my proposals of copy-deletion, the deletion of copies meets Full Interpretation rather than the Chain Uniformity Condition. Furthermore, the deletion mechanism I propose makes no reference to the kind of position the copy occupies but rather to whether or not the copy involves the checking of a feature of $\alpha$.

Lee (1995:3–5) questions the validity of maintaining the Chain Uniformity Condition, arguing that such uniformity conditions are properly stated as conditions on computational *derivation* rather than on representation. Pointing out that Chomsky (1995:253) himself adopts this approach with his postulation that "chains be uniform with respect to phrase-structure status", Lee points out that maintaining both conditions is redundant. Furthermore, if last-resort deletion is allowed, then not only can it target a derivationally nonuniform chain and render it uniform, it can also rescue cases of L- and L-bar chain interleaving by deleting the offending L-bar link.

If the Chain Uniformity Condition is a derivational condition, copy-deletion can then be exclusively motivated for convergence with respect to the requirements of Full Interpretation. The question then is how the argument-adjunct extraction symmetry is to be derived. My analysis actually follows Lee's quite closely, who proposes the following criterion on the economy of representation:

(5)    THE CHECKING MEASURE ON CHAINS
       An element $\alpha_i$ cannot be a member of the legitimate LF chain C= $(\alpha_1, \ldots, \alpha_n)$ if it does not mark the checking history of the chain C.

Lee (1995: ch. 2) makes three important assumptions. The first is that Shortest Move forces XP-movement to proceed through adjunction to XP, as only that will ensure short chain links. The second assumption assimilates adverbs into the checking system, as they are licensed by checking their formal features in adjunction positions of a head X. Finally, Lee also holds that once the formal features of an argument (e.g., [Case]) or an adverb (e.g., [ADV]) are checked, the argument cannot target positions of that type in the course of the derivation. This has the result that once the Case feature of an argument is checked, it cannot move through L-specifiers, and further, once the [ADV]-feature of an adverb is checked, adjunct extraction cannot proceed through any adjunction positions. These three assumptions yield the LF representations in (6) for the examples in (4), where I use traces as mnemonics for copies:

(6)　(a)　$[_{CP}$ [which car] did $[_{TP}$ t$''''$ $[_{TP}$ John leave New York $[_{CP}$ t$'''$ $[_{CP}$ before $[_{TP}$ t$''$ $[_{TP}$ he $[_{VP}$ t$'$ $[_{VP}$ fixed t]]]]]]]]]]

　　(b)　$[_{CP}$ how did $[_{TP}$ John leave New York $[_{CP}$ before $[_{TP}$ he fixed the car t]]]]]

By Lee's proposals, because all the adjoined argument traces in (6a) do not record any part of the checking history of the argument chain, they will delete by (5), the example being a Subjacency violation because of the trace $t''$. In (6b), on the other hand, the only trace (which is the source of the ECP violation) cannot delete.

　　I find all three of Lee's assumptions problematic. The interpretation of Shortest Move as requiring argument movement to proceed via adjunction to XP, I believe, must be entirely dispensed with, as it blurs the distinction between ECP and Subjacency violations. For example, it would lead us to consider superraising in (7) as at worst a Subjacency violation rather than the violation of the relativized minimality that it is:

(7)　(a)　*John seems it is certain to go home.

　　(b)　John seems $[_{CP}$ $[_{TP}$ t$''''$ $[_{TP}$ it is certain $[_{CP}$ t$'''$ $[_{TP}$ t$''$ to $[_{VP}$ t$'$ $[_{VP}$ t go home]]]]]]]]

I will therefore assume that the extraction of arguments does not involve movement through adjunction positions.

　　Although I agree with Lee that adjoined positions can be feature-checking positions, the postulation that the formal features of adverbs are checked by inflectional heads and/or the verb is stipulatory. Checking theory does not surely necessitate the syntactic validation of each and every lexical feature, and it is unclear as to exactly why inflectional projections L-related to the verb are the ones that check the adverb's features. I will therefore assume that adverbs are outside the checking process in their base-generated adjoined positions.

My position also differs from Lee's with regard to the positions targeted by adjunct movement. Although I accept her suggestion that adjunct movement can target only adjunction positions, I generalize it to apply even if the feature of the adjunct have been checked lower down. The fact that I allow feature checking from adjoined positions overcomes any problems that the WH-extraction of adjuncts may pose. The WH-feature of *why* in (8a) will be checked in a broadly L-related position to $C^0$, as in (8b).

(8)    (a)  Why did you say that?

       (b)  $[_{CP}$ why $[_{CP}$ $[_{C}$ did $[_{TP}$ you say that t]]]]

These assumptions come together to yield LF representations for the argument-adjunct asymmetry in (4) quite distinct from the ones that Lee's analysis provides. In (9a), the argument WH-phrase will have to move to the matrix [Spec, CP] in one fell swoop, whereas in (9b) the (VP-) adjunct raises through adjunction-to-XP:

(9)    (a)  $[_{CP}$ [which car] did $[_{TP}$ John leave New York $[_{CP}$ before $[_{TP}$ he $[_{VP}$ fixed $[_{TR}$ which car]]]]]]

       (b)  $[_{CP}$ how $[_{CP}$ did $[_{TP}$ John leave New York $[_{CP}$ $[_{TR}$ how] $[_{CP}$ before $[_{TP}$ he $[_{VP}$ fixed the car $[_{VP}$ $[_{TR}$ how]]]]]]]]]

Copy-deletion by (1) cannot delete any of the copies in either representation, because neither movement leaves any copies in a position where a feature of the WH-phrase is checked. Whereas (9a) forms a legitimate object (that derivationally violates Subjacency), (9b) does not. Because the adjunct chain will consist of an operator and three variables, (9b) will thus violate Full Interpretation.

If these speculations are on the right track, the elimination of the ECP as a condition on representations appears to be at hand, as some aspects of the ECP may reduce to Full Interpretation. However, as there are many complex issues at stake here, I set the matter aside for further research, turning now to the issues of the derivation of XP-adjunction constructions.

## 6.3    The Economy of Derivation

Let us now examine how the grammar enforces the distinction between landing sites targeted in the course of a derivation, i.e., to the minimalist interpretation of the PUB, repeated in (10). At the end of chapter 2, I sought to give it a Chain Uniformity account, but since that condition has now been recast as a derivational one, let us examine whether the PUB too can be accorded a similar reinterpretation.

(10) PRINCIPLE OF UNAMBIGUOUS BINDING
   A variable that is α-bound must be β-free in the domain of the head
   of its chain (where α and β refer to different types of A-bar
   positions).

With the assimilation of XP-adjunction, and especially scrambling, into the
feature-checking system, much of the burden on the PUB is distributed over
the last resort condition on movement and configurations in which Greed
can be fulfilled. For example, the fact that neither DP-scrambling nor topicalization can target [Spec, CP] follows trivially from Greed because such
raising will not result in a checking relation with $C^0$, and thus it will not
take place. Similarly, the fact that WH-phrases cannot be topicalized follows from the fact that WH-phrases and topics target the same projection,
and that topicalization requires $Top^0$ to be the designated head. Because
this is not a head that can license a checking relation with the [+WH]
feature of the WH-phrase, such raising will not be tolerated.

   However, because the Greed account of the PUB relies on the assumption
that no checking takes place in [Spec, CP/TopP], it lacks the empirical
coverage that the PUB has. As recent proposals (Chomsky 1995:269–70)
about checking phrase it in terms of the attraction of α by the features of
a functional head, a checking relation could be established that is not a
consequence of the needs of α but of the needs of the functional head itself.
Thus, for example, it is plausible that a WH-phrase in [Spec, TopP] enters
into a checking relation with $Top^0$ because $Top^0$ must check its [strong]
D-feature in the overt syntax against an identical categorial feature in its
SPEC. As the WH-phrase is so categorially specified, it may raise to [Spec,
TopP], but then we would predict that [Spec, TopP] should be able to serve
as an escape hatch for WH-movement beyond this position. However, as
we discussed at length in chapter 2, such a situation never actually obtains,
not only in this particular case but in all other similar ones—movements
with distinct morphosyntactic imperatives can never use the L-bar landing
sites of others.

   The other economy of derivation principles (in the form presented here)
are similarly ill-equipped to capture the effects of the PUB. Chomsky's
(1995:253) proposal about the derivational uniformity of chains just cited
is of no special value in this regard because it makes reference only to the
phrase-structure status of raised elements, which is not at issue here, all
the raised elements being XPs. Collins's (1994) version of the Economy of
Derivation is a more plausible candidate, but because it assumes a strictly
binary typology of L- and L-bar movement, it cannot in its present form rule
out chains that involve the use of [Spec, TopP] as an escape hatch for XP-
adjunction. In addition, because it makes crucial use of the number of nodes

traversed and number of operations of Form-Chain in computing economy, it may be that it will be unable to determine the most optimal derivation for chains that relate two L-bar positions. For example, in the two possible derivations of long-distance WH-movement using [Spec, TopP] as an escape hatch represented schematically in (11), both derivations involve the same number of nodes traversed and applications of Form-Chain:

(11)   (a)  ...  [CP [WH] [TP ... [TopP [WH] [TP [WH]...]]]]

       (b)  ...  [CP [WH] [TP ... [CP [WH] [TP [WH]...]]]]

Given the unsatisfactory nature of a derivational account of the PUB, let us then explore whether the effects of the PUB can be subsumed under Full Interpretation. In the revised checking theory outlined previously, the checking of features of α can target either those features that are typically its morphosyntactic properties, such as Case, number, [+WH], etc., or only its categorial features, such as D, V, etc. The basic intuition I wish to capture is that deletion in L-bar chains affects only those bound variable copies that involve the checking of a morphosyntactic feature intrinsically associated with α itself by the numeration. Following Marantz (1997), I assume that categorial features are not lexical/morphological properties of lexical items. Then, L-bar copies that involve the checking of a categorial feature will not be deleted, and such derivations will not converge at the interface.

(12)  DELETION OF COPIES
      Delete every bound variable copy of α in which a feature of α is checked, where:

      (a) In an L-bar chain, the feature of α that is checked must be a noncategorial feature.

      (b) In an L-chain, the feature of α that is checked can be either a categorial or a noncategorial feature.

The proposal here assumes a distinction between categorial and noncategorial features that is contested by Chomsky (1995:232). I hold that in the checking of features associated with α, primary reference is made to noncategorial features such as [Case], [number], [FOCUS] etc., but in cases in which an XP raises from an XP-adjoined position to [Spec, TopP], checking will make reference only to its categorial feature and will therefore not provide sufficient ground for copy-deletion. This distinction then ensures that of the two derivations in (11), only (11b) will converge, because it is only here that checking accesses a noncategorial feature (the [+WH] feature) of the bound variable copy. The fact that in (11a) checking in [Spec,

TopP] will only target the categorial D-feature of the WH-phrase ensures the preservation of the copy at the C-I interface and a consequent violation of Full Interpretation. Similar arguments can be constructed to explain the various asymmetries noted between L-bar movements in chapter 2, in interaction with language-particular constraints regarding possible adjunction sites, etc.

The issue of the projectivity of the PUB now receives a different analysis. Note first that the mechanism in (12) does not preclude chains formed by covert movement from, say, a scrambled position to a topic position, if that movement targets a noncategorial feature of the raised XP. My proposal has been that QR and raising to [Spec, CP/TopP] from a scrambling position is driven by exactly such requirements, so chains formed by overt scrambling and covert raising to satisfy a [+Q] or a [+topic] feature (e.g., where the scrambled XP is a *-to*-topic) will always satisfy Full Interpretation at the interface.

I had earlier suggested that the reason why languages such as German do not have scrambling of WH- in situ is that such WH- in situ can be licensed as operators only if they remain in their base position in the LF derivation. Let us assume that this licensing is done by local unselective binding by a Q operator at LF (Chomsky 1995:291), with the result that the configuration required for WH- in situ licensing must be that in (13a). In a configuration involving WH-scrambling, however, this basic configuration will not be instantiated. The copy-deletion mechanism in (12) will preserve both the TP-adjoined copy as well as the trace, as in (13b):

(13)   (a) ... $[_{CP}$ WH$_1$ Q $[_{TP}$ $[_{VP}$ WH$_2$]]]

      (b) ... $[_{CP}$ WH$_1$ Q $[_{TP}$ [WH$_2$] $[_{TP}$ $[_{VP}$ $[_{TR}$ WH$_2$]]]]]

In this LF representation, the Q operator does not locally bind the WH-in situ, and hence it cannot be licensed an operator. If, on the other hand, the definition of binding adopted in chapter 4 applies in unselective binding as well, WH-scrambling in German will result in a Full Interpretation violation—because the TP-adjoined copy cannot count as a binder, the Q operator will be associated with two bound variables.

## 6.4   The L-/L-Bar Distinction

In the introductory chapter I suggested that this book can also be seen as a discussion of the role that the L-/L-bar distinction plays in the grammar. At various points in the book, I have suggested that the L-/L-bar distinction should actually reduce to the kind of feature that is checked in a particular position, and it is time now to examine whether we can actually achieve this objective.

Looking back, my approach makes reference to the L-/L-bar distinction in a way that does not reduce to the morphosyntactic imperative in two major instances: In the definition of syntactic binding that the binding theory employs, repeated in (14), and in the definition of the copy-deletion mechanism, in (12):

(14) DEFINITION

A node $\alpha$ is bound by a node $\beta$ iff $\beta$ is not a variable, $\alpha$ and $\beta$ are coindexed and $\beta$ c-commands $\alpha$, where,

(i) if $\beta$ is an L-bar position, $\beta$ must involve the checking of a [+Q] feature, or

(ii) if $\beta$ is an L-position, $\beta$ must involve the checking of a Case feature.

In both cases, the reference to the L-/L-bar distinction is with the explicit intention of distinguishing between positions on the basis of the L-relatedness distinction rather than between the morphosyntactic feature that is checked. In (14), this reference has a twin objective: The first is to ensure that only [+Q] elements qualify as L-bar binders, and the second is to prevent dative-shifted IOs from acting as binders for elements contained in the DO. Similarly, in (12), the L-/L-bar reference is to derive the fact that we want an internal differentiation between the class of L-bar copies.

The ideal case would be one that eliminates these references to the L-/L-bar distinction and engineers a situation in which the binding properties of positions and the deletion of copies are conditioned purely by the kind of morphosyntactic feature that is checked. This task is easier for (12) than for (14), because it is possible to argue that there are no instances of checking in L-movement which access *only* a categorial feature: Even when a DP raises to [Spec, TP] in satisfaction of only the [strong] D-feature of Tns (the EPP), the noncategorial features of that DP (e.g., the φ-features) also get implicated in the checking relation. If this is uniformly the case, then (12) can be rephrased as (15):

(15) DELETION OF COPIES

Delete every bound variable copy of $\alpha$ in which a noncategorial feature of $\alpha$ is checked.

A similar redefinition of (14) is much tougher, as the only possible revision appears to be that in (16):

(16) DEFINITION

A node $\alpha$ is bound by a node $\beta$ iff $\beta$ is not a variable, $\beta$ must involve the checking of a [+Q] feature or a [Case] feature, and $\beta$ c-commands $\alpha$ and is coindexed with it.

Whereas the elimination of the reference to the L-/L-bar distinction in clause (14)(i) can be justified by the assumption that [+Q] features can only be checked in L-bar positions, clause (14)(ii) must be retained to explain the fact that dative-shifted IOs do not pattern with other Case-checking positions in acting as binders. The way (14) did this was by allowing dative-shifted IOs to slip through the cracks as it were, between the definitions of legitimate binders given by the two clauses. Then, in order to replace (14) with (16), alternative explanations must be found for the binding properties of IOs. Happily, there appears to be some hope of rescue from the LF raising approach to pronominals and reflexives I adopted earlier in chapter 4.

To see this, recall the two cases of the failure of dative-shifted IOs to induce Principle B violations and bind reflexives in the DO:

(17) mɛ̃-ne  ram$_i$-ko   ʊski$_i$  kɪtab       di
     I        Ram(IO)   his      book(DO)  gave

   'I gave Ram$_i$/his$_i$ book.'

(18) *ram$_i$-ne   sita$_j$-ko   əpne-ap$_{i/*j}$-ko   dɪk$^h$aya
      Ram(SU)   Sita(IO)   self(DO)                 showed

   'Ram showed Sita himself/*herself.'

Considering first (17), recall that Hindi-Urdu pronominals raise to $D^0$ at LF. This will identify the element in [Spec, TP] as the only possible antecedent for the pronominal, from which it correctly obviates. Consequently, coreference of the pronominal with the IO is perfectly licit. The account for (18) is similar, as XP-reflexive raising to adjoin to AGR-oP will raise the DO reflexive out of the domain of the IO.

It thus appears possible to completely eliminate references to the L-/L-bar distinction from the definition of binding, and indeed, from the binding theory completely, which will then read as follows:

(19) THE BINDING THEORY

    (a) DEFINITION
        A node α is bound by a node β iff β is not a variable and β
        must involve the checking of a [+Q] feature or a [Case] feature,
        and β c-commands α and is coindexed with it.

    (b) TRANSLATION DEFINITION:
        A DP is a variable iff either (i) or (ii) hold.

        (i) It is a copy that is locally bound by the closest minimally
            c-commanding copy,

(ii) It is locally bound by a category that checks a [Case] feature, lacks independent reference and is in a checking relation with its licensing functional head.

Other cases of DP-coindexation are uninterpretable.

(c) PRINCIPLES

A: A reflexive must be bound in its binding domain.

B: A pronominal must be free in its binding domain.

(d) BINDING DOMAIN

(i) The binding domain for a reflexive is the smallest CFC where it could potentially be bound.

(ii) The binding domain for a pronominal is the smallest CFC where it could potentially be free.

(iii) A CFC is a domain in which all the grammatical functions compatible with its head are realized.

## 6.5 Conclusion

The assimilation of derived XP-adjunction into the theory of movement has led to some significant conclusions about the architectural design of Universal Grammar. This book has argued that XP-adjunction as syntactic movement requires us to revise many of the current assumptions about the theories of binding, coreference, and reconstruction. This chapter demonstrates that many of these revisions have significant consequences for the theory of economy in Universal Grammar. Not only do our proposals facilitate a simplification of the statements of economy principles such as Full Interpretation, they also reduce the distance between the principles that enforce an economy of derivation from those that ensure economy of representation. Because the economy of representation forces the deletion of copies, and because that mechanism in turn makes reference to the kind of morphosyntactic feature that is checked in a derivation, the economy of representation ends up enforcing a kind of derivational economy as well. Finally, the elimination of the references to the L-/L-bar distinction in the theories of binding and copy-deletion serves the minimalist objective of installing morphosyntactic features at the heart of conjectures about the nature and organization of UG.

# Notes

## Chapter 1

1. Although Hindi and Urdu are both standard forms of a common dialect of Western Hindi, the two languages are officially and popularly considered to be two distinct languages in India and Pakistan. Because the distinction between the two languages does not derive from ethnicity, religion, or culture, and because they are identical with respect to syntactic description, I refer to this common language as Hindi-Urdu. The data reported in this book is based on my own dialect, spoken by the educated middle-classes in Delhi and the urban centers in Uttar Pradesh.

2. Actually all possible orderings of the four constituents in (1) are allowed, as Hindi-Urdu also attests V-scrambling. We limit our attention to argument scrambling in this book.

3. The WCO filter has received distinct formulations in Chomsky (1977), Koopman and Sportiche (1982), and Lasnik and Stowell (1991), but our discussion here is unaffected by the specifics of its formulation.

4. The choice of the terms NP-movement and WH-movement and XP-adjunction over the terms A- and A-bar movement is significant here only at the level of descriptive clarity. Because I wish to avoid the confusion around the A/A-bar distinction caused by the incorporation of the VP-internal subject hypothesis into the theory (see Mahajan 1990 and chapter 2 for a discussion), as well as to argue that we need a refinement of the typology of A-bar movement that distinguishes between adjunction and WH-movement, I adopt this terminology.

5. Neither the claim that scrambling is derived XP-adjunction nor the conclusion that the standard theories of binding and reconstruction are at least part of the problem in a uniform analysis of scrambling can be claimed to be original. For work that makes similar correlations, see Gurtu (1985), Saito (1989, 1992), Sengupta (1990), den Dikken and Mulder (1991), Dayal (1993), and Davison (1995).

# Chapter 2

1. Although Mahajan offers no explicit definition of what he considers to be lexical Case, the notion roughly corresponds to arguments that bear Case-markers, such as the ergative Case-marker on transitive subjects in the perfective past (excluding, however, the dative/accusative Case-marker *-ko*, which he argues to be structural Case).

2. Alternatively, it could be argued that UG permits chains to bear a dual Case if and only if one of the Cases is structural and the other lexical. Mahajan entertains both possibilities and does not explicitly choose between the two.

3. Hindi-Urdu verb agreement is determined by the following principles. (a) The verb agrees with the subject in case it is unmarked for lexical Case. (b) If the subject is lexically Case-marked, the verb agrees with the direct object if that is unmarked for lexical Case. (c) If both subject and direct object arguments are marked, the verb is in the default third person masculine singular form.

In the perfective past, Hindi-Urdu transitive subjects bear the lexical ergative Case-marker *-ne* and therefore do not control verb agreement.

4. Actually, characterizing (4b)/(5b) as a word order variant is like claiming that passive or raising is an instance of word order variation in English. The way Mahajan's system is constructed, an OSV order is perfectly 'normal', because only the argument that requires structural Case moves out of the VP. In fact, it is to derive the normal SOV order that an 'optional' movement of the lexically Case-marked subject must take place. This analysis predicts that native speakers should make no distinction between SOV and OSV orders in the perfective past and preferably consider the OSV order as the default. Unfortunately, neither conclusion is supported by native speakers—Hindi-Urdu speakers have a very strong intuition about a basic SOV word order, and they consider OSV (and other) orders as context-bound variations from the norm.

5. At this point, Mahajan assumes a UG clause structure that is different from the one he overtly professes to elsewhere in the dissertation. In the discussion of the properties of scrambling in his dissertation (chapter II), he adopts a Pollockian view of the hierarchical ordering between TP and AGR-sP in that TP dominates AGR-sP, while in the discussion of Hindi-Urdu verb agreement, he ascribes to the position that AGR-sP dominates TP. Presumably this is an error, and one that would appear minor but for the fact that for each of the two analyses, the hierarchy of the inflectional phrases they individually assume turns out to be quite significant.

For the analysis of Hindi-Urdu verb agreement, AGR-sP must dominate TP; otherwise neither can the right order of auxiliaries and main verbs be derived, nor can subject-verb agreement be effected. For the Case-driven movement analysis of scrambling, on the other hand, TP must dominate AGR-sP, because the analysis needs a landing site for scrambled DOs and IOs that will precede and c-command the subject argument in the [Spec, AGR-sP].

6. As it is, Mahajan's analysis is already too expensive in that it generates a number of competing derivations which are all licit. Consider examples (i) and (ii):

(i) kɪtab       ram-ne      pəʈʰi
    book(DO)   Ram(SU)    read

    'The book, Ram read.'

(ii) kɪtab      ram         pəʈʰega
     book(DO)   Ram(SU)    will read

     'The book, Ram will read.'

By Mahajan's proposals, (i) differs from (ii) in that (i) must involve raising of the DO to [Spec, AGR-oP] (because it involves the perfective participle). This yields the representations in (iii):

(iii) (a) [$_{AGR-oP}$ kɪtab$_i$ [$_{VP}$ ram-ne t$_i$ [$_{AGR-o}$ pəʈʰi]]]

     (b) [$_{AGR-sP}$ kɪtab$_i$ [$_{VP}$ ram t$_i$ [$_{AGR-s}$ pəʈʰega]]]

Mahajan also proposes that lexically Case-marked DPs need not stay in situ at S-structure because lexical case is adequate for the S-structure Case Filter in *any* position. This means that in (i), the subject could very well be in a functional projection outside VP, and the object would have scrambled to a position *higher* than that of the subject. This yields another representation in (iv)(a). Example (ii) could also have another representation, given Mahajan's assumption that specific DPs are assigned Case in [Spec, AGR-oP]—as a specific interpretation is available to the object, the S-structure representation of (ii) could be (iv)(b):

(iv) (a) [$_{XP}$ kɪtab$_i$ [$_{TP}$ ram-ne [$_{AGR-oP}$ t$_i$ [$_{VP}$ t$_{SU}$ t$_{DO}$ t$_v$]]] pəʈʰi]

     (b) [$_{XP}$ kɪtab$_i$ [$_{AGR-sP}$ ram [$_{AGR-oP}$ t$_i$ [$_{VP}$ t$_{SU}$ t$_{DO}$ t$_v$]]] pəʈʰega]

In fact, more derivations are possible, and the theory provides no adequate means of choosing between them.

7. Mahajan also claims that VP-level DO leftward scrambling has the ability to license a monomorphemic reflexive in the IO:

(i) (a) ram-ne$_i$    apne$_{i/*j}$  bəccõ-ko      šer$_j$      dɪkʰaya
        Ram(SU)     self's      children(IO)   tiger(DO)   showed

    'Ram$_i$ showed a tiger$_j$ to self's$_{i/*j}$ children.'

(b)  ram-ne$_i$     šer$_j$      əpne$_{i/j}$  bəccõ-ko      t$_{DO}$  dɪk$^h$aya
     Ram(SU)    tiger(DO)  self's    children(IO)            showed

'Ram$_i$ showed a tiger$_j$ to self's$_{i/j}$ children.'

Mahajan's intuitions do not appear to be that of the majority dialect, as
all the speakers I have consulted sharply reject (i)(b) on the coindexation
intended.

8. And also overtly, viz., the grammaticality of (i):

(i)  ty     znaes  [$_{CP}$ Petr  Ivanyč  [$_{CP}$ čto  [$_{IP}$ t$_i$  uže
     you    know            Peter  Ivanich        that          has come
     priexal]]]
     already

'Do you know that Peter Ivanich has already come?'

9. In Dayal's analysis, scrambling is allowed out of finite clauses because
scrambling precedes the extraposition of the finite clause. Her account
thus does not assume the strict distinction I maintain between the locality
constraints on XP-adjunction versus those on WH-movement.

10. Note that the status of the PUB as nonprojective is not at issue with
regard to the question why the scrambling of a WH-phrase in a multiple
WH-question results in superiority-type effects in (i)–(ii):

(i)  (a)  [$_{IP}$ kɪsne  kya    k$^h$aya]?
               who    what   ate

     'Who ate what?'

     (b)  ?*[$_{IP}$ kya$_i$  [$_{IP}$ kɪsne  t$_i$  k$^h$aya]?
               what           who          ate

     'What did who eat?'

(ii) (a)  [$_{IP}$ kɔn  kyũ  ayega]?
               who  why  will come

     'Who will come why?'

     (b)  ?*[$_{IP}$ kyũ$_i$  [$_{IP}$ kɔn  t$_i$  ayega]]
               why           who          will come

     'Why will who come?'

Generally, WH-phrases can scramble as freely as DPs, so the ungrammaticality of the (b) examples in (i) and (ii) does not stem from a restriction
on WH-scrambling. Neither can the nonprojectiveness of the Hindi-Urdu
PUB be at stake, as a projective PUB would rule out all licit cases of
WH-scrambling as well.

The illegitimacy of these derivations then follows from some other principle of the grammar. Because these violations so closely resemble Superiority
violations in English, I propose that these too can be accounted for by the
ECP. To confirm this, consider the LF representations of (i)(b) and (ii)(b)
in (iii) and (iv) (assuming right-adjunction in [Spec, CP]):

(iii) $[_{CP}$ [kɪsne$_i$ [kya$_j$ ]] $[_{IP}$ t$_i$ t$_j$ k$^h$aya]]

(iv) $[_{CP}$ [kya$_j$ [kɪsne$_i$ ]] $[_{IP}$ t$_i$ t$_j$ k$^h$aya]]

Assuming the traditional version of the ECP, by which complements
must be head-governed and noncomplements antecedent-governed, we find
that representation in (iii) does not constitute an ECP violation: The trace
of *kya* 'what' is lexically head-governed, and the trace of the subject is antecedent governed. In (iv), on the other hand, although lexical government
of the trace of *kya* still holds, antecedent government of the subject trace
no longer obtains, as the subject WH-phrase, being right-adjoined to [Spec,
CP], does not c-command its trace. Thus, (iv) is an ECP violation rather
than a PUB violation.

11. A natural question that arises at this point is as to why last-resort
deletion cannot delete the intermediate XP-adjoined link at LF, thereby
allowing the chain to satisfy the Chain Uniformity Condition. I return to
this issue in chapter 6, where I suggest that the Chain Uniformity Condition
(as a distinct principle) must be abandoned altogether.

12. The occurrence of *-to* with the possessor nominal appears to be less
marked in an appropriate context, which typically involves a contrastive
reading of the XP-*to*. Example (i) is much better than (35c):

(i) tʊmhara-to  sɪrf  dɪl    ʈuʈa    hɛ,  meri-to   zɪndəgi  xətəm
    yours-TOP   only  heart  broken  is   my-TOP    life      finish
    ho  gəyi  hɛ
    be  went  is
    'YOU'VE only broken your HEART, I'VE ruined my LIFE!'

Interestingly, the contrastive focus spreads over from the *-to* subjects
in these clauses. Bayer (1996) has noted that it is a property of focusing
particles to take multiple foci. It remains for future research to determine
whether such uses fall within the scope of an analysis of *-to* as a topic
particle.

13. See Bhaya-Nair (1991) for a pragmatic account of the 'sentence-final'
use of *-to* as a tag question. See also fn. 15.

14. The intervention of other factors such as intonation may play a part
in licensing multiple topics. For example, some speakers accept (49b) with

a heavy pause in between the two DPs. I suggest that the DP following the pause is a kind of 'afterthought topic' in the sense of Dwivedi (1994).

15. The fact that (i) is better than (48c) has to do with the fact that *-to* here is used as a sentential tag question, or as an answer to a negated interrogative. In either case, the set to which the topic particle (exhaustively) refers ranges over two propositions, rather than just one, in which the one is contrasted with the other:

(i)  ??[ ram-to kɪtab pəʈʰ rəha hɛ]-to

   (a) 'Ram is reading a book, isn't he?'

   (b) 'Ram is reading a book, I tell you!'

The sentential tag use of *-to* appears to conform to the way in which Japanese WH-*wa* questions are interpreted. Miyagawa suggests that *-wa* questions are, like other instances of contrastive *wa*, interpreted by partitioning the set shared by the speaker and the hearer into two or more subsets, "the members of one subset being associated with a property that can be contrasted with the property explicitly or implicitly associated with the members of the other subset(s)" (Miyagawa 1987:205). This set-contrast analysis can be extended to *-to* tag questions on the assumption that the shared set ranges over the affirmation and negation of a particular proposition. Then, because the tag question picks out only one of the two members of the set, the other can get represented only if the relation of IS IN CONTRAST TO is established.

16. The default option, it appears, must be $C^0$ as the designated head. Designated $Top^0$ heads are more marked and appear to require an additional licensing condition in complement position—"a designated embedded $Top^0$ must be head-governed by a lexical category" (MS 1993:491). This licensing condition explains why embedded topicalization is prohibited with nonbridge predicates, because they do not lexically head-govern their CP complements.

17. To completely distinguish QR from scrambling, it may be possible to identify a functional head above IP and VP for scope interpretations. I do not consider the alternative here, but nothing in the analysis I propose here precludes it. The basic conclusion that I do make is that (58) must be incorrect, and the facts that lead to its formulation must be accounted for in some other way.

18. Japanese may be considered a language in which QR over a scrambled QP is possible. As Aoun and Li (1993:189) have shown, a Japanese sentence of the form $[QP_1, \ldots, QP_2]$ is unambiguous only in its base order. If $QP_1$ is a scrambled QP, then the sentence is ambiguous:

(i) dareka-ga    daremo-o    semeta      (*unambiguous*)
   someone      everyone    criticized

   'Someone (*wide scope*) critized everyone.'

(ii) dareka-o$_k$   daremo-ga   t$_k$   semeta      (*ambiguous*)
    someone       everyone           criticized

   'Someone, everyone criticized.'

This difference in relative scope interpretations cannot be derived by (58). The nonambiguity in (i) follows from the intuition that syntactic linear order is responsible for scope interpretation in Japanese. That same intuition, however, would predict that scrambling should switch the relative scope interpretations around in (ii) rather than lead to an ambiguity. Assuming that a Case-movement analysis of scrambling is not an option (*contra* Aoun and Li), it would then appear that scrambling is not QR. In order to derive the wide scope reading of the subject QP, it must therefore be assumed that QR over the scrambled QP can and must take place.

19. Some speakers suggest that examples such as (i) and (ii), involving a distributive indefinite quantifier, also exhibit the same pattern as (61), in that scrambling of the QP containing the indefinite distributive quantifier allows it to receive a specific reading:

(i) hər    admi   kɪsi-na-kɪsi      ɔrət-ko   pyar   kərta   hɛ
   each   man    some-not-some    woman    love   does   is

   'Every man loves some woman or the other'.

(ii) [$_{IP}$ [kɪsi-na-kɪsi      ɔrət-ko]$_i$ [$_{IP}$ hər    admi   t$_i$   pyar   kərta
        some-not-some    woman              each   man           love   does

    hɛ]]
    is

   'SOME woman is loved by every man.'

This specific interpretation follows from the analysis for the specificity effects noted with scrambling in chapter 5.

20. Aoun and Li (1993:56) assume the proposals of Aoun and Hornstein (1985) that variables left by QPs are not subject to Principle C.

## Chapter 3

1. The one reason the structure in (1) may be viewed with suspicion is that a functional projection intervenes between θ-projections. Although it is unclear that the traditional understanding of all functional projections being VP-external is actually a principled position, it is obvious that

minimalism certainly cedes this theoretical position by the adoption of the Larsonian structure of ditransitives. The empty head position in the VP-shell structure proposed by Larson is more of a functional than a lexical position—it is never the site of lexical insertion of the (main) lexical head of the predicate and is always targeted by substitution.

Recent suggestions by Chomsky (1995) and Ura (1995) may also be used to explain the reason why AGR-oP intervenes between two θ-projections. Given that the descriptive property of [strength] is that a strong feature triggers an overt operation to eliminate it by checking (Chomsky 1995:233), and my suggestion that at least one of the features of AGR-o are always [strong], AGR-o (as the checker that eliminates the [strong] feature) will have to intervene between the VPs containing the external and internal arguments, respectively.

2. As Mahajan (1991) himself notes, this is not tenable under current assumptions about Case checking. While he attempts to link specificity effects to the fact that AGR is pronominal and therefore specific, that proposal cannot be maintained if AGR is essentially a parasitic Case-assigner. In addition, minimalism does not allow verbs to be structural Case-assigners (although Laka [1993] attempts to incorporate the idea of a $V_{Case}$ into the system). Even if this were allowed, this attempt to link specificity effects to Case-checking positions is bound to face empirical problems. As we shall see later, neither do objects Case-marked by V always receive a nonspecific reading, nor is this specific reading always available to all objects that are supposedly Case-marked by AGR-o.

3. As for the difference between (6b) and (7b), the choice of habitual aspect in the former appears to be crucial in determining the relative acceptability of the two.

4. Maintaining the analysis in Travis (1988) regarding the possible adjunction sites of adverbs in the split-VP I propose in (1) does not pose any problems, because process adverbs could very well attach to the lower VP, $VP_2$, or the AGR-oP projection itself. However, as I argue that derived adjunction to Case and verb agreement checking positions is only possible if that adjunction is itself feature-driven, I maintain that process adverbs attach to $VP_2$.

5. A goal NP in a DOC may be more 'affected' than a PDC goal, but the roles remain the same. See Koizumi (1993) and Hale and Keyser (1991).

6. Larson does attempt to account for languages that have only the PDC by proposing a link between the DOC and the possibility of P-stranding: Languages that do not allow P-stranding will also lack the DOC. Zhang (1990) demonstrates that this prediction is incorrect, because the dative alternation is attested in many languages that lack P-stranding altogether.

7. Dayal's arguments for a redefinition of the notion of binding originate

in part from the fact that her analysis of the structure of Hindi-Urdu ditransitives is located within a discussion of the coreference effects in scrambled
constructions. As a consequence, though she also considers the two LF-
movement approaches to Principles A and B that I address in the next
chapter, she eventually settles on the above hypothesis, as it allows the
binding theory to be sensitive to linear order.

8. The theoretical consequences of considering preposition insertion to
be cheaper than Shortest Move violations may turn out to be unpleasant,
because preposition insertion could achieve the status of an economy escape-
hatch. See Kidwai (1998) for an analysis of this insertion phenomenon in
a model of UG that assumes Halle and Marantz's (1993) postsyntactic
morphology.

9. Note that assuming QR of the IO quantifier *over* the QR'd DO does
nothing to save the derivation, because the trace of the QR'd IO will still
be the closest potential A-bar binder for the variable left behind by the
QR'd DO.

10. The only way that these Hindi-Urdu Case OCP effects can be seen
as (at best, weak) arguments for the overtness of Case-checking adjunction
operations (in Hindi-Urdu) is on the adoption of Halle and Marantz's (1993)
postsyntactic Morphology component, with its attendant assumption that
inflectional morphology is available presyntactically only as features, which
are spelled out in this component. Then, in the Hindi-Urdu DOC both
objects enter the Morphology component specified for the feature [dative]
and [accusative], respectively. The decision that only the [dative] feature is
to be spelled out by the Case-marker *-ko* is made in accordance with the
adjacency requirement imposed by the Hindi-Urdu Case OCP (plus some
formalization of the intuition that Case-checking specifier positions tolerate
zero morphology better than Case-checking XP-adjoined positions). Then,
because the configurations created by XP-adjunction are relevant for determining the morphological shape of lexical items, we can thus consider it
to be driven to target Morphology, and hence necessarily overt.

11. See also Hornstein (1995:154) for the proposal that only the lexical
link of an argument chain is evaluated by the principle of Full Interpretation
at the C-I interface, with the consequence that all but one member of an
argument chain are deleted at LF.

# Chapter 4

1. It appears that the Hindi-Urdu XP-reflexive can also have what appears to be a 'monomorphemic' form *əpne-(P)*, which is in free variation
for many speakers with *əpne-ap-(P)*. The crucial test for the identity of

two forms comes from nonfinite complements. If the form *əpne-P* is truly a monomorphemic reflexive, it should be able to take long-distance antecedents, but, as (i) and (ii) show, it actually behaves like an XP-reflexive:

(i) ram$_i$-ne     sita$_j$-se     [PRO$_j$ əpne-ap$_{*i/j}$-ko marne-ko]     kəha
    Ram(SU)   Sita(DO)            self(EDO)          to-hit-DAT   said
    'Ram told Sita$_j$ to hit self$_{*i/j}$.'

(ii) ram$_i$-ne sita$_j$-se [PRO$_j$ əpne$_{*i/j}$-ko marne-ko] kəha

It seems that at least in dialects such as mine, the reflexive *əpne-(P)* is just a phonological variant of the XP-reflexive.

2. Cole and Sung (1994) derive the prohibition against long-distance binding of XP-reflexives such as *himself* from the ECP. Consider the LF representation of (3a) on the illegitimate reading:

(i) [$_{CP1}$ [$_{IP1}$ John [$_{VP1}$ himself [$_{VP1}$ thinks [$_{CP2}$ that [$_{IP2}$ Bill [$_{VP2}$ t′ [$_{VP2}$ likes t]]]]]]]]]

According to Chomsky's (1986a) suggestions that the use of adjunction to IP/CP as an escape-hatch for further movement is disallowed, *himself* must move directly from the lower VP to the matrix one. Because this movement crosses CP$_2$, a barrier by inheritance, the ECP is violated.

3. Dayal (1997) actually argues that nonfinite complements in Hindi-Urdu have the categorial status of DPs rather than CPs. In a theory of the licensing of PRO that implicates a Tns head in DPs as well, the analysis I present here would not require significant modification.

4. The data in (i)–(iv) also establishes the central role played by the φ-features of [Spec, TP] elements in licensing Hindi-Urdu X$^0$-reflexives:

(i) ram$_i$-ne     sita$_j$-ko     [PRO$_j$ əpni$_{i/j}$ gaṛi lane-ko]     kəha
    Ram(SU)   Sita(DO)            self's   car   to-bring-DAT   said
    'Ram$_i$ told Sita$_j$ to get self's$_{i/j}$ car.'

(ii) ram$_i$-ne     sita$_j$-se     [PRO$_i$ əpni$_{i/*j}$ gaṛi lane-ka]
     Ram(SU)   Sita(DO)            self's   car   to-bring-GEN
     vada    kiya
     promise did
     'Ram$_i$ promised Sita$_j$ to get self's$_{i/*j}$ car.'

(iii) ram$_i$-ne     sita$_j$-ko     [PRO$_j$ ghər  jane-ke-liye] [PRO$_j$ əpni$_{i/j}$
      Ram(SU)   Sita(DO)            home  to-go-for     self's   car
      gaṛi              lane-ko] kəha
      to-bring-DAT   said
      'Ram$_i$ told Sita$_j$ to get self's$_{i/j}$ car for going home.'

(iv) ram$_i$-ne   sita$_j$-se   [PRO$_j$ ghər jane-ke-liye] [PRO$_j$ əpni$_{i/*j}$
     Ram(SU)  Sita(DO)       home to-go-for         self's
     gaṛi lane-ka]     vada kiya
     car to-bring-GEN   promise did
     'Ram$_i$ promised Sita$_j$ to get self's$_{i/*j}$ car for going home.'

The predicates *say* and *promise* are object and subject control predicates, respectively. Examples (i) and (ii) demonstrate that long-distance raising of $X^0$-reflexives is dependent on object control because it is only in such an environment that the $X^0$-reflexive is ambiguous in reference. Examples (iii) and (iv) show that the pattern generalizes to purposive adjunct clauses as well. The effect is certainly a curious one: If the most embedded PRO bears the φ-features of the matrix subject, then the embedded reflexive cannot raise to the matrix clause, but if PRO bears the φ-features of the matrix object, $X^0$-reflexive raising is allowed. Although I have no convincing explanation for this *feeding* effect with object control, the point to be noted is that because PRO must necessarily be in [Spec, TP], it is the φ-features of PRO that are relevant in determining the possiblity of $X^0$-reflexive successive cyclic raising.

5. In Hindi-Urdu, for example, the Norwegian (20a) can be expressed using either a *jo-vo* relative clause or the *-wala* construction:

(i) vo  jo    vahā   cəl   rəha   hɛ
    he  who  there  walks  PROG  is
    'He who is walking there'

(ii) vo  vəhā   cəlnewala
     he  there  walking-one
     'He who is walking there'

It is, however, a matter of debate whether either of these constructions actually involves restrictive modification at $X^0/X'$ levels. Dayal's (1997) study of the Hindi-Urdu correlative construction would suggest not, although the Hindi-Urdu *-wala* construction has not been investigated in any depth to substantiate a claim one way or the other.

6. I assume that the Hindi-Urdu genitive DP invokes the same configuration at Spellout as the Russian one. Bhattacharya and Dasgupta's (1996) proposals that genitives and deictic elements are not $D^0$ elements in either Hindi-Urdu or Bangla can be harnessed as support for this analysis, but the occurrence of agreement between the possessor and the possessum in Hindi-Urdu DPs may appear to pose some problems. According to Abney (1987), agreement in the DP involves an AGR in $D^0$, but this would require $D^0$ to be head initial in what is a head-final language.

Also note that Hindi-Urdu possessor–possessum agreement does not pattern with subject-verb agreement (gender, number, person) but rather with modifier agreement (number and gender). As we do not traditionally assume a parasitic Case-assigning AGR head for adjective–noun agreement, there is little reason to postulate it for other categories that behave just like adjectives. I will therefore assume that the mechanisms that ensure modifier agreement in the Hindi-Urdu noun phrase also effect possessor–possessum agreement, and that these mechanisms do not make reference to an AGR in $D^0$.

7. Actually, Chomsky (1995:272–76) makes available a more elegant solution to the problem of covert raising to $D^0$ in Hindi-Urdu and Russian, as it is argued that covert checking involves the raising of just the formal feature complex of a lexical item to adjoin to the checking head. This is just what we need to incorporate raising to $D^0$ into a Greed-driven grammar. Notice that Avrutin's analysis specifically requires covert raising of possessors to $D^0$ rather than to [Spec, DP] and is therefore forced to classify this movement as driven by considerations of interpretation. In Chomsky's system, however, covert raising of the possessor targets $D^0$ for the checking of its genitive Case.

8. XP-reflexives provide further evidence for the special properties of [+Q]-driven movements, be they overt or covert. Recall that an XP-reflexive raises to be licensed in a position broadly L-related to (one of) the head(s) that licenses its antecedent; this movement could in principle result in a configuration such as [TP *himself* [TP *John likes*]]. Now if we were to assume that covert L-bar movement is insensitive to the [±Q] distinction, the reflexive should induce a coindexation violation by its antecedent. It is therefore necessary to argue that the LF-raised XP-reflexive does not count as a binder for the subject R-expression, a result achieved by assuming that only [+Q] elements have L-bar binding properties.

9. I propose that, unlike possessive pronominals, English [±WH] pronominals are not in [Spec, DP] by LF and raise to $D^0$ at LF. The IP is then the binding domain in which the pronominal must be free.

10. The proposals here are reminiscent of those in Lasnik and Stowell (1991). Lasnik and Stowell seek to derive the fragility of WCO violations from their distinction between 'true' quantifiers and 'untrue' quantifiers: While a true quantifier binds a variable, a nontrue quantifier binds a 'null epithet'. My own position is, in conceptual terms, very close to Lasnik and Stowell's, as my proposals too typologize L-bar elements in terms of their binding properties. However, since this difference is not a lexical difference, my proposals do not require the extra empty category that Lasnik and Stowell's analysis does.

11. These proposals also have a partial explanation for the facts noted

by Huang (1993). He notes that SCO effects with R-expressions are considerably weakened when the R-expression is sufficiently deeply embedded in the WH-phrase (examples from Huang 1993:106):

(i) *Whose$_i$ mother does he$_i$ love?

(ii) ??Which pictures of John$_i$ does he$_i$ like most?

In my approach, the binding theory will apply to the copy of the moved element. In (i), this will yield a Principle B violation as the WH-pronominal will be L-bound, but in (ii), it will yield a coindexation violation, as the R-expression in the copy *John* cannot be translated as a bound variable because it does not lack independent reference. Now, if coindexation violations are somehow less marginal than binding violations, as we see with WCO effects, then the difference in acceptability is accounted for.

12. There are, however, two problems with these proposals, which do not find resolution within this approach. First of all, crosslinguistically, it is simply not that IOs cannot license reflexives in DOs—in English they clearly can, as in *I showed Mary$_i$ herself$_i$*. Second, it is expected under this analysis that DOs should be able to license reflexives in the IO, an expectation that is not confirmed in either English or Hindi-Urdu but is in German (cf. Müller and Sternefeld 1994b:360). At present I have no real analysis for these facts.

13. As noted in chapter 2, Mahajan (1990) reports judgments of certain native speakers who allow $X^0$-reflexives to be bound by IO antecedents as well as subjects:

(i) ram-ne$_i$    mohən$_j$-ko    əpni$_{i/j}$ kıtab      lɔṭa      di
    Ram(SU)   Mohan(IO)   self's    book(DO)   return   gave

'Ram$_i$ returned Mohan$_j$ self's$_{i/j}$ book.'

The majority of native speakers, it will be remembered, force the $X^0$-reflexive to be subject-oriented. Even though the judgments reported here are marginal, it is possible to derive these judgments from either of two sources. The first hypothesis traces this use to the fact that such speakers use the $X^0$-reflexive referentially, a use permitted by the fact that the raised reflexive will not c-command the IO in its base position. As I argue in the next chapter, Hindi-Urdu possessive reflexives can be used referentially in the subject position of a matrix clause, and these speakers can be seen as generalizing this strategy further.

The second solution uses the binding theory—assume that head movement leaves copies. Therefore, the *copy* of the reflexive in the DO is translated as a bound variable. Now, a reflexive must satisfy Principle A, and because Cased positions are L-positions, the IO *Mohan* serves as the antecedent for the reflexive in the copy.

14. An important consequence of this elimination of L-bar binding from the theory of grammar is that we no longer have an adequate account for resumptive pronouns. In the literature, resumptives are traditionally defined as locally L-bar bound variables, but this would be ruled out as a coindexation violation in my approach. Although I am grateful to an anonymous reviewer for bringing my attention to this point, I must confess that I can see no way other than stipulation to incorporate the resumptive facts into the binding theory proposed here. The fact that resumptive pronouns are immune to WCO effects (Safir 1996) will then presumably follow from the account I give here, but the issues involved are far more complex than just this.

# Chapter 5

1. I do not engage in the extensively discussed problematics of defining what counts as [FOCUS] (see Chafe 1976, Chomsky 1971, Jackendoff 1972, Culicover and Rochemont 1991, Rochemont 1986, Firbas 1964, Kuno 1972, Rooth 1985, Prince 1981, Lambrecht 1994, Erteschik-Shir 1998, Zubizarreta 1998, etc.), because the ways and means by which foci are interpreted does not affect my basic claim that [FOCUS] is a feature accessed by the computational system.

2. This restriction to non-discourse-initial questions does not necessarily weaken the claim that Hindi-Urdu has a preverbal focus position, as this appears to be a more universal restriction than suggested by the literature on positional focus. Presumably, the fact that the scrambled XP simultaneously receives a strongly 'already-mentioned'/presuppositional interpretation is the limiting factor, as discourse-initiating utterances cannot felicitously contain such material.

3. An alternative approach to the link between scrambling and positional focus could be along the lines of Cinque (1993). Cinque proposes that the link between syntactic position and prosodic prominence follows from his null theory of phrasal stress, whereby phrasal stress is entirely determined by the direction in which the Head Parameter is set and the depth of syntactic embedding in a language. Then, because Hindi-Urdu is a head-final language it is expected that prosodic prominence should be assigned to the immediately preverbal position in a clause, as that will constitute the most deeply embedded constituent in the clausal configuration. In structures with scrambling, because the operation moves away constituents from this deeply embedded position, the phrasal stress will be assigned

to the next item that qualifies as the most deeply embedded one. DO scrambling thus renders the SU or the IO as the most 'deeply embedded', and hence the greater prominence is assigned to either of these in situ categories as compared to the scrambled DO.

Even if we ignore the fact that Hindi-Urdu lacks the Nuclear Stress Rule altogether, adopting Cinque's approach cannot be adequate as an analysis of scrambling. First, it makes too strong a correlation between prosodic prominence and positional focusing, as it has been demonstrated by Kenesei and Vogel (1989) that even in a language such as Hungarian that has both the Nuclear Stress Rule as well as a preverbal focus position, the main prosodic prominence does *not* necessarily fall on the preverbal focus position. Second, this analysis essentially implies that the oft-noted link between scrambling and what is called preverbal focusing is a fortuitous rather than rule-governed correlation. Scrambling takes place for whatever reasons XP-adjunction in general takes place and has nothing to do with *triggering* the focusing effect observed in scrambled configurations—that is, Cinque's proposals result in a scenario isomorphic to the one that gave birth to the discussion in this book, in which scrambling lacks a syntactic motivation.

4. My proposals resemble those of Jayaseelan (1989/1995) in only these details, as his account equates scrambling with topicalization. For a discussion of the problems with Jayaseelan's analysis, see Kidwai (1995).

5. Although I establish a strict correlation between WH-licensing and head activation in the overt syntax, in fact WH-phrases in Hindi-Urdu in discourse-initial questions as well as in DO questions may be licensed without scrambling. This suggests that the dormancy of FP is perhaps relevant only to discursive/pragmatic [FOCUS], and that [Spec, FP] may be targeted freely by intrinsically focused lexical items, such as WH-phrases and focusing particles (Bayer 1996). DO WH-focusing (without scrambling) must then be analyzed as originating from a numeration that does not contain the free feature [PFOCUS], DO WH-foci simply raising to [Spec, FP] for the checking of intrinsic focus.

Note that this analysis has the welcome consequence of excluding WH-constructions from automatic membership of the class of discursively motivated focus constructions: Although all WH-phrases elicit an indexical assertion as a response, only those WH-constructions in which this indexical assertion is necessarily relevant for the ensuing discourse can be considered to be focus constructions. In other words, scrambling for head-activation in WH-constructions only takes place when the focus denoted by the WH-phrase(s) is discursively relevant.

6. The Case-marker *-ko* is the most robust marker of definiteness in the Hindi-Urdu Case paradigm. Case marking by *-ko* is subject to some

restrictions—humans are preferably *-ko* marked, with the requirement being absolute for names and address terms. Nonhuman objects may optionally take this marking, and when they do, the DP is necessarily interpreted as specific/definite and, in some cases, as an *affected* object. See Singh (1993) for some discussion of this last point.

7. This analysis remains unchallenged even if the chain at LF also includes the chain of covert raising to [Spec, CP] or [Spec, TopP], because this will be a distinct chain and will be calculated separately by the mapping to semantic representation.

8. As Diesing's proposals subsume definite and specific interpretations under an overarching notion of presuppositionality, the facts of Hindi-Urdu definiteness effects also find an explanation within this approach. Consider first the fact that Case-markers such as *-ko* as well as deictic pronouns induce definite readings of the XPs they mark. Even as I assume, following Bhattacharya and Dasgupta (1996), that the Hindi-Urdu $D^0$ is the Case-marker, I also suggest that definiteness may spread over to the site of modifying determiners as well. Following suggestions by Diesing herself (1992:149; n. 39), let us assume that this Case-marker or the deictic pronoun is a *strong* quantifier (Milsark 1974) that triggers the LF QR of the DP in which it is contained. Thus, Case-marked DPs and DPs bearing a deictic pronoun will always be accorded a presuppositional interpretation. The fact that bare DPs usually receive an indefinite interpretation also follows the broad parameters set by Diesing's proposals—presumably the null determiner in Hindi-Urdu is, in the Milsarkian sense, only *weakly* quantificational, and therefore cannot trigger the LF QR of its containing DP.

# Bibliography

Abney, S. P. 1987. *The English Noun Phrase in Its Sentential Aspect*. Ph.D. thesis, Massachusetts Institute of Technology.

Aoun, J. and E. Benmamoun 1996. Minimality, Reconstruction and PF-Movement. *Linguistic Inquiry* 29:568–97.

Aoun, J. and L. Choueri 1997. Resumption and Last Resort. To appear in J. Ouhalla and U. Shlonsky (eds.) *Semitic Syntax*. Dordrecht: Kluwer.

Aoun, J. and N. Hornstein 1985. Quantifier types. *Linguistic Inquiry* 16:623–36.

Aoun, J. and Y. A. Li 1993. *The Syntax of Scope*. Cambridge MA: MIT Press.

Avrutin, S. 1992. Movement of Bound Variables in Russian. In *Proceedings of the Leiden Conference of Junior Linguists 3*, pages 1–16. University of Leiden.

Avrutin, S. 1994. The Structural Position of Bound Variables in Russian. *Linguistic Inquiry* 25:709–28.

Baker, M. 1988. *Incorporation: A Theory of Grammatical Function Changing*. Chicago: University of Chicago Press.

Baltin, M. 1982. A Landing Site Theory of Movement Rules. *Linguistic Inquiry* 13:1–38.

Barss, A. 1986. *Chains and Anaphoric Dependencies: On Reconstruction and Its Implications*. Ph.D. thesis, Massachussetts Institute of Technology.

Barss, A. and H. Lasnik 1986. A Note on Anaphora and Double Objects. *Linguistic Inquiry* 17:347–54.

Bayer, J. 1990. *Directionality of Government and Logical Form: A Study of Focusing Particles and WH-Scope*. Habilitation thesis, University of Konstanz.

Bayer, J. 1996. *Directionality of Government and Logical Form: On the Scope of Focusing Particles and WH- in situ*. Dordrecht: Kluwer.

Bayer, J. and J. Kornfilt 1991. Against Scrambling as an Instance of Move-α. In *Proceedings of North-Eastern Linguistic Society 22*, pages 1–15. GLSA, Amherst.

Bayer, J. and J. Kornfilt 1994. Against Scrambling as an Instance of Move-α. In N. Corver and H. van Riemsdijk (eds.) *Studies in Scrambling* pages 17–60. Berlin: Mouton de Gruyter.

Bhattacharya, T. and P. Dasgupta 1996. Classifiers, Word Order and Definiteness in Bangla. In V. Swarajya Lakshmi and A. Mukherjee (eds.) *Word Order in Indian Languages*, pages 73–94. Hyderabad: CASL, Osmania University, and Booklinks.

Bhaya-Nair, R. 1991. Expressing Doubt and Certainty: The Tag Question and the -TO Particle in Some Indian Languages. In A. Abbi (ed.) *Language Sciences* 13, pages 19–28. Oxford: Pergamon Press.

Bures, A. 1992. Re-Cycling Expletives and Other Sentences. Unpublished generals paper, Massachussetts Institute of Technology.

Chafe, W. 1976. Givenness, Contrastiveness, Subjects, Topics and Point of View. In C. N. Li (ed.) *Subject and Topic*, pages 25–56. New York: Academic Press.

Chomsky, N. 1955. *The Logical Structure of Linguistic Theory*. Chicago: University of Chicago Press 1985.

Chomsky, N. 1971. Deep Structure, Surface Structure, and Semantic Interpretation. In D. Steinberg and L. Jakobovits (eds.) *Semantics: An Interdisciplinary Reader in Philosophy, Linguistics, and Psychology*, pages 183–316. Cambridge: Cambridge University Press.

Chomsky, N. 1977. On WH-Movement. In P. Culicover, T. Wasow, and A. Akmajian (eds.) *Formal Syntax*, pages 71–132. New York: Academic Press.

Chomsky, N. 1981. *Lectures on Government and Binding*. Dordrecht: Foris.

Chomsky, N. 1986a. *Barriers*. Cambridge MA: MIT Press.

Chomsky, N. 1986b. *Knowledge of Language: Its Nature, Origin and Use*. New York: Praeger.

Chomsky, N. 1989. Some Notes on the Economy of Derivation and Representation. In I. Laka and A. Mahajan (eds.) *Functional Heads and Clause Structure*, pages 43–74. *MIT Working Papers in Linguistics* 10.

Chomsky, N. 1992. A Minimalist Program for Linguistic Theory. *MIT Occasional Papers in Linguistics* 1.

Chomsky, N. 1993. Bare Phrase Structure. *MIT Occasional Papers in Linguistics* 2.

Chomsky, N. 1995. *The Minimalist Program*. Cambridge MA: MIT Press.

Chomsky, N. and H. Lasnik 1993. Principles and Parameters Theory. In J. Jacobs, A. von. Stechow, W. Sternefeld and T. Venneman (eds.) *Syntax: An International Handbook of Contemporary Research*, pages 506–89. New York: Walter de Gruyter.

Cinque, G. 1990. *Types of A-Bar Dependencies*. Cambridge MA: MIT Press.

Cinque, G. 1993. A Null Theory of Phrase and Compound Stress. *Linguistic Inquiry* 24:239–98.

Cole, P., G. Hermon and L.-M. Sung 1990. Principles and Parameters of Long-Distance Reflexives. *Linguistic Inquiry* 21:1–22.

Cole, P., and L.-M. Sung 1994. Head-Movement and Long-Distance Reflexives. *Linguistic Inquiry* 25:355–406.

Collins, C. 1994. Economy of Derivation and the Generalized Proper Binding Configuration. *Linguistic Inquiry* 25:45–62.

Collins, C. and H. Thráinsson 1993. Object Shift in Double Object Constructions and the Theory of Case. In C. Phillips (ed.) *Papers on Case and Agreement II*, pages 131–74. *MIT Working Papers in Linguistics* 19.

Culicover, P. and M. Rochemont 1991. *English Focus Constructions and the Theory of Grammar*. Cambridge: Cambridge University Press.

Davison, A. 1995. Lexical Anaphora in Hindi/Urdu. To appear in K. Wali, K.V. Subbarao, B. Lust, and J. Gair (eds.) *Lexical Anaphors and Pronouns in Some South Asian Languages: A Principled Typology*. Berlin: Mouton de Gruyter.

Dayal, V. 1993. Binding Facts in Hindi and the Scrambling Phenomenon. In T. Holloway King and G. Ramchand (eds.) *Theoretical Perspectives on Word Order in South Asian Languages*, pages 237–61. Stanford: CSLI Press.

Dayal, V. 1997. *Locality in WH-quantification: Questions and Relative Clauses in Hindi*. Dordrecht: Kluwer.

Diesing, M. 1990. *The Syntactic Roots of Semantic Partition*. Ph.D. thesis, University of Massachusetts at Amherst.

Diesing, M. 1992. *Indefinites*. Cambridge MA: MIT Press.

den Dikken, M. and R. Mulder 1991. Double Object Scrambling. In J. Bobaljik and T. Bures (eds.) *Proceedings of the Student Conference in Linguistics*, pages 67–81. *MIT Working Papers in Linguistics* 14.

Dwivedi, V. 1994. *Syntactic Dependencies and Relative Phrases in Hindi*. Ph.D. thesis, University of Massachusetts at Amherst.

Erteschik-Shir, N. 1998. *The Dynamics of Focus Structure*. Cambridge: Cambridge University Press.

Firbas, J. 1964. On Defining the Theme in Functional Sentence Analysis. *Travaux Linguistiques de Prague* 1:267–80. Prague: Academia.

Fukui, N. and M. Speas 1986. Specifiers and Projections. *MIT Working Papers in Linguistics* 8:128–72.

Gambhir, V. 1981. *Syntactic Restrictions and Discourse Functions of Word Order in Standard Hindi*. Ph.D. dissertation, University of Pennsylvania.

Gurtu, M. 1985. *Anaphoric Relations in Hindi and English*. Ph.D. thesis, Central Institute of English and Foreign Languages.

Haider, H. 1988. Matching Projections. In A. Cardinaletti, G. Cinque and G. Giusti (eds.) *Constituent Structure*, pages 101–23. Dordrecht: Foris.

Hale, K. and J. Keyser. 1991. On the Syntax of Argument Structure. *Lexicon Project Working Paper 34*. Center for Cognitive Science, Massachussetts Institute of Technology.

Halle, M. and A. Marantz. 1993. Distributed Morphology. In S. J. Keyser and K. Hale (eds.) *The View From Building 20*, pages 111–76. Cambridge MA: MIT Press.

Hestvik, A. 1990. *LF-Movement of Pronouns and the Computation of Binding domains*. Ph.D. thesis, Brandeis University.

Hestvik, A. 1992. LF-Movement of Pronouns and Antisubject Orientation. *Linguistic Inquiry* 23:557–94.

Hornstein, N. 1995. *Logical Form*. London: Basil Blackwell.

Horvath, J. 1981. *Aspects of Hungarian Syntax and the Theory of Grammar*. Ph.D. thesis, University of California at Los Angeles.

Huang, C.-T. J. 1993. Reconstruction and the Structure of VP: Some Theoretical Consequences. *Linguistic Inquiry* 24:103–8.

Iwakura, K. 1987. A Government Approach to Double Object Constructions. *Linguistic Analysis* 17:78–98.

Jackendoff, R. S. 1972. *Semantic Interpretation in Generative Grammar*. Cambridge MA: MIT Press.

Jackendoff, R. S. 1990. On Larson's Treatment of the Double Object Construction. *Linguistic Inquiry* 21:427–56.

Jayaseelan, K. A. 1989/1995. Question-Word Movement to Focus in Malayalam. Ms. Central Institute of English and Foreign Languages.

Jonas, D. and J. Bobaljik 1993. Specs for Subjects. In J. Bobaljik and C. Phillips (eds.) *Papers on Case and Agreement I*, pages 59–98. *MIT Working Papers in Linguistics* 18.

Jones, D. 1994. *Binding as an Interface Condition: An Investigation of Scrambling*. Ph.D. thesis, Massachussetts Institute of Technology.

Kayne, R. 1989. Facets of Past Participle Agreement in Romance. In P. Beninca (ed.) *Dialect Variation and the Theory of Grammar*, pages 85–103. Dordrecht: Foris.

Kenesei, I. and I. Vogel 1989. Prosodic Phonology in Hungarian. *Acta Linguistica Hungarica* 39:149–93.

Kidwai, A. 1995. *Binding and Free Word Order Phenomena in Hindi-Urdu*. Ph.D. thesis, Jawaharlal Nehru University.

Kidwai, A. 1998. Indirect Objects in Hindi-Urdu: Dative Shift as PF-movement. Talk at Seminar on Agreement, Delhi University.

Kidwai, A. 1999. Word Order and Focus Positions in Universal Grammar. In G. Rebuschi and L. Tuller (eds.) *The Grammar of Focus*, Amsterdam: John Benjamins.

Kim, A. 1988. Preverbal Focusing and Type XXIII Languages. In M. Hammond, E. Moravscik, and J. Wirth (eds.) *Studies in Syntactic Typology*, pages 147–69. Amsterdam: John Benjamins.

Kiss, K. 1987. *Configurationality in Hungarian*. Dordrecht: Reidel.

Koizumi, M. 1993. Object Agreement Phrases and the Split-VP Hypothesis. In J. Bobaljik and C. Phillips (eds.) *Papers on Case and Agreement I*, pages 99–148. *MIT Working Papers in Linguistics* 18.

Koopman, H. and D. Sportiche 1982. Variables and the Bijection Principle. *The Linguistic Review* 2:139–60.

Kuno, S. 1972. Pronominalization, Reflexives, and Direct Discourse. *Linguistic Inquiry* 3:161–95.

Kuno, S. 1973. *The Structure of the Japanese Language*. Cambridge MA: MIT Press.

Laka, I. 1993. Unergatives That Assign Ergative, Unaccusatives That Assign Accusative. In J. Bobaljik and C. Phillips (eds.) *Papers on Case and Agreement I*, pages 149–72. *MIT Working Papers in Linguistics* 18.

Lambrecht, K. 1994. *Information Structure and Sentence Form*. Cambridge: Cambridge University Press.

Larson, R. 1988. On the Double Object Construction. *Linguistic Inquiry* 19:335–91.

Larson, R. 1990. Double Objects Revisited: Reply to Jackendoff. *Linguistic Inquiry* 22:589–632.

Lasnik, H. and M. Saito 1992. *Move-α*. Cambridge MA: MIT Press.

Lasnik, H. and T. Stowell 1991. Weakest Crossover. *Linguistic Inquiry* 22:687–720.

Laxmibai, B. 1994. Question-Word Fronting in Hindi: An Experimental Study. Ms., University of Osmania.

Leben, W. 1973. *Suprasegmental Phonology*. Bloomington: Indiana Linguistics Club.

Lee, K. R. 1995. *Economy of Representation*. Ph.D. thesis, University of Connecticut at Storrs.

Mahajan, A. 1990. *On the A/A-Bar Distinction and Movement Theory*. Ph.D. thesis, Massachussetts Institute of Technology.

Mahajan, A. 1991. Clitic Doubling, Object Agreement and Specificity. In *Proceedings of the Twenty-first Annual Meeting of the North-Eastern Linguistics Society*, pages 263–277. GLSA, Amherst.

Mahajan, A. 1992. Specificity Condition and the CED. *Linguistic Inquiry* 23:510–16.

Manzini, M. R. and K. Wexler 1987. Parameters, Binding Theory and Learnability. *Linguistic Inquiry* 18:413–44.

Marantz, A. 1997. No Escape from Syntax: Don't Try Morphological Analysis in the Privacy of Your Own Lexicon. *UPenn Working Papers in Linguistics* 4:201–23.

Milsark, G. 1974. *Existential Sentences in English*. Ph.D. thesis, Massachussetts Institute of Technology.

Miyagawa, S. 1987. WH-phrase and -WA. In J. Hinds, S. Maynard, and S. Iwasaki (eds.) *Perspectives on Topicalization: The Case of Japanese 'wa'*, pages 185–217. Amsterdam: John Benjamins.

Mohanan, T. 1992. Case OCP: A Constraint on Word Order in Hindi. In T. Holloway King and G. Ramchand (eds.) *Theoretical Perspectives on Word Order in South Asian Languages*, pages 186-223. Stanford: CSLI Press.

Müller, G. 1992. In Support of Dative Movement. *Proceedings of the Leiden Conference of Junior Linguists 3*, pages 201–17. University of Leiden.

Müller, G. and W. Sternefeld 1993. Improper Movement and Unambiguous Binding. *Linguistic Inquiry* 24:461–507.

Müller, G. and Sternefeld 1994a. A-Bar Chain Formation and Economy of Derivation. Ms., Universitat Tübingen.

Müller, G. and Sternefeld 1994b. Scrambling as A-bar Movement. In N. Corver and H. van Riemsdijk (eds.) *Studies in Scrambling*, pages 311–385. Berlin: Mouton de Gruyter.

Pandit, I. 1985. Exceptions to Weak and Strong Crossover in Hindi. *Linguistic Inquiry* 16:678–81.

Pica, P. 1987. On the Nature of the Reflexivization Cycle. In *Proceedings of North-Eastern Linguistic Society*, pages 483–99. GLSA, Amherst.

Pollock, J.-Y. 1989. Verb Movement, UG and the Structure of IP. *Linguistic Inquiry* 20:365–424.

Postal, P. 1993. Remarks on Weak Crossover Effects. *Linguistic Inquiry* 24:539–56.

Prince, E. 1981. Toward a Taxonomy of Given–New Information. In P. Cole (ed.) *Radical Pragmatics*, pages 223–56. New York: Academic Press.

Reinhart, T. 1986. Center and Periphery in the Grammar of Anaphora. In B. Lust (ed.) *Studies in the Acquisition of Anaphora* 1. Dordrecht: Reidel.

Reinhart, T. 1991. Binding and Coreference Revisited. Ms., Tel Aviv.

Reinhart, T. 1994. WH- in situ in the Framework of the Minimalist Program. Ms., Tel Aviv.

Reinhart, T. and Y. Grodzinsky 1993. The Innateness of Binding and Coreference. *Linguistic Inquiry* 24:69–102.

Rizzi, L. 1990. *Relativized Minimality*. Cambridge, MA: MIT Press.

Rizzi, L. 1996. Residual Verb-Second and the WH-Criterion. In A. Belletti and L. Rizzi (eds.) *Parameters and Functional Heads: Essays in Comparative Syntax*, pages 63–90. New York: Oxford University Press.

Rochemont, M. 1986. *Focus in Generative Grammar*. John Benjamins: Amsterdam.

Rooth, M. 1985. *Association with Focus*. Ph.D. dissertation, University of Massachusetts at Amherst.

Rothstein, S. 1991. Syntactic Licensing and Subcategorization. In S. Rothstein (ed.) *Perspectives on Phrase Structure: Heads and Licensing*, pages 139–58. San Diego: Academic Press.

Safir, K. 1996. Derivation, Representation and Resumption: The Domain of Weak Crossover. *Linguistic Inquiry* 27:313–39.

Saito, M. 1989. Scrambling as Semantically Vacuous A-bar Movement. In M. Baltin and A. Kroch (eds.) *Alternative Conceptions of Phrase Structure*, pages 182–200. Chicago: University of Chicago Press.

Saito, M. 1992. Long-Distance Scrambling in Japanese. *Journal of East Asian Linguistics* 1:69–118.

Sengupta, G. 1990. *Binding and Scrambling in Bangla*. Ph.D. thesis, University of Massachusetts at Amherst.

Singh, M. 1993. Thematic Roles, Word Order and Definiteness. In T. Holloway King and G. Ramchand (eds.) *Theoretical Perspectives on Word Order in South Asian Languages*, pages 225–45. Stanford: CSLI Press.

Snyder, W. 1992. The Chain Condition and Double Object Constructions in Albanian. *Proceedings of the Leiden Conference of Junior Linguists 3*, pages 265–77. University of Leiden.

Travis, L. 1988. The Syntax of Adverbs. *McGill Working Papers in Linguistics, Special Issue on Comparative Germanic Syntax*, pages 280–310.

Travis, L. 1991. Derived Objects, Inner Aspect and the Structure of VP. In *Proceedings of North-Eastern Linguistics Society 22*. GLSA, Amherst.

Tuller, L. 1992. The Syntax of Postverbal Focus Constructions in Chadic. *Natural Language and Linguistic Theory* 10:303–34.

Ura, H. 1995. *Grammatical Function-Splitting in an AGR-less Case Theory*. Ph.D. thesis, Massachusetts Institute of Technology.

Vikner, S. 1985. Parameters of Binder and Binding Category in Danish. *Working Papers in Scandinavian Syntax* 23. University of Trondheim.

Vikner, S. 1990. *Verb Movement and the Licensing of NP-Positions in the Germanic Languages*. Ph.D. thesis, University of Geneva.

Watanabe, A. 1993. *AGR-based Case Theory and Its Interaction with the A-bar System*. Ph.D. thesis, Massachussetts Institute of Technology.

Webelhuth, G. 1989. *Syntactic Saturation Phenomena and the Modern Germanic Languages*. Ph.D. dissertation, University of Massachusetts at Amherst.

Zhang, A. 1990. Relations between Double Object Constructions and Preposition Stranding. *Linguistic Inquiry* 21:312–15.

Zubizarreta, M. L. 1998. *Prosody, Focus and Word Order*. Cambridge: Cambridge University Press.

# Index